THE HELMSMAN

Leading with Courage and Wisdom

THE
HELMSMAN

Leading with Courage and Wisdom

Kenneth S. Coley, Ed.D.

purposeful design®
p u b l i c a t i o n s
A Division of ACSI
Colorado Springs, Colorado

Purposeful Design Publications is the publishing division of the Association of Christian Schools International and is committed to the ministry of Christian school education, to enable Christian educators and schools worldwide to effectively prepare students for life. As the publisher of textbooks, trade books, and other educational resources within ACSI, Purposeful Design Publications strives to produce biblically sound materials that reflect Christian scholarship and stewardship and that address the identified needs of Christian schools around the world.

Unless otherwise indicated, all Scripture quotations are taken from the HOLY BIBLE, NEW INTERNATIONAL VERSION® (NIV®), © 1973, 1978, 1984 by International Bible Society. All rights reserved worldwide. The "NIV" and "New International Version" are trademarks registered in the United States Patent and Trademark Office by International Bible Society. Use of either trademark requires the permission of International Bible Society.

Scripture quotations marked (NASB) are taken from the New American Standard Bible®, © 1960, 1962, 1963, 1968, 1971, 1972, 1973, 1975, 1977, 1995 by the Lockman Foundation. Used by permission.

Scripture quotations marked (NKJV) are taken from the Holy Bible, New King James Version (NKJV), © 1982 by Thomas Nelson, Inc. Used by permission. All rights reserved.

Scripture quotations marked (KJV) are taken from the Holy Bible, King James Version.

Printed in the United States of America
14 13 12 11 10 09 08 07   2 3 4 5 6 7

Library of Congress Cataloging-in-Publication Data

Coley, Kenneth S., 1952-
   The helmsman : leading with courage and wisdom / by Kenneth S. Coley.
      p. cm.
   ISBN 978-1-58331-073-1 Catalog #6536
   1. Christian leadership--Biblical teaching. 2. School administrators. 3. Leadership--Biblical teaching. I. Title.
   BS680.L4C65 2006
   268'.3—dc22
                              2006017774

Editorial team: Gina Brandon, John Conaway, Karen Friesen
Designer: Chris Tschamler

Purposeful Design Publications
A Division of ACSI
PO Box 65130 • Colorado Springs, CO 80962-5130
Customer Service: 800/367-0798 • Website: www.acsi.org

To Kathy, my loving wife, who is a remarkable combination of Irish wit, intelligence, character, and beauty ...

"An excellent wife ... her worth is far above jewels.
The heart of her husband trusts in her,
And he will have no lack of gain."
Proverbs 31:10–11, NASB

Contents

Foreword

What I know most about Ken Coley derives from reading what he has written in this book. Such is the common relationship between readers and an author: We pick up a book and see the author's name but have no personal acquaintance with that name; instead, we come to know him or her only through the text before us. An author reveals himself through his *style*—for as Georges-Louis Leclerc, Comte de Buffon, declared in 1753, "The style is the man himself." An author's *rhetoric*—the choice and arrangement of language and the effect of those choices upon us—creates for each of us an imagined voice, a speaker who addresses us in a tone we recognize as friendly and fraternal, or hostile and haughty, or erudite and excluding, or intimate and inviting. We also recognize the speaker's attitude toward the subject matter and the attempt to argue with opponents and persuade them or to encourage supporters to advocate that same attitude.

From these rhetorical clues, we are able to identify an author's worldview, the platform on which she stands, the vantage point from which he looks out and sees the world. So, then, *who* is Kenneth S. Coley and *why* is his book worth reading? Setting aside the biographical details, I perceive that the human voice speaking to us through the pages of this book belongs to someone deeply committed to faith in the Lord Jesus Christ as the living Word of God and to the integrity and authority of the Bible as the written Word of God. In submission to the living Lord and to the Scriptures, he has responded to a call to serve in the vocation of teaching—in his home as husband and father, in his church as an elder, and in institutions to students at various levels of learning. Now, after sufficient years of experience—including many of the ups and downs that are normal to this vocation—he offers us his lesson plan for leadership.

Coley's tone is warm toward an audience of colleagues; it is informed yet informal, without being folksy. He does not pontificate in arcane language nor insult his audience with either current professional jargon or clichés. He addresses us as if we were gathered around a seminar table for a symposium, a meeting of equals for which he serves as facilitator of the discussion.

The speaker's attitude toward the subject of leadership in Christian schooling is ardent in its advocacy, critical of its defects, and constructive in pointing to ways of strengthening the weaknesses he perceives. Like any effective teacher, he avoids both cynicism and sarcasm, even as he leaves no doubt that some of his students are failing to achieve the best possible results through inept or inadequate methods and means.

He speaks to us in the voice of an experienced classroom teacher, appealing to whatever intellectual curiosity we may possess by using pedagogy's most reliable method of instruction—storytelling. Each chapter of this book begins with a vignette—a slice-of-life experience familiar to any professional educator—that provides the context and setting of the chapter's exposition and argument.

Coley conducts his narrative as if from the wheelhouse of a stately ship—his primary metaphor for a Christian school. Perhaps *metaphor* is not the adequate term; perhaps *analogy* or even *synecdoche* might be more appropriate, since in the early chapters he examines the school-as-ship and shows in some detail how the helmsman—the responsible officer at the wheel or helm—steers the rudder and pilots the ship-as-school. From this teacher, I've learned an interesting nuance to the New Testament Greek word *kybernetes*, translated as "helmsman" in both Acts 27:11 and Revelation 18:17 (NKJV). It is sometimes also translated as "administrator." But no matter how seasoned the reader may be or how seaworthy one's own stomach, Coley leaves no doubt as to who—according to his worldview—is Captain of our ship.

Coley deals extensively with the crisis created by the vacuum that exists when no one is prepared to succeed the present leader. This author also outlines a process for filling that void, citing John Maxwell and other leadership experts to encourage a biblical philosophy of succession planning, based on the example of the Lord Jesus Himself, who trained His apostles to lead the early Church and prepare those who would follow them.

Perhaps the most revealing portrait of the author comes in the final two chapters on "Legal Issues" and "Shore Leave." In chapter 11, Ken Coley condenses an entire course in school law and liability into a few pages of practical information, case law precedents, and recommended steps to avoid litigation and prepare for its almost certain inevitability. Here, he speaks in preventive and warning tones about the stewardship of a school and its personnel in avoiding or dealing with the entanglements and effects of legal disputes.

But in chapter 12, he expresses the concern of an elder brother—even a father—for someone whose personal life and professional well-being are precious to him. Coley is frank and direct in holding Christian school leaders accountable for their obligation to conserve their spiritual, physical, and emotional health. He offers "the common signs that have been positioned by God in our lives to protect us from reaching the point of exhaustion"—itself often a cause leading to covert or even overt sinful behavior—and offers recommendations for restoring joy in our calling through spiritual cleansing, physical exercise and rest, and emotional balance.

Who, then, is Dr. Kenneth S. Coley, author of this book? He is someone whose biblical worldview informs his understanding of the purpose of Christian schooling and whose professional experience equips him in his vocation to teach others.

D. Bruce Lockerbie
Chairman, Paideia Inc.
Stony Brook, New York

Acknowledgements

During my thirty-plus years of professional experience, the Lord has brought many people into my life to assist directly or indirectly in my understanding of leadership and administration. For their immeasurable contributions, I would like to recognize the following:

Albert and Sara Coley, my parents, who continue to teach me about servanthood leadership.

Dr. David C. Coley, my brother, for his generosity in sharing with me his own professional insights in educational administration.

Leon F. Hughes, my first principal, who challenged me to pursue school leadership and modeled all the concepts for this text.

James Anthony, my longtime board chair, who offered me my first principalship and never wavered in his support.

Rev. Robert D. Crowley, my father-in-law, whose consistent demonstration of spiritual leadership expanded my understanding beyond academic pursuits.

Dr. Gilbert Austin, my dissertation advisor, who was one of the early pioneers in the effective schools movement but was never too famous or too occupied to shepherd his students.

Phyllis Jackson and Laura White, both of whom worked tirelessly with me on this manuscript during its early stages as if it were their own.

Special thanks to ACSI leaders Derek Keenan and Cynthia Daniels for sharing my passion for developing effective helmsmen, and to Steve Babbitt and Gina Brandon of Purposeful Design Publications for their creativity and craftsmanship in the publishing of this book.

Introduction

This book has been more than thirty years in the making! I have a deep love for Christian schools and a passion (which God has been developing in me during my many and varied years in the field) to assist the pastors, board members, headmasters, and administrators who lead them. As I crafted each chapter, I included concepts that I believe will inspire you both personally and professionally.

In each chapter, you will find something for your *heart*. Proverbs 4:23 states, "Keep your heart with all diligence, For out of it *spring* the issues of life" (NKJV). I have been blessed over the years as the Holy Spirit has led me to passages of Scripture that have given me discernment, insight, and solace. First and foremost, I want to build on the foundation of God's Word. I hope that these Scriptures will touch your heart, transform your life, and shape your ministry.

Second, I have presented what I believe to be challenging concepts for your *mind*—for both inexperienced and veteran administrators. There is a rich heritage in the field of school administration that needs to be passed on to a new generation of leaders of Christian schools. In addition, you are involved in a profession that has a significant body of literature dedicated to it. While this book is short on discussions of statistical research, I think that the presentations of scholarly material will strengthen your understanding of the critical issues in the field. In each chapter, I have included numerous references to scholarly work that I hope you will pursue on your own.

Finally, I have built into each chapter something for your *hands*. I hope that you will encounter strategies that will compel you to begin scribbling notes and designing new approaches for your ministry. Go ahead; call this a practical textbook. I accept the label as a badge of honor.

The chapters of this text are divided into five sections, one introductory section and four sections that represent four biblical roles that are essential for the head administrator in any school, but especially in a Christian school. The first role or persona is that of the helmsman as *administrator*. As will be detailed in chapter 1, this characterization comes from the Greek word that is translated both "helmsman" and "administrator" in Paul's writings. In this role, the leader of the school guides the development and progress of the school's philosophy and governance in the same way his or her counterpart is responsible for the guidance of a ship at sea. No one would possibly mistake the seafarer's task as mundane or routine; and in the same way, the oversight of the welfare of a school in the turbulence of today's postmodern culture should not be viewed as making hollow speeches and counting paper clips.

The next section places the helmsman in a different setting and metaphor—that of *community builder*. Nehemiah, widely thought of as one of Scripture's greatest models of leadership, serves as the biblical basis for these chapters involving leadership theory.

The third section presents the important task of the helmsman as a *builder of the body*, on the basis of the Ephesians 4 exhortation for spiritual leaders to equip the Body of Christ. Certainly, the helmsman must view himself or herself as dependent on other saints who contribute to the overall ministry that the Lord has called them to complete. In the school setting, this means training teachers to effectively lead their classrooms, while the teachers themselves are challenged to grow professionally as educators and community leaders.

The fourth section of chapters presents the biblical picture of the helmsman as a *steward*, the manager of the resources that God has given to the school for the training of His children. Jesus and other human authors throughout Scripture discuss the eternal significance of being trustworthy in the administration of the finances, facilities, and resources placed in our care.

Throughout the book, you will be challenged to take your turn at the helm. I hope you do so with enthusiasm, yet with humility. It will demand your complete reliance on the Lord and all the strength that He can provide. Christ is your Captain and your North Star, and He promises to be there by your side, even in the strongest gale. Are you restless to board the ship and try your hand at the wheel? Perhaps you can imagine the heart of Ulysses as he prepares for his leave-taking. In the imagination of the poet Alfred, Lord Tennyson, the famous sailor is thought to have said, "There lies the port; the vessel puffs her sail: There gloom the dark, broad seas.... To strive, to seek, to find, and not to yield."

Are you ready for the adventure of a lifetime? Climb aboard!

Principles for Guiding Principals

Principles for Guiding Principals are truly that ... statements or principles that give clear directions for those in administration. Think of them as navigational tools that provide wisdom for planning and problem solving for principals who must make a multitude of decisions each day.

The effective administrator articulates the biblical mandate for a Christ-centered education that will lead each child to a biblical worldview.

The effective administrator accepts the challenge of being a courageous helmsman who has Christ as his or her guide.

The effective administrator understands the traditional roles of administration from a historical perspective.

The effective administrator reflects on the importance of a special call to ministry, educational training and experience, and a correct philosophy of education and develops a clear articulation of the school's mission.

The effective administrator establishes healthy, productive working relationships with others involved in school governance in order to maintain a harmonious school climate.

The effective administrator leads the school and community in a never-ending "curriculum dialogue" in an effort to meet all students' needs and reveal God's truth in the school's curriculum.

The effective administrator seeks to expand the spectrum of students who can be successfully ministered to by the faculty and the school community.

The effective administrator demonstrates the characteristics of a transformational leader who builds a community by inspiring followers to become leaders.

The effective administrator creates a climate of motivation for the faculty by making use of the six forces of leadership.

The effective administrator inspires others to become moral leaders of the school by demonstrating "leadership by outrage" when the community's core values are violated.

The effective administrator equips the faculty to grow professionally by developing a positive, trusting relationship with each teacher and by carrying out meaningful supervisory activities.

The effective administrator intentionally mentors faculty members so that they may become effective leaders themselves.

The effective administrator oversees the financial practices of the school to ensure integrity and stability.

The effective administrator demonstrates wisdom and discernment in legal matters in order to protect the name of Christ, the safety and well-being of the students and faculty, and the resources of the ministry.

The effective administrator cares for his or her own spiritual, physical, and emotional health.

I. Perspectives and Personas

# Biblical Perspective

Principles for Guiding Principals:

The effective administrator articulates the biblical mandate for a Christ-centered education that will lead each child to a biblical worldview.

The effective administrator accepts the challenge of being a courageous helmsman who has Christ as his or her guide.

The newly appointed administrator was looking forward to spending a few quiet moments alone in the building after the open house was over and everyone had gone home. As he walked the deserted hallways, he was overwhelmed by the gratitude he felt because God had entrusted him with this special assignment. Was he prepared to lead this faculty and student body? As he passed empty classrooms with teachers' names posted outside each door, he wondered if his leadership style would be the right one for this time and this place. Would he become the spiritual leader this community so eagerly awaited?

He paused at the bronze plaque that listed the original school board members—men and women who were instrumental in the creation of this campus and who had sacrificed much to birth this young school. Many of them were still active, and most he had met. Several had greeted him and his family enthusiastically, but others were cautious after the unrest the previous administrator had left behind.

The light reflecting off the nearby trophy case caught his attention, and he took a moment to reflect on the traditions and accomplishments that were already established in the school's brief history. He studied these symbols of the past and considered how these pieces would fit in the landscape of the vision the Lord was painting in his mind. And he had to admit, at that moment, a hint of fear pricked his heart. Could he lead these people?

As he turned to go, he discovered that he had been standing in a shadow. His eyes followed the silhouette until they rested on the wooden cross that stood magnificently at the entrance of the building. The Holy Spirit brought to his mind the words of the Lord to Joshua: "Now then, you and all these people, get ready.... Be strong and courageous.... Be careful to obey all the law.... Do not let this Book of the Law depart from your mouth.... Do not be terrified; do not be discouraged, for the Lord your God will be with you wherever you go" (Joshua 1:2–9).

In those moments in the shadow of the cross, the young school leader recommitted his life to Christ and to preparing to the best of his ability to fulfill this special calling. As did so many before him, this young administrator sensed the exhilaration of a new journey in much the same way a helmsman does before his vast ship leaves the harbor. The helmsman has no idea what storms await, but he knows he must prepare himself and the crew for what lies ahead.

When considering our calling and our career responsibilities, it is crucial to begin with the rudiments of defining who we are and to transition to this as a profession and what we are as individual servants to the Lord in the ministry that He has called us to. Without this fundamental understanding, we will lack the confidence and direction that comes from knowing precisely who we are as we fulfill our calling. So we begin … *What does it mean to be a Christian school administrator?*

First and foremost, a Christian school administrator is a Christian. This individual has settled in his or her mind that Christ is God made flesh (John 1:14) and must be preeminent in all things (Colossians 1:18). The leader of any family, group, or ministry must base his or her life and decision making on this foundation; otherwise fissures will immediately form that will rob the ministry of its integrity (Luke 6:48). You must be convinced of this truth before you face the traditions of your community, the allure of academic pursuits, or the fads of leadership trends.

How can a captain call the sailors to the deck and ask them to give all their energies to the storm if the captain is not convinced of the importance of the struggle? How can the captain move forward through uncharted waters with confidence that is not based on self-aggrandizement or arrogance but on a clear plan from the Holy Spirit? On what basis does the captain speak decisively when his or her decision making is called into question or when painful choices must be made?

Jesus challenges all who aspire to be involved in Christian education in the following parable: "Can a blind man lead a blind man? Will they not both fall into a pit? A student is not above his teacher, but everyone who is fully trained will be like his teacher" (Luke 6:39–40). In *The Pattern of God's Truth*, Frank Gaebelein expresses the urgency of a Christ-centered life in this way: "The fact is inescapable; the worldview of the teacher, insofar as he is effective, gradually conditions the worldview of the pupil. No man teaches out of a philosophical vacuum. In one way or another, every teacher expresses the convictions he lives by, whether they be spiritually positive or negative" (2002, 37).

At this point, a word of caution is in order for those on school boards who wish to consider a retired administrator who may be a member of their church and an established leader in the community but who has been trained as an educator for non-Christian schools. I always raise this question: Is he or she willing to retool to be the spiritual leader that is necessary in this ministry? Through the excellent seminars and educational resources that are available, such an experienced educator can reorient his or her approach to be an effective leader. But the caution is this: there is a learning curve, and the philosophical/theological basis for everything that is done must be different, or the result will be a secular school housed in a local church.

You Take the Helm

List specific ways administrative tasks are performed differently in a Christian school as opposed to other schools in your community (for example, your approach to student discipline or curriculum planning).

Second, the leader is involved in "schooling." This term can mean many different things, but the leader must fully grasp its meaning for the community that God has called him or her to. This understanding is especially important as the mission and vision statements are constructed. Unfortunately, some confuse schooling with a Sunday morning Bible study, a youth meeting, or summer camp. While all these activities are educational, they lack the form and style necessary to be effective throughout a 180-day school year with all the expectations our society has for the total development of a child. However, later in this discussion I will make a crucial distinction between the current demands on schooling, as dictated by a number of forces in American culture, versus a biblical view of education.

Another misunderstanding occurs when people approach the administration of a school as they would the administration of any other organization. In subsequent chapters, I will explore in more detail the fundamental difference between a school community and other organizations.

Before this discussion moves to the third word in our job title, we must first make several distinctions that are vital when one places the first two qualifiers together—Christian school, as opposed to a host of other schools such as government school, charter school, military school, or independent private school. Each label carries with it significant distinctives that communicate to everyone in its community and the public at large what type of school it is and that at least hint at the mission of the school.

In *Kingdom Education,* author Glen Schultz defines *Christian education* as the lifelong, Bible-based, Christ-centered process of leading a child to Christ, building a child in Christ, so that the child will serve Christ (1998, 25). Schultz argues that the responsibility of the education of a child rests squarely on the shoulders of the parents, on the basis of the scriptural mandates of Deuteronomy 6 (6). (A thorough understanding of this Bible passage should be required of all those in leadership in your ministry.) Schultz goes on to develop the metaphor of the three-legged stool that rests on the family, the church, and the school. Even educational texts written from a secular viewpoint have acknowledged the importance of harmony among these three. Schultz concludes that the result of a Christian school education should be that the young adult will have developed a *Christian worldview* (29). (This simple goal or outcome is worthy of separate text all by itself. See Frank Gaebelein's *The Pattern of God's Truth* and Martha MacCullough's *How to Develop a Teaching Model for World View Integration.*)

Many members of evangelical churches still have serious reservations about Christian schools and their importance for Christian education today. It is incumbent upon all Christian educators to become familiar with their perceptions in order to be able to articulate the importance of a biblical mind-set about educating the next generation. Ken Smitherman, president of ACSI, says:

A number of years ago, ACSI surveyed evangelical pastors. The results verified that it is a small minority of them who enroll their own children in Christian schools. The overwhelming majority who did not enroll their own children responded to what they considered the critical issues regarding Christian schools. In descending order, the top four critical issues were identified as poor quality, legalism, exclusivity, and overkill on Bible and religion. Such perceptions will clearly not enhance pastoral support for Christian schooling. And we do know that when pastors support Christian schooling, the families under their leadership, almost without exception, support and participate in Christian schooling.

Our challenge is significant. First, we must make certain that Christian schools are effective enough to be considered essential; and second, we must develop strategies that clearly and honestly make that essentialness evident. Sometimes the latter is as challenging as the former. We encourage you to join with us in prayerfully pursuing the highest levels of effectiveness within your individual school—effectiveness that will in due time be viewed as essential—necessary, indispensable, fundamental, and intrinsic within our Christian culture. (2004–05, 5)

Many Christians during the past two decades have been candid with me about personal reservations they have about enrolling their children in a Christian school. Because the possibility of considering a Christ-centered education is something new to many believers, I have selected the ten most frequently asked questions and the responses I have given over the years to people who ask, Why should I have my child in a Christian school?

1. Doesn't God expect Christian children to attend public school where He wants them to witness to unsaved classmates?

Deuteronomy 6 and many other passages of Scripture clearly establish God's mandate for His people—train the next generation to love the Lord with all their heart, mind, soul, and strength. Many Christian school leaders have called this training the development of a Christian worldview. Our ultimate goal for our children must be for each one to view all of life from a Scripture-centered perspective rather than a human-centered perspective that is taught in secular schools.

A frequently used analogy is the comparison of training troops for war, an apt one in light of the apostle Paul's admonition to prepare ourselves for battle. What if the United States were to gather its best eighteen-year-olds together and send them to Russia to be trained for four years in the very best military schools in that nation? Could we then confidently commission them four years later to be United States Marines, soldiers who are ready to fight and die in accordance with their training? Such a plan is ludicrous! Aren't Christian parents approaching the education of their children in this way, however, when they send God's soldiers for the twenty-first century to be taught in schools that have removed His Word and His standards?

2. If we focus on the training of our children and decide to remove them from secular schools, are we not abandoning the unsaved children left behind?

Absolutely not! We must approach this arena as we do any mission field. Certainly there are Christian teachers who have a special call to teach in public schools. Many other adults use their God-given abilities to lead school clubs such as Fellowship of Christian Athletes and Young Life. Many churches are involved with successful after-school tutoring programs. Others have chosen to become active in the political arena in an effort to effect change in local schools. Special occasions should be set aside for the commissioning of all those who serve Christ in this way. Christians must not abandon public schools! But I won't give them my children! God has entrusted them to me.

3. Aren't Christians removing their children from reality?

God's truth and His instruction in the Bible are the realities Christians must pursue. Anything that opposes these is deception. Satan beckoned Eve to experience a new perspective and gain new knowledge. We all see this as counterfeit and confront daily the consequences of the sin of Adam and Eve because they were deceived. Our children must grow in an environment that presents a Christian worldview of God's one and only reality. One Christian educator wrote:

> The responsibility for educating children belongs to parents, who received them as a gift from God. Psalm 127:3 (KJV) notes that "children *are* an heritage of the Lord *and* the fruit of the womb is *his* reward." The word *heritage* means "something inherited; an estate inherited from one's father or ancestor" (Strong 1886). Each child is created by God in His own image (Genesis 1:27) and then given to parents, who are responsible to educate the child according to God's Word. While parents may elect to use the assistance of other people in educating their children, the responsibility clearly belongs to them—not to the government,

the church, or the school. This means that parents are responsible to God for the educators they choose to assist them in the education process. (Hartzler 2004–05)

4. Aren't Christian schools like hothouses sheltering kids from harsh or unpleasant experiences?

Many Christian school leaders simply point to the strong advantages of a special plant raised in the nurturing environment of a greenhouse. Such a setting provides the much-needed opportunity for the development of a strong, unshakable root system to be established so that when the plant is placed in a hostile setting it will be healthy enough to survive. Our children must have an opportunity to be firmly grounded in God's Word.

5. Will my child have the opportunity to know non-Christians and witness to them?

This issue can be approached in a number of ways. Few Christian schools would claim that all of their students are saved. Most will admit students who are unsaved or unchurched as long as they have a positive attitude. Beyond the interaction they have with their classmates, students have weekly opportunities to witness to others their own age at school athletic events with other schools, at church-sponsored events, at community recreational activities, as well as to kids in their own neighborhoods.

6. If public school was good enough for past generations, why is it not acceptable today?

This concern is perhaps at the core of most people's objections to enrolling their children in a Christian school and is easily the most volatile. Many parents and church leaders today look back to their high school days with rich nostalgia and wonder why anyone would call into question the school systems that helped produce so many fond memories. I attended a public high school in North Carolina. Our head custodian was a bivocational pastor who preached to us and shared the gospel on every occasion. Every Christmas, over the high school public address system, Pastor Andrew read the account in the Gospels about the birth of Christ to the entire student body. Andrew is no longer there, and that is not the only thing that has changed! The Bible is out; condoms are in. My strong urging to every adult who has been out of school longer than five years is to investigate for himself or herself. If you find that your local schools are a positive environment for a growing Christian teenager, then express thanks to the Lord and encourage them to continue. However, such is not the case for the vast majority of the secular schools that I am aware of.

7. Aren't some Christian teenagers successful in public school?

Without a doubt, some Christian teenagers are successful in public schools. Such a situation reminds me of Daniel and his three friends standing firm in the face of opposition in a hostile land. These young men were ready for the challenges to their faith. In much the same way, Esther was confronted with the challenge of standing against a culture that opposed her Lord. My response is, If your child is a Daniel or an Esther, then he or she may be ready for challenges if he or she believes God is leading that way. However, those types of kids are rare indeed. Also, parents must consider the amount of deprogramming that must occur as children are confronted with nonbiblical teaching.

8. Can graduates of Christian high schools gain acceptance into the college of their choice?

The track record of Christian school graduates is so well established that this is no longer a serious concern for most parents. My first response to parents is to encourage them to check with the admissions office of any college or university they are interested in. I have never heard a negative response from an admissions committee when asked about admitting graduates from Christian schools. I also tell parents to consider Matthew 6:33 and be confident that God's best awaits our children if we teach them to put Him first.

9. Aren't some students prevented from attending a Christian school because of high tuition costs?

Unfortunately, yes, some students are. But this is a concern that the Body of Christ can actively do something about. One approach is to challenge every church in the area to establish a scholarship fund. Each church would administer its own fund that could be used to support students in kindergarten through twelfth grade, homeschooling, college, and seminary. Imagine if each church made a one-thousand-dollar scholarship available for a student who attends a Christian school.

10. What Scripture passage supports the decision to send children to Christian schools?

There are numerous passages that support the decision to send children to Christian schools, including Deuteronomy 6 discussed earlier in this chapter. Proverbs 22:6 instructs parents to "train a child in the way he should go." The Hebrew wording for *training* literally means "touch the palate," which refers to the practice of a Hebrew mother placing on her baby's tongue bits of food that she had chewed. As the baby was fed, he or she not only received nourishment but also developed an appetite for nutritious foods. In the same way, each of us is to lead our children to develop godly appetites as they grow. As we commit ourselves to raising the next generation for Christ, the Holy Spirit will bless our efforts to develop a Christian worldview in the minds and hearts of the children God has entrusted to us.

Derek Keenan, vice president of academic affairs at the Association of Christian Schools International (ACSI), uses the phrase, "teaching our kids to swim beyond the buoys." In the final analysis, isn't that what we want? We must plan for our graduates of Christian schools to leave the confines of our homes, churches, and schools prepared to meet the rough currents of workplaces and the open hostility found on most college campuses.

You Take the Helm

Which of the questions or issues listed above do you believe is raised most often in your community? Can you identify other concerns that you must be prepared to discuss?

Now to the third word in our job title—*administration* or *administrator.* The Latin etymology is the word *administrare*, a combination of the prefix *ad*, which means "to," with the infinitive *ministrare*, which means to "serve." In its core essence, the concept of administration is about service. To be an effective leader in a Christian school community, or any organization for that matter, the primary goal of the leader is Christlike servanthood. During my fifteen years as an administrator, I wanted to communicate to students as well as to my staff that the head administrator is not above stooping to clean up a mess.[1] As a part of my day, I regularly ate lunch in the school cafeteria. I'm sure we can all recall the embarrassment of dropping a tray and having a horrible mess for someone to pick up. Whenever this accident occurred in our lunchroom, I attempted to be the first one to arrive at the humiliated child's side to mop up the milk and peach juice.

And now for the most exciting dimension of being a Christian school administrator ... The apostle Paul lists the word *administrations* in 1 Corinthians 12:5 (KJV) in his discussion concerning the gifts. The word in 1 Corinthians 12:28 (NIV) that is translated "administration" comes from the Greek word *kybernesis*. Another form of this Greek word, *kybernetes*, is translated "helmsman," which is used in Acts 27:11 (NKJV) when Paul refers to the pilot of the ship. (The word also appears in Revelation 18:17 and once again refers to the man steering the ship.) It has been argued by many that the office of administration in the church may have developed in times of emergency from within and without, just as the importance of the helmsman increases in a time of storm. A helmsman has to know the nature and direction of storms, the habits of air and water currents, and the process of steering by the stars and sun. For the proper discharge of this gift, the charisma of God is indispensable (Kittel 1985, 1036).

The uses of *kybernesis* in the Old Testament (Septuagint) appear mostly in Proverbs. Its uses are closely related to the concept of wisdom, denoting the ability of the leader to offer proper direction to a group (Gangel 1997, 51; see also Proverbs 1:5, 11:14, 24:6; Ezekiel 27:8).

All too often, leaders approach the notion of administration with a less-than-excited, even negative mind-set about policies, paperwork, and personnel matters. The Holy Spirit inspired the apostle Paul to select a term that means anything but that. Put away your notions about mindless hours of filing forms and consider the dynamic opportunities that await an administrator who steers the course of a school for the glory of God's kingdom. In *Leading in a Culture of Change*, Michael Fullan describes leadership in this way: "I have never been fond of distinguishing between leadership and management: they overlap and you need both qualities. But here is one difference that it makes sense to highlight: leadership is needed for problems that do not have easy answers. The big problems of the day are complex, rife with paradoxes and dilemmas." He continues: "We demand that [leaders] solve, or at least manage, a multitude of interconnected problems that can develop into crises without warning; we require them to navigate an increasingly turbulent reality that is, in key aspects, literally incomprehensible to the human mind; we buffet them on every side with bolder, more powerful special interests that challenge every innovative policy idea; we submerge them in often unhelpful and distracting information; and we force them to decide and act at an ever faster pace" (2001, 2).

In *AquaChurch*, Leonard Sweet describes the complex skills Christian leaders need in order to navigate their ministries in a day and age when road maps are obsolete. We are no longer traveling static highways, but we are leading ministries into uncharted waters that have shifting currents and unpredictable winds. What is needed for this postmodern seascape is a helmsman. Sweet concludes about this biblical sailor: "The captain of the ship was called in Greek *kubernetes*. A captain was one who (1) knew from experience the ways of the sea; (2) could perform all the diverse duties on board the ship; (3) could set and keep a true course; (4) assumed responsibility for the welfare of the ship's passengers and cargo. The captain was the "navigator" with skills that could take a ship from where it was docked to where it was destined to go" (1999, 19).

Is the Lord calling you to climb aboard and take the wheel? Just as ancient sailors depended on the North Star amid a host of heavenly bodies, you must depend on Christ as your constant companion. Just as they needed wind for power, you will need the Holy Spirit as your source of power. Just as they studied navigational charts, you will use His Word as your manual to help you lead your crew.

Notes

1. I wish to acknowledge the influence of the following leaders on the preparation of this discussion: Glen Schultz, *Kingdom Education;* Paul Kienel, Ollie Gibbs, and Sharon Berry, *The Philosophy of Christian School Education;* and Claude Schindler, *Educating for Eternity.*

Historical Perspective

2

Principle for Guiding Principals:

The effective administrator understands the traditional roles of administration from a historical perspective.

The administrator examined her new office on the Saturday before school started. Her desk was oddly bare, and the empty shelves were barricaded by boxes of books. She took a seat in a new chair that had none of the usual scars on the mahogany arms, fresh wood that would soon be scratched from the wear of worry. But this day, while all was quiet, she sat back in her chair and gazed out the window while she reflected on her "mindscape"—where she had come from, what she had been trained to do, and which way she should go. She asked the Holy Spirit to help define in her what type of leader she should be. Some schools at one time needed an effective manager. Others used to depend on their administrator to take the lead in instructional matters. More recently, she had been taught that changing times demanded that she become the leader of a larger community. She leaned over to pick up a textbook. Perhaps a look back would tell her what she needed to know to move forward.[1]

A brief look at a historical perspective on administration is both professionally instructive and academically beneficial. This review will begin with the turn of the last century and establish the major movements that have occurred in the last one hundred years. In each time period, there will be discussion of one or two theorists who defined the thinking at that time.

Most texts divide the discussion into four major divisions that are dated in broad categories as follows:

> **Classical Schools of Management Theory**
> Scientific Management and Administrative Management—1900
> Human Relations—1930
> Behavioral Science—1950
> Human Resources—1960

The focus of this discussion will shift from these general theories of organizational thought to the theories associated specifically with educational administration beginning with the 1960s. The changes throughout the last half of the twentieth century have been labeled as follows:

> Program Manager—1960s and 1970s
> Instructional Leader—1980s
> Transformational Leader—1990s
> Community Leader—early 2000s

In later chapters, we will explore significant trends in leadership theory that are certainly related to the upcoming discussion on historical perspectives of management theory. Following an examination of the evolving role of the administrator in the last half of the twentieth century, we will take a closer look at the effective schools movement that has made such an important impact over the last thirty-five years. I encourage you to ask two vital questions as you take this whirlwind tour of a century of change: What are the strengths and weaknesses of each period? What is obviously missing in the discussion of modern secular theories that is mandatory for your leadership of a Christian school?

Scientific Management

Patrick Montana and Bruce Charnov, authors of a thorough text that discusses management theory from a historical perspective, note that since the time of Moses and Jethro in Exodus 18 there have been discussions of effective management and the successful management of people and projects. However, not until recently has there been a body of literature that examines these processes in a scientific way (1993, 8). The beginning of the scientific management era is generally marked by the influence of Frederick W. Taylor (1856–1915). Montana and Charnov wrote, "Created by engineers, scientists, and practicing managers concerned with the improvement of worker efficiency (the amount a worker produces in a given period of time), this approach assumed two major forms: management of work and management of organizations" (9). Taylor, called the Father of Scientific Management, and his associates thought that workers, motivated by economics and limited by physiology, needed constant direction. This approach and other theories were published in *The Principles of Scientific Management* in 1911. Taylor's writings, which were influenced by his experiences in companies such as Bethlehem Steel, continue to influence concepts such as job design, work layout, and task scheduling.

Taylor believed that maximum production was tied to maximum efficiency of the worker. Such efficiency was possible only by having a "management scientist" redesign tasks for employees who were not to be trusted with structuring the work themselves. For instance, on the basis of these observations of the military, Taylor coined the term *soldiering* for workers who were slacking off. It was believed that the manager must provide the following for each worker (Hoy and Miskel 1982, 2):

- *A large daily task.* Each person in the establishment, [whether of] high or low [status], should have a clearly defined task. The carefully circumscribed task should require a full day's effort to complete.
- *Standard conditions.* The worker should be given standard conditions and the appliances to accomplish the task with certainty.
- *High pay for success.* High pay should be tied to successful completion of that day's task.
- *Loss of pay in case of failure.* Failure should be personally costly.
- *Expertise in large organizations.* As organizations become increasingly sophisticated, tasks should be made so difficult as to be accomplished only by a first-rate worker.

Administrative Management

Traditional or classical organizational thought, often called administrative management theory, concentrates on the broad problems of departmental division of work and coordination. While Taylor's human engineers worked from the individual workers upward, the administrative managers worked from the managing director downward. Their focuses were different, but their contributions complemented one another (Hoy and Miskel 1982, 3).

Henri Fayol (1841–1925) was a trained engineer who used a scientific approach to administration and is therefore known as the developer of administrative theory. He developed his concepts of management while leading a large French coal-mining company and published them in his book *General and Industrial Management* (1929). In this text, Fayol is credited with several major contributions to administrative theory. First, he distinguished between supervisory and managerial responsibilities, assigning more importance and recognition to managing as opposed to supervising workers. Second, he defined what the managers did as *functions of management*, which served as tools for the classification and evaluation of management. He also developed general principles that offered practical advice on how to function as a manager. Finally, Fayol departed from contemporary thought to argue that these principles could be learned, as opposed to the notion that managers are born with these abilities (Montana and Charnov 1993, 13–14). Hoy and Miskel list Fayol's five functions of administrative behavior, which consisted of the following (1982, 3):

- To *plan* means to study the future and arrange the plan of operations.
- To *organize* means to build up material and human organization of the business, organizing both people and materials.
- To *command* means to make the staff do their work.
- To *coordinate* means to unite and correlate all activities.
- To *control* means to see that everything is done in accordance with the rules which have been laid down and the instructions which have been given.

Another theorist, Luther Gulick (1892–1992), later amplified these functions as he developed his response to the question, "What is the work of the chief executive?" He listed seven administrative procedures that have been reduced to the well-known acronym POSDCoRB: planning, organizing, staffing, directing, coordinating, reporting, and budgeting. He emphasized the principle of division of labor. He believed that the more a task could be broken down into its components, the more specialized, and therefore the more effective, the worker would be in performing the task. A second principle was span of control, or the number of workers supervised. In subdividing from the top downward, each work unit had to be supervised and coordinated with other units. The span of control considered to be most effective was five to ten subordinates. The major features of this era can be summarized in the following list of concepts presented by Hoy and Miskel (1982, 4):

1. *Time and motion studies.* Is a task carried out in a way that minimizes time and effort required?
2. *Division of labor and specialization.* Efficiency can be attained by subdividing any operation into its basic components.
3. *Standardization of task.* Breaking tasks into component parts allows for routinized performance.
4. *Unity of command.* Decision making is centralized, with responsibility flowing from top to bottom.
5. *Span of control.* Each supervisor at any level has a limited number of subordinates (five to ten) to direct.
6. *Uniqueness of function.* Functions performed by one department are not duplicated by another.
7. *Formal organization.* The focus of analysis is on the official organizational blueprint; informal structures involving the interaction of individuals within the organization are not evaluated.

Human Relations Movement

As noted in the preceding list, the management theory of the early decades of the last century was totally focused on the formal structure of the organization and gave no thought to the dynamics at work in the informal structure. A growing awareness of this powerful but unexamined dimension of any organization gave rise to the human relations movement. During a time of transition, the work of Mary Parker Follett (1868–1933), one of the first researchers and authors who focused on the human side of administration, pointed managers to the importance of developing and maintaining dynamic and harmonious relationships. Specifically, she focused on how managers deal with conflict. She developed what she called "a collaborative approach to problem solving," in which she advocated the involvement of workers in the everyday conflicts and the use of compromise in management disputes (Montana and Charnov 1993, 13). Despite her work, the development of the human relations approach is usually traced to what has become some of the most famous studies done in the first half of the century—the studies conducted at the Hawthorne plant of the Western Electric Company in Chicago.

The Hawthorne studies, from 1927 to 1932, began with three experiments that were conducted to study the relation of quality and quantity of illumination to efficiency in industry. The initial results revealed that the production rates increased in the test group until the light became so poor that the workers complained that they could no longer see what they were doing. Elton Mayo, an Australian industrial psychologist, and Fritz Roethlisberger, a social psychologist, were Harvard professors who were hired by the company to investigate further concerning the relationship between physical conditions of work and productivity. The company thought that both psychological as well as physiological factors were involved. The researchers asked a series of questions:

1. Do employees actually get tired out?
2. Are rest pauses desirable?
3. Is a shorter working day desirable?
4. What are the attitudes of employees toward their work and toward the company?
5. What is the effect of changing the type of working equipment?
6. Why does production fall off in the afternoon?

In an effort to isolate the variables they were examining, the researchers isolated six women in a special working environment and began to manipulate work conditions such as payment systems, rest breaks of various sorts and lengths, variations in the length of the workday, and the provision of food and refreshments during the workday. These women were under the watchful eye of a supervisor, who became more like a friendly observer than a disciplinarian. After a five-year period, these workers returned to the main workforce; however, a totally unexpected set of findings had occurred. Output increased, but the increase was independent of any change in rest pauses or working hours. Both the daily and weekly production levels rose to a point much higher than under the nearly identical conditions of the preexperimental setting (Hoy and Miskel 1982, 6). After interviewing these workers, researchers discovered that the test room was an enjoyable place to work, the relationship between the employees and their supervisor was more positive during the experimental period, and participating in the experiment had created a special bond or group identity for them. In addition, the women responded to the realization that they were taking part in a meaningful experiment. (The researchers identified this tendency to react differently because they were being observed as the "Hawthorne Effect." Though this one phrase is often quoted as the primary finding in these studies, there was a much more significant result.)

Patrick Montana and Bruce Charnov summarize the work of the Hawthorne studies: "Mayo and his colleagues concluded that factors other than the physical aspects of work had the power of improving production. These factors related to the interrelationships between workers and individual worker psychology were termed, after much additional investigation, human relations factors" (1993, 20). These experiments changed forever the importance and awareness of the informal dimensions that are significant when considering the motivation of participants in an organization and the interpersonal dynamics that influence productivity.[2]

Behavioral Science Movement

The theoretical movements and corresponding periods following the human relations movement of the thirties and forties have been classified in a variety of ways by different authors who have generally agreed on the theorists who have made the most significant contributions, though some names may appear in more that one category.[3] The third major movement of the twentieth century is usually designated to have occurred around 1950, and it is considered a reaction to the overemphasis on formal structure by the classical approach on the one hand and the concern by the human relations approach for social relations on the other. What resulted was the behavioral science approach, which focused on work behavior in formal organizations. New theories in the fields of psychology, sociology, political science, and economics influenced thinking. Included in the behavioral science approach, also called management science (Montana and Charnov 1993), are the writings of Chester Barnard, Douglas McGregor, and Herbert Simon.

Barnard originated much of the thinking of the movement with his analysis of organizational life in *Functions of the Executive*, which was published in 1938. The product of Barnard's years as president of Bell Telephone Company of New Jersey, this book provides a comprehensive theory of cooperative behavior in formal organizations (Hoy and Miskel 1982, 9). He maintained that employees form organizations to achieve goals and emphasized "cooperative effort as a key to organizational productivity and managerial effectiveness." This concept of cooperation is further developed as Barnard discusses workers' reactions to a managerial order they consider legitimate and acceptable. His "acceptance theory of authority" argues that the leader's authority or power is defined not by his position but by the acceptance of the followers (Montana and Charnov 1993, 19).

Herbert Simon (1916–2001), in *Administrative Behavior* (1947), extended Barnard's work and discussed the concept of organizational equilibrium as a focal point for a formal theory of work motivation. The organization was seen as an exchange system in which inducements are exchanged for work. Employees remain in the organization as long as they perceive the inducements as larger than their efforts and contributions. In addition, Simon is known for his analysis of decision making and information processing. Because managers seldom process the optimum amount of information regarding a problem, executives invariably search for *satisfactory* results in their decision making. Simon termed this process *satisficing*. He argued that, though there is no one best solution, some solutions are more satisfactory than others (Hoy and Miskel 1982, 10).

You Take the Helm

Keeping in mind the first two categories of administrative theory introduced in the twentieth century, consider from a biblical perspective what qualities from each era you wish to emulate in your administrative style.

Table 2.1 The Development of Administrative Science

Era	Movement	Theorist	Publication
1900	Scientific Management and Administrative Management	Frederick Taylor	*The Principles of Scientific Management* (1911)
		Henri Fayol	*General and Industrial Management* (1929)
		Luther Gulick	Papers on the Science of Administration (1937)
1930	Human Relations	Mary Parker Follett	*Creative Experience* (1924)
		Elton Mayo	The Hawthorne Studies (1927–1932)
1940-1950	Behavioral Science	Chester Barnard	*Functions of the Executive* (1938)
		Herbert Simon	*Administrative Behavior* (1947)
1960	Human Resources	Douglas McGregor	*The Human Side of Enterprise* (1960)
		Rensis Likert	*New Patterns of Management* (1961)
		Chris Argyris	*Integrating the Individual and the Organization* (1964)
		Frederick Herzberg	*Work and the Nature of Man* (1966)

Human Resources Movement

In the mid-1960s, Raymond Miles, a writer for the *Harvard Business Review*, posed a question in the title of his article that would suggest a new era. He suggested a distinction that took hold: "Human Relations or Human Resources?" One of the theorists of this new movement, Chris Argyris, articulated the focus of this approach: "We're interested in developing neither an overpowering manipulative organization nor organizations that will 'keep people happy.' Happiness, morale, and satisfaction are not going to be highly relevant guides in our discussion. Individual competence, commitment, self-responsibility, fully functioning individuals, and active, viable, vital organizations will be the kinds of criteria that we will keep foremost in our minds" (1964, 4).

Another well-known figure at this time, Rensis Likert, expressed that the leader characterized by this movement would be neither directive nor patronizing but instead supportive: "The leader and other processes of the organization must be such as to ensure a maximum probability that in all interactions and in all relationships within the organization, each member, in light of his background, values, desires, and expectations, will view the experience as supportive and one which builds and maintains his sense of personal worth and importance" (1961, 103).

Perhaps the best known of the representatives is Douglas McGregor, who pointed out that administrative decisions are influenced by the leader's attitude toward his or her workers. Some executives view their employees as lacking potential for growth, being disinterested in the productivity of the organization, and unable to put forth meaningful effort unless they are closely supervised. This generally negative view is held by a leader McGregor designated as Theory X. In his book *The Human Side of Enterprise* (1960, 132), he lists these assumptions held by a Theory X leader:

1. Average people are by nature indolent—they work as little as possible.
2. They lack ambition, dislike responsibility, prefer to be led.
3. They are inherently self-centered, indifferent to organizational needs.
4. They are by nature resistant to change.
5. They are gullible, not very bright, ready dupes of the charlatan and demagogue.

Theory Y leaders, on the other hand, believe that managers must take the responsibility to establish workplace environments where workers feel valued and trusted. In such environments, they become motivated to be productive and even to desire professional growth. McGregor lists the following assumptions about people associated with Theory Y (1960, 132):

1. Management is responsible for organizing the elements of productive enterprise—money, materials, equipment, people—in the interest of economic (educational) ends.
2. People are not by nature passive or resistant to organizational needs. They have become so as a result of experience in organizations.
3. The motivation, the potential for development, the capacity for assuming responsibility, the readiness to direct behaviors toward organizational goals are all present in people; management does not put them there. It is a responsibility of management to make it possible for people to recognize and develop these human characteristics for themselves.
4. The essential task of management is to arrange organizational conditions and methods of operation so that people can achieve their own goals best by directing their own efforts toward organizational objectives.

The impact of this thinking is certainly instructive for school leaders. It is vital to view each faculty member as a called out and gifted team member. Ephesians 2:10 reminds each believer and each leader that "we are God's workmanship." Each educator, though fallible, must be encouraged in light of God's Word and His grace. Even beyond the positive qualities attributed to teachers by a Theory Y administrator, this verse goes on to say, "created in Christ Jesus to do good works, which God prepared in advance for us to do." Imagine the powerful influence of a Christian school administrator who views his or her interaction with the staff from the perspective of eternity—to facilitate the carrying out of each teacher's "good works" that have been orchestrated by the Master Designer.

The writings of the fourth theorist of the human resource movement, Frederick Herzberg, further highlight the emphasis on developing an individual's potential, as can be seen in Herzberg's discussion of his two-factor theory, also called the motivation hygiene theory. Herzberg's research led him to believe that there are certain factors associated with work that may be considered *maintenance factors*. As these needs are met (see table 2.2), the worker is not "dissatisfied." He or she basically comes to work in a neutral state, that is, a neutral state of motivation since his or her maintenance needs have been met. Herzberg argues that as the motivator factors are provided, then the worker is satisfied or positively motivated (see table 2.2). He described the influence of the two-factor theory in the following way: "To feel that one has grown depends on achievement of tasks that have meaning to the individual, and since the hygiene factors do not relate to the task, they are powerless to give such meaning to the individual. Growth is dependent on some achievements but achievement requires a task. The motivators are task factors and thus are necessary for growth" (1966, 78).

Table 2.2 (Herzberg 1966, 78)

Motivating and Demotivating Factors in the Work Situation (According to Herzberg)	
Motivators (Satisfiers)	**Maintenance Factors (Dissatisfiers)**

Achievement
Recognition
Work itself
Responsibility
Advancement
Growth
	Organizational policy and
	  administration
	Supervision
	Working conditions
	Interpersonal relations (with superiors,
	  subordinates, and peers)
	Salary
	Status
	Job security
	Personal life

You Take the Helm

While continuing to consider Herzberg's two-factor theory, read Philippians 4:11–20 and construct a biblical response to the theory.

Next, consider what you as a spiritual leader can do to exhort your colleagues to desire Paul's spirit of contentment in their lives.

Finally, since we work with struggling saints, what are factors in a Christian school that serve to discourage or demotivate teachers and administrators? Have you identified those factors that inspire and encourage?

The Changing Role of the School Administrator

During the time periods mentioned in the previous discussion, there was relatively little change in the basic responsibilities of a school administrator. The role that he or she played has been characterized as that of *administrative manager*. Because of various trends in the corporate world, among other pressures of the position, the leader of a local school attempted to maintain the status quo and generally avoided being drawn into political or instructional matters. This began to change for public school administrators in the 1960s and 1970s as federally mandated programs were being funded to assist various types of special student populations. In addition, new and innovative curriculum concepts were being developed and implemented across the country. During this time, the administrator's position could be described as *program/curriculum manager.* Looking back at these decades, researchers view the administrative role as implementing programs that were imposed from external sources and monitoring the school's compliance with the standards prescribed by others (Hallinger 1992, 35–48).

The 1980s marked a new emphasis on the administrator as *instructional leader.* The effective schools movement, presented later in this chapter, heralded this enormous change in the principalship. "By the mid-80s professional norms deemed it unacceptable for principals to focus their efforts solely on maintenance of the school or even on programme management. Instructional leadership became the new educational standard for principals" (Hallinger 1992, 35–48). Despite the listing of various qualities or leadership behaviors, some critics of this new emphasis claimed that administrators were continuing to manage changes that were still being mandated from outside the local school. With the move toward giving administrators and faculties more say in the creation and implementation of plans for their schools (called site-based management and school restructuring), the administrator's role once again expanded in the late '80s and into the '90s to include the major leadership role of uniting teachers, parents, and students. This role is referred to as *transformational leadership.* (This role is of vital importance to administrators of Christian schools and is the focus of chapter 6.)

Effective Schools Movement

With the increase in emphasis on standardized testing in the 1970s, researchers such as Gilbert Austin at the University of Maryland examined the performance of elementary school children in language arts and mathematical skills. In search of statistical *outliers*—schools that performed significantly higher or lower than other schools did—Austin looked at the test scores from each school and compared them with those from other schools in the state of Maryland. Having identified eighteen high-achieving schools and twelve low-achieving schools, Austin and his colleagues asked, "What are characteristics of schools whose students perform better than their peers in other schools?" As they and other researchers around the country sought to identify and discuss what happens in classrooms in high-achieving schools, the effective schools movement was born (Austin n.d.). Numerous lists of the characteristics of high-achieving schools may be found in the literature that is based on various projects, but most findings include some or all of the following characteristics that are listed in "The Quiet Revolution in Educational Research," an article in *Phi Delta Kappan* magazine (Walberg, Schiller, and Haertel 1979, 179–83):

> Teachers in effective schools consistently …
> - establish classroom rules that allow pupils to attend to personal and procedural needs without having to check with the teacher.
> - communicate high expectations of high achievement.
> - start off each class by reviewing homework and by reviewing material covered in the previous few classes.
> - make the objective(s) of the new instructional episode clear to the students.
> - directly teach the content or skill that will be measured on the test.
> - after teaching the new material, assess student comprehension through questions and practice.
> - provide uninterrupted successful practice that is monitored by the teacher moving around the classroom.
> - maintain direct engagement by the student on the academic task.
> - assign homework to increase student familiarity with material.
> - hold review sessions weekly and monthly.

In addition to the classroom characteristics discussed in the effective schools literature, the impact of the administrator's leadership was another significant finding. In higher-achieving schools, administrators exerted strong leadership, participated frequently and directly in instructional matters, communicated high expectations for staff and students, and were oriented toward academic goals (Austin n.d.). This project and others clearly reveal the vital role that the school's key leader plays in the students' success in the classroom.

In the 1980s, widespread interest continued concerning the administrator's role in the school. Joan Lipsitz, program officer for elementary/secondary education at the Lilly Endowment, conducted case studies of four successful middle schools and reached the following conclusions (1984):

> - The principals led the schools by making clear and powerful statements about the school's purpose.
> - The principals were able to define what was possible in the school's mission, and the students and teachers rallied around these goals.

- Principals had a driving vision and articulated why things were done the way that they were.
- The principals took an active role in instruction and set performance standards.
- The principals had a driven, energetic style, and their authority was derived from their acknowledged competence.
- The school environment was noticeably caring, and there was a striking lack of adult isolation. Rather, there was considerable teamwork and common planning.
- The teachers had high expectations for themselves and were given a high degree of autonomy.

For an excellent discussion on the effective schools movement, see chapter 1 of *What Works in Schools: Translating Research into Action* by Robert J. Marzano.

In the 1990s, Lawrence Lezotte (n.d.), spokesperson for effective schools research and implementation and the founder of the Effective Schools League, developed what he termed the "the second generation" of effective schools characteristics, building on the first twenty years of research and the changing needs of schools at the close of the twentieth century. He included the characteristics listed below:

1. Safe and Orderly Environment

The First Generation: In the effective school, there is an orderly, purposeful, businesslike atmosphere which is free from the threat of physical harm.

The Second Generation: In the first generation, the safe and orderly environment correlate was defined in terms of the absence of undesirable student behavior. The second generation will place increased emphasis on the presence of certain desirable behaviors. These second-generation schools will be places where students actually help one another.

2. Climate of High Expectations for Success

The First Generation: In the effective school, there is a climate of expectation in which the staff believe and demonstrate that all students can attain mastery of the essential school skills, and the staff also believe that they have the capability to help all students achieve that mastery.

The Second Generation: High expectations for success will be judged, not only by the initial staff beliefs and behaviors, but also by the organization's response when some students do not learn.

3. Instructional Leadership

The First Generation: In the effective school, the principal acts as an instructional leader and effectively and persistently communicates that mission to the staff, parents, and students.

The Second Generation: In the second generation, instructional leadership will remain important; however, the concept will be broadened and leadership will be viewed as a dispersed concept that includes all adults, especially the teachers. With the democratization of organizations, especially schools, the leadership function becomes one of creating a "community of shared values."

4. Clear and Focused Mission

The First Generation: In the effective school, there is a clearly articulated school mission through which the staff shares an understanding of and commitment to the instructional goals, priorities, assessment procedures, and accountability.

The Second Generation: The focus will shift toward a more appropriate balance between higher-level learning and those more basic skills that are truly prerequisite to their mastery. Designing and delivering a curriculum that responds to the demands of accountability and that is responsive to the need for higher levels of learning will require substantial staff development.

5. Opportunity to Learn and Student Time on Task

The First Generation: In the effective school, teachers allocate a significant amount of classroom time to instruction in the essential skills.

The Second Generation: Teachers will have to become more skilled at interdisciplinary curriculum, and they will need to learn how to comfortably practice "organized abandonment." They will have to be able to ask the question, "What goes and what stays?"

6. Frequent Monitoring of Student Progress

The First Generation: In the effective school, student academic progress is measured frequently through a variety of assessment procedures. The results of these assessments are used to improve individual student performance and also to improve the instructional program.

The Second Generation: First, the use of technology will permit teachers to do a better job of monitoring their students' progress. Second, this same technology will allow students to monitor their own learning and, where necessary, adjust their own behavior. In the area of assessment, the emphasis will continue to shift away from standardized norm-referenced, paper-pencil tests and toward curricular-based, criterion-referenced measures of student mastery…. The monitoring of student learning will emphasize "more authentic assessments" of curriculum mastery.

7. Home-School Relations

The First Generation: In the effective school, parents understand and support the school's basic mission and are given the opportunity to play an important role in helping the school to achieve this mission.

The Second Generation: The relationship between parents and the school must be an authentic partnership between the school and home. The best hope for effectively confronting the problem—and not each other—is to build enough trust and enough communication to realize that both teachers and parents have the same goal—an effective school and home for all children!

Twenty-First Century and Beyond

In *What Works in Schools: Translating Research into Action,* one of the most thorough looks at educational research that has been published, Robert Marzano organizes thirty-five years of research into three general factors that influence student academic achievement: (1) school-level factors, (2) teacher-level factors, and (3) student-level factors (see table 2.3 for a further breakdown of these factors). After a review of the literature, Marzano chose those recommendations that could be implemented without a drastic addition of resources. Changes that would require a drastic increase in the time spent in school or additional personnel or equipment were not included (2003, 10).

Included under the first school-level factor heading of a "Guaranteed and Viable Curriculum" is the factor reported to have the strongest relationship with student achievement: opportunity to learn. Marzano recommends that leaders (1) identify and communicate the content considered essential for all students versus the content that is considered supplemental, (2) ensure that the essential content can be addressed in the amount of time available for instruction, (3) sequence and organize the essential content in such a way that students have ample opportunity to learn it, and (4) ensure that teachers address the essential content, while protecting the instructional time that is available (Marzano 2003, 25–31). Within the concept of "Challenging Goals and Effective Feedback," Marzano highlights the importance of clearly defining obtainable goals and the necessity of implementing an assessment system that provides timely feedback on specific knowledge and skills for specific students (39). Under the heading "Parent and Community Involvement," Marzano discusses the importance of meaningful parent involvement by establishing vehicles for communication, ways to involve parents in the day-to-day running of the school, and governance structures that encourage the participation of parents and community members (49–51). The fourth category, "Safe and Orderly Environment," challenges administrators to establish and enforce appropriate consequences for violations of rules and procedures and the teaching of self-discipline and responsibility. The fifth school-level factor, "Collegiality and Professionalism," includes the expectation that administrators find meaningful ways to involve faculty members in the governance of the school and the design of staff development activities (65).

Table 2.3 (Marzano 2003, 10)

Factors Affecting Student Achievement	
Factor	**Example**
School	Guaranteed and Viable Curriculum Challenging Goals and Effective Feedback Parent and Community Involvement Safe and Orderly Environment Collegiality and Professionalism
Teacher	Instructional Strategies Classroom Management Classroom Curriculum Design
Student	Home Atmosphere Learned Intelligence and Background Knowledge Motivation

Ten Traits of Highly Effective Administrators

Elaine McEwan (2003), a former teacher, librarian, principal, and assistant superintendent for instruction in a Chicago school district, and author of more than thirty books for parents and educators, used an exceptionally innovative research design to develop a list of ten traits that she presents as being descriptive of effective administrators. First, she began with thirty-seven traits gleaned from extensive reading in the literature about administrators. Next, she selected 175 educators around the country and asked them to name ten traits that they believed were essential to being a highly effective administrator. She describes the 108 respondents as "a sample of convenience" who were part of her email network and were willing to participate. McEwan then discovered natural clusters around which the traits with the most votes tended to fall. Finally, she took her list of ten best traits and "tested" them in interviews with administrators (21 women and 16 men), each of whom had a proven track record of success as an administrator. The final list, presented below, was fine-tuned during the interview process.

Table 2.4 (McEwan 2003, 175)

Ten Traits of Highly Effective Principals

Trait Number 1: The Communicator

The highly effective principal is a communicator—a genuine and open human being with the capacity to listen, empathize, interact, and connect with individual students, parents, and teachers in productive, helping, and healing ways, as well as the ability to teach, to present, and to motivate people in larger group settings.

Trait Number 2: The Educator

The highly effective principal is an educator—a self-directed instructional leader with a strong intellect and personal depth of knowledge regarding research-based curriculum, instruction, and learning who motivates and facilitates the intellectual growth and development of self, students, teachers, and parents.

Trait Number 3: The Envisioner

The highly effective principal is an envisioner—an individual who is motivated by a sense of calling and purpose, focused on a vision of what schools can be, and guided by a mission that has the best interests of all students at its core.

Table 2.4 *continued*

Trait Number 4: The Facilitator
The highly effective principal is a facilitator—a leader with outstanding human relations skills that include the abilities to build individual relationships with parents, teachers, and students; collaborative teams with staff members and parents; and a schoolwide community of leaders.

Trait Number 5: The Change Master
The highly effective principal is a change master—a flexible, futuristic, and realistic leader, able to motivate as well as manage change in an organized, positive, and enduring fashion.

Trait Number 6: The Culture Builder
The highly effective principal is a culture builder—an individual who communicates (talks) and models (walks) a strong and viable vision based on achievement, character, personal responsibility, and accountability.

Trait Number 7: The Activator
The highly effective principal is an activator—an individual with gumption (e.g., drive, motivation, enthusiasm, energy, spunk, and humor) enough to share with staff, parents, and students.

Trait Number 8: The Producer
The highly effective principal is a producer—a results-oriented individual with a strong sense of accountability to taxpayers, parents, students, and teachers who translates high expectations into intellectual development and academic achievement for all students.

Trait Number 9: The Character Builder
The highly effective principal is a character builder—a role model whose values, words, and deeds are marked by trustworthiness, integrity, authenticity, respect, generosity, and humility.

Trait Number 10: The Contributor
The highly effective principal is a contributor—a servant-leader, an encourager, and an enabler whose utmost priority is making a contribution to the success of others.

McEwan's list is instructive for Christian school leaders, but the spiritual dimension of a Christian leader is noticeably missing, though points of intersection may occur in some of the traits she discusses. The Association of Christian Schools International (ACSI) is committed to developing highly effective leaders and schools along with ways to assess the performance of both. To that end, a "Matrix for Effectiveness" has been designed to communicate a high standard of excellence for member schools. Point one of this matrix states, "We believe that Christian schools exist to support parents in fulfilling their biblical responsibility to educate children. It is our intent not to define each school's philosophy but to provide a starting point, a framework consisting of five essential elements—truth, intellectual development, Christian educators, potential in Christ, and operational integrity—upon which a school can build and implement its own philosophy" (ACSI 2004).

The remainder of this book is crafted to assist all administrators in achieving the highest levels of effectiveness for God's glory as they lead their faculties to fulfill the sacred stewardship He has given them.

Notes

1. Thomas Sergiovanni has challenged educators to "change our metaphors" (1995). He writes, "Because traditional management theory does not work well in nonlinear and loosely structured situations or under conditions that require extraordinary commitment and performance, a great deal is at stake in developing a new and better-fitting theory. For this to happen, our metaphors for management, leadership, and schooling must change. Subsuming 'instructional delivery system' as a tactical option under the more encompassing and strategic 'learning community' is an important beginning. What would schools be like if community was indeed the metaphor of choice?" See chapter 6 in this text. For us we must ask, What would our schools look like if we used "Christian community" as our metaphor?

2. For additional information on the specifics of the Hawthorne studies, please go to one of these websites:

    http://www.revision-notes.co.uk/revision/795.html
    www.accel-team.com/motivation/hawthorne_02.html
    www.geocities.com/Athens/Forum/1650/hawthorneppt.htm
    http://www.library.hbs.edu/hc/wes/indexes/alpha/content/1001955886.html

3. For an interesting discussion on the varying influence these movements had on the development of supervision as opposed to the practices in administration, see "The Evolution of Clinical Supervision" in Edward Pajak's *Approaches to Clinical Supervision* (Norwood, MA: Christopher-Gordon, 1993).

II. The Helmsman as Administrator:
1 Corinthians 12:28

Designing Your School's Philosophy

Principle for Guiding Principals:

The effective administrator reflects on the importance of a special call to ministry, educational training and experience, and a correct philosophy of education and develops a clear articulation of the school's mission.

The administrator was new to the community and decided to take a sightseeing drive around the communities surrounding his new assignment. Nearby was a shopping center with a big-box store and a crowded parking lot. Not far from that block was a public school that appeared to have been built in the late 1970s and that was in need of renovation. Farther down the main road were the immaculate grounds of a popular golf course surrounded by the houses of many people who appeared to have the means to easily afford a private education. After a short drive, he made his way back to the campus by another route that included a neighborhood of families living in small brick homes that were prevalent after World War II. These ranch-style homes were well maintained for the most part, but whether their owners could afford a quality education was a question that nagged at his heart along with questions about how best to communicate to families who do not have significant means the importance of making the sacrifice to enroll their children in a Christian school. Throughout his prayer walk around his new surroundings, the new leader passed a wide variety of churches representing many denominations. Could he join hands with the families who worshiped the Lord in these local congregations to assist them in training their children? He knew that it was paramount to discover the answers to these questions.

Approaching the topic of philosophy can be both confusing and intimidating. The background of the word *philosophy* indicates that it means "love of wisdom," which starts you in the right direction. But you might feel as if you just stepped off the edge of a pool into very deep water that you were not prepared for. So maybe it is best to start at the other end and wade in.

On your way to the other end, you pass some marks indicating the depth of the challenge: What is truth? What is real? And what is beauty? Still too deep? Just keep going to the steps that allow you to wade into this discussion. Here you see the question, What are the beliefs, convictions, or ideas you base your life and ministry on? Consider the broad principles in your life that influence the everyday decisions that you make. For some, this time of reflection will be much like an inexperienced swimmer needing some coaching in the basics and some practice time alone in the pool to prepare for deeper waters.

For a Christian educator, there are several basic concepts, which some call *core values*, that strongly influence every dimension of one's decision making. The answer to the foundational philosophical question, What is truth? is that it is God's Holy Word. His Word becomes the source from which the leader can receive inspiration and guidance as he or she develops the remainder of his or her philosophy. Let's wade out a little deeper and apply this philosophical insight in an examination of the philosophies of three of the "fathers" of education as we know it today. The central point in looking briefly at these educators is to recognize that, without an unerring allegiance to God's Word, even the good intentions of a well-meaning educator become quickly misguided and corrupted.

Three well-known educators—Johann Amos Comenius, Horace Mann, and John Dewey—serve to illustrate the interrelation of faith, philosophy, and educational psychology. Before these three are examined, it will be helpful to frame the discussion by briefly examining three verses of Scripture:

> Behold, children are a gift of the Lord, The fruit of the womb is a reward. (Psalm 127:3, NASB)

People were bringing little children to Jesus to have him touch them.... "Let the little children come to me." (Mark 10:13–16)

Fathers, do not exasperate your children; instead, bring them up in the training and instruction of the Lord. (Ephesians 6:4)

Long before the permissive, child-centered thinking of our day, King Solomon wrote of the special "gift" our children are and that the Creator of the universe has carefully chosen to bless each household where He places these children. We are not to view children as the center of our world but as a special reward given to us as a part of our stewardship with the Designer and Sustainer. Jesus called His disciples to bring the little ones to Him. Should we do any less? Paul reminds us that we are to care for and nurture the children in our care. Unlike educators who have touted care and compassion to the exclusion of boundaries and correction, the apostle challenges educators and parents to make biblical standards the focus of our educational philosophy.

Johann Amos Comenius

Johann Amos Comenius (1592–1670) was the first proponent of many educational concepts that are customary in modern classroom instruction today across our country and around the world. Despite his strong Christian convictions and appreciation for biblical truth, many secular educators refer to him as the Father of Modern Education. Comenius was born on March 28, 1592, in Moravia, which is now in the modern-day Czech Republic. The name *Comenius* is Latin, the original language in which he wrote. His family name is Komensky in their native language. He grew up as a part of the Unity of the Brethren, a small Protestant denomination. Religious persecution and political wars (such as the Thirty Years' War) forced him to move from Moravia to Poland. Continued political and religious unrest then caused him to relocate to England, Prussia, and the Netherlands. Though there are no documents to confirm the fact, it has been stated that Comenius was offered the first presidency of Harvard College.

Comenius wrote extensively about methodologies and developmental concepts that are still significant today. He described the importance of a child's developmental readiness for learning and the importance of sequencing material in ways that are organized for each stage of development. He also argued that teaching and learning should proceed slowly and not be forced or hurried. His book *Orbis Pictus*, the World in Pictures, is believed to be one of the first textbooks for young readers that included pictures and illustrations (Gutek 2000, 51–52). His methodologies include the use of repetition and review, the practical application of subject content, the value of demonstration and direct observation, and the importance of integrating spiritual, philosophical, and scientific learning (Christian History Institute 1999).

Horace Mann

Two hundred years later, a second "father" who influences education today was born in Franklin, Massachusetts. Horace Mann (1796–1859) has been referred to as the Father of American Public Schools because of his influence on the philosophical and organizational foundations of our schools today. He had mastered the tenets of Calvinism by the age of ten but abandoned them for the liberal theology of Unitarianism at twenty-three. His community school curriculum, the *New England Primer*, the *Westminster Assembly Catechism*, and methodologies consisted mostly of recitation and memorization. His achievements as a lawyer, an educator, and a politician include becoming the first secretary of the Massachusetts Board of Education, establishing the first Normal School for Teachers in 1839, serving as the editor of *Common School Journal*, and serving as the president of Antioch College.

Mann brought increased public attention to the poor condition of school buildings, the low salaries of teachers, the limited scope of the curriculum, and the widespread delinquency of children in some neighborhoods. As he skillfully worked to build consensus for increasing taxes for these needed improvements, Mann built consensus among diverse groups by encouraging Protestants to accept the "morality" that would be taught while omitting the doctrines of Christianity (Gutek 2000, 103–107). The seeds of today's opposition to biblical teachings in our public schools were first sown by Horace Mann.

John Dewey

Another "father" who influenced the further removal of eternal truth from modern classrooms began approximately 100 years after Mann's influence. America's Father of Progressive Education, John Dewey (1859–1952), is the third example in our examination of the influence of philosophy on an educator's approach to education. Born and raised in Burlington, Vermont, Dewey, along with his family, attended a congregational church where his mother was especially active. His education at the University of Vermont and Johns Hopkins University, along with his interest in the writings of Charles Darwin, led to his philosophical identification with American pragmatists who argued that philosophy should deal with real human problems rather than metaphysical speculation. Dewey, therefore, rejected universal and eternal truths. "He believed that human beings can arrive at tentative warranted assertions. These assertions are developed as we test and verify our ideas by acting upon them to resolve problems" (Gutek 2000, 170).

Dewey is best known for the establishment of the Lab School at the University of Chicago from 1896 to 1904 as an experimental setting to test his ideas. Many of the following terms so prevalent in education today were first used at the Lab School: *child-centered education, self-expression, realizing potential, integrated curriculum, constructing knowledge, cooperative study groups, hands-on experience*, and *critical thinking* (Eakin 2000). In "Giants of American Education," an article by Sybil Eakin, one researcher comments about a time when Dewey was challenged about some of his students' apparent lack of basic skills: "Dewey seemed serenely unconcerned by doubts about his school's success in teaching basic skills. In 1896 he wrote, 'It is one of the great mistakes of education to make reading and writing constitute the bulk of the school work the first two years.' Claiming that language is 'the outgrowth of social activities' and 'the mean of social communication,' Dewey pointed out that traditional teaching of reading provides no stimulus for expression or communication."

James Wilhoit summarizes the significant impact that Dewey's educational philosophy had on shaping religious values:

> In essence, Dewey applied to education the tenets of several of the then fashionable schools of thought—pragmatism, thoroughgoing empiricism, and Darwinian evolutionism. Dewey himself was an open antagonist of supernaturalism. While he considered himself religious, his understanding of religion and divinity was vastly different from an orthodox understanding of the Christian faith. He dabbled in religion and religious education throughout his life and in the end developed his own peculiar and thoroughly "scientific" faith. His educational philosophy, however, is only incidentally connected to his religious views.
> (Anthony and Benson 2003, 344)

Jack Layman offers more detail about the destructiveness of Dewey's philosophy: "Dewey's obvious and immediate influence was on classroom methods, but his philosophical base was more significant. He rejected religion based on revelation, and he was strident in his denial of God, the Bible, or anything else that transcended the natural world. Religious values, he argued, are useful only if they arise from nature and are not attached to the existence of God or divine revelation; 'supernaturalism … stands in the way' of human progress (Dewey 1964, 80)" (Layman 2003, 38).

Table 3.1

Johann Amos Comenius	Father of Modern Education
Horace Mann	Father of American Public Schools
John Dewey	Father of Progressive Education

The School's Mission

In the life of the Christian educator, the realization that Christ is preeminent in all things (Colossians 1:18) means that the *Lordship of Christ is the foundation of every aspect of the school program.* Consistency is extremely important as each dimension is added. The school's founder (or founders) should be motivated by a special call, passion, or burden, such as a heartfelt compassion for the teenagers in a community who are apart from God and struggling with destructive influences in their lives. Such compassion may lead one or more leaders to begin a school that will be established on Christian principles but that will admit students who are not members of a church at the time of enrollment. In another case, the key leader (or leaders) of a school may have an awareness that the local school alternatives for children are detrimental to the healthy growth of Christian students and may choose to establish a school expressly for the discipleship of youth who already know the Lord. In another situation, a particular church may wish to strengthen Christian families who worship with their congregation and may choose to make membership in their church a prerequisite for admission. Certainly, there are pluses for each of these motivations, and many fine schools fall into each of these categories. However, the point here is that the initial reason or motivation for establishing the school is *influenced by the philosophy of the founder.* From the passion to create a school comes the hammering out of a mission statement. Such a statement must answer the basic questions, Who are we? Whom do we serve? What do we do?

Who Are We?
The answer to the first question, Who are we? must clearly articulate to someone unfamiliar with the school the identity of the group that establishes and maintains the school. Frequently the name of the school, such as First Baptist Academy, succinctly communicates this information. In other cases, the mission statement may include a phrase such as "a ministry of" a particular church or the phrase "a parent-run" school, to indicate that a group of parents from no specific church or denomination united to begin the school. (See table 3.2 for examples.)

Table 3.2

Burden/Passion/Need	Philosophy	Resulting Admission Requirements
Teens needing a Christian environment	Students can be saved in a learning environment	Admit unchurched families who agree to support the school's policies
Christian students struggling to grow as disciples	Students need a strong Christian peer group	Admit students from families who have at least one parent who is a believer
Young families in the local church body needing support in rearing their children	Family units and their children benefit from working in harmony with like-minded believers	Admit students from families who worship at their local church

Whom Do We Serve?

The second question of the mission statement, Whom do we serve? communicates to potential families the target audience for the ministry. Phrases that are typically used include "partnering with Christian families" or "committed to the discipleship" of students. Such statements appear to indicate that the school was created to minister to children of families who are already believers and in some cases even require that older students be able to express their Christian testimony. Other schools enthusiastically admit students who are not saved and/or who come from unchurched families, and express this in their mission statements by using phrases such as "salvation and discipleship" or "ministering to all families" in a particular geographic area. The efficacy of the position to admit students in the hope of evangelizing them or the position to minister to only church families is not at issue here. The point is that *one's passion for the existence of the school will be influenced by his or her philosophy concerning the students whom he or she wishes to minister to.* If it is not, then a disconnect occurs between the motivation for the founding of the school and the actual ministry it intends to carry out. In addition, the information about which grades are included in the school is very helpful.

To illustrate, a group of people once approached me about establishing a school in their community. They spoke of the heartbreak of teenagers who experience drug addictions, pregnancies out of wedlock, and sexually transmitted diseases; they spoke of rising crime in the community and a severe high school dropout rate. In general, they communicated that there was "a darkness that had settled" on their community. They spoke enthusiastically about including on their board a local pastor who had an evangelistic zeal. For the first founders' day celebration, one man mentioned a well-known preacher who would attend, and this leader shared his dream of seeing children and their families come to Christ. However, as we talked further, those in the group expressed their intention to admit only students from Christian families. I had to point out that there was a disconnect or apparent inconsistency between their motivation to begin their ministry and the clientele that they hoped to attract. Had they really considered who would actually be at their school activities? What would an unbeliever's expectations be for attending a Bible conference or a meeting with an evangelistic intent? In addition, during the first year of the school's existence, they planned to admit only students in grades nine through twelve. I pointed out that this was another inconsistency between their motivation for beginning the school and the students they wanted to minister to. They had not thought through the difficulty of wanting to conquer the prevalence of drugs, disease, and dropout rates by accepting at the school's inception older teenage students who had already established lifestyles and habits in conflict with the deepest burdens of the school's leaders. I suggested that they consider growing their traditions and standards by beginning with younger students and families, rather than trying to fight through the inevitable conflicts that come when a school admits large numbers of older students who have not been in a Christian school environment.

Though I have stated the previous warnings, I have observed that a leader's philosophy may be that a committed group of Christian administrators and faculty can overcome these obstacles by the strength and direction of the Holy Spirit. If that is the case, then admitting entire grade levels of students who have not previously been in a Christian school may be appropriate. One further comment is needed at this point. A genuine tragedy occurs when administrators admit students who, for whatever reason, do not meet the established admission requirements or in general do not fit with the school's mission statement but are allowed to attend because of the *school's financial needs*. This violation of the school's core values dooms the school from reaching its goals that are based on the third question (What do we do?).

Should we admit students who have a troubled past? This is a serious question that must be wrestled with by the leaders of every school. No matter what the standards for admission are, a clear response to this dilemma must be prayed about very thoroughly. Moving too quickly to rescue young people in difficult situations may overburden a faculty and administration that are not prepared to lend the needed support to the family and student. Fair or not, the reality is that a school can quickly gain a reputation in the community for being filled with students who are not qualified to attend other schools in the area. Such a perception can be managed, if not avoided altogether, if the administrator develops carefully worded procedures that lead to building up a family and a child in need without becoming detrimental to the child's peer group or the energies of the faculty.

A fourteen-year-old girl and her mother came to our school to admit the girl into the ninth grade. Both voiced their commitment to Christ, though they each admitted to a lack of obedience in certain areas. The young woman expressed her deep desire for a fresh start away from her current friends and bad habits. When I asked her to elaborate, she openly shared that she frequently cut class and would have difficulty breaking the habit if she continued in her present school. In addition, she tearfully described a recent stay in a local hospital's detox unit in an effort to break her addiction to alcohol—all of these things by the age of fourteen! I was moved by her candor and remorse, but how could I be assured of her sincerity and her willingness to do what was necessary to allow the Holy Spirit to work in her life while the faculty discipled this young Christian?

Following our established procedures, I requested that she write a 250-word essay stating why she wanted to attend our Christian school. Since this was an unusual situation, I presented her with a difficult challenge: Would she meet with an admissions committee consisting of teachers who would be her ninth-grade instructors and give her testimony and answer questions? (This meeting is a part of written policy and procedures.) I will never forget this young teenager's courage as she bravely expressed her regrets for her recent sins and her desire for a change in her life—all of this in front of five adults whom she had never met. The committee voted to admit her on probation for one quarter, an option in our admissions procedures. I am delighted to report that she became a B honor-roll student that year and committed only one minor discipline-related violation during the entire school year. May God receive all the glory! Below is the note she wrote to me in a card to express her appreciation:

Dear Mr. Coley:

I wanted to thank you for everything you've given me. At my interview, the first time we met, I was almost positive that you wouldn't accept me into your school because of my past history. But I was wrong. Other schools would have turned me down for sure, thinking I would bring a bad name for them and influence their kids.

At your school, I've learned a lot of things. I've learned about pride, honor, respect, and God. Those things I will carry on for the rest of my life, and I thank you and all my teachers. I'm going to be proud to say I graduated and that you were my principal.

In the next three years that I go to your school, I'm sure there will be many doors opening for me so I may learn more, and I can't wait!

I just wanted to say thank you, and I appreciate how you don't look at kids' past records, even though they may be long and great. You have a great gift that God gave you. God bless.

You Take the Helm

Make a list of procedures that you and your staff can follow to ensure the orderly admission of students who are qualified for a particular type of school. How can you avoid upheaval and hard feelings, while at the same time be able to step out in faith to share Christ's grace and mercy with those in need?

What Do We Do?

Most school leaders today have spent time intently meditating on God's Word during the process of answering the question, What do we do? Many conclude that the most significant accomplishment the school can make in the lives of its students is to train them to think and live in a way that reflects the influence of Scripture and the Holy Spirit in their lives. For that reason, schools include phrases such as "biblical worldview" or "Christian worldview." These are certainly appropriate goals when we consider the mandate given to us in Deuteronomy: "Love the Lord your God with all your heart and with all your soul and with all your strength" (6:5). Other educators wish to include an emphasis on making an impact on more than just the child's intellectual development. They often reflect on Luke 2:52, which says, "Jesus grew in wisdom and stature, and in favor with God and men." This conviction may be articulated by using phrases such as "ministering to the whole child" or "the growth of the student academically, physically, spiritually, and socially." Other broad educational purposes can include the desire to prepare students for ministry to the community or in the Body of Christ. In addition, many schools include the intention to prepare students for their pursuit of college or a vocation.

Figure 3.1 summarizes the relationship between the influence of a person's philosophy, the unique motivation one has to participate in the creation of a Christian school, and the development of the school's mission statement.

Figure 3.1

| A special burden, passion, or call to ministry in Christian education | + | The influence of the person's philosophy | → | The development of a more precise or focused statement that defines the who, the what, and the why in ministry |

You Take the Helm

Has the Lord placed a special desire in your life to minister to a particular group of people, or has He perhaps given you a special burden (or responsibility) to teach students with unique needs? If so, begin now to fashion a mission statement for your career. Can you identify verses of Scripture that give you a biblical underpinning for your life's direction?

Developing Educational Goals

Flowing logically from the school's mission statement is a set of educational goals that give a general direction to the development of the school's curriculum. (The specifics of curriculum development will be described in chapter 5.) These goals are broad, not limited to a particular time frame for completion, and not worded in such a way that the assessment of the statement is easily measured. They are, in fact, general statements of what the school seeks to accomplish as it carries out its mission statement in light of its intended community. For instance, as a Christian school desires to prepare students for participation in the life of the Body of Christ, it may focus on music training so that students can effectively participate in a variety of musical activities in worship. Many schools wish to emphasize the preparation for serving Christ around the world, and in doing so develop educational goals regarding foreign language or participation in international mission trips. As a part of preparing students for college, educational leaders also develop goals for the preparation and presentation of advanced placement courses.

As these goals are developed, another dimension of philosophy comes into play—a leader's philosophy of education, or in other words, what the person believes about teaching and learning. If we return to our swimming pool analogy in the beginning of this chapter, complete answers to questions that arise at this point require thorough research in the deep water of educational theory and hours of practice to establish consistency throughout the school program. For example, the question, What do you believe about the learner? is a critical piece to a philosophy of education.

Educator and author Janet Lowrie Nason recounts a conversation with another Christian that began with the question, What is Christian education? Nason responded:

> It is the Holy Spirit directing a born-again teacher to meet the needs of a learner. When that learner is also a believer, the Holy Spirit in the life of the learner works in dynamic interaction to apply and relate truth. We maximize Christian education when the teacher and learner are both believers, clean channels for the Holy Spirit and depend on Him for direction. The exciting reality in Christian education recognizes that the teaching and learning process works in reverse! The Holy Spirit may direct a student to make a comment or a point that meets the need of the teacher. Christian education takes place when the Holy Spirit activates the teaching and learning process, regardless of the subject. (2002, 5)

Nason's response powerfully illustrates the relationship between her spiritual convictions and her philosophy of teaching and learning. However, we conclude this portion of our discussion with a strong challenge from Jack Layman, professor at Columbia International University and former member of the executive board of ACSI: "Educational philosophy has degenerated into a smorgasbord of conflicting speculations and a shift of focus from metaphysics to methodology. Most public educators cannot articulate their philosophy clearly because they are not sure what it is. Christian educators, however, need to be able to understand, articulate, and apply a biblical philosophy of education. The Christian school movement will thrive or fail to the extent that they do" (2003, 49). What do you believe about the God-given uniqueness of each child He has created? Perhaps the following discussion will help you articulate your beliefs.

Helping Students Discover Their Unique Gifts

The Gold Rush was a fascinating and exciting time in our nation's history. During this period of westward expansion, prospectors moved to the West and risked everything, including their lives, for the opportunity to discover gold hidden in the earth. They spared no effort and gave themselves fully for just the prospect of success. History tells us that many miners in the last century died empty-handed despite their best efforts; there simply was not any treasure.

As Christian educators, are we convinced that God has placed special treasure within each student? Are we as passionate to discover the precious talents that have significance for God's kingdom as the prospectors were to discover gold? Several passages in the New Testament inspire us to focus on helping students discover their God-given talents.

Ephesians 2:10 assures us of the unique giftedness of each child: "For we are God's workmanship." The word *workmanship*, which can also be translated as "craftsmanship," comes from the Greek word *poiema*, which gives us our English word *poetry*. Imagine the potential outcomes if a Christian educator views each child as God's poetry! The verse goes on to say that we are "created in Christ Jesus to do good works, which God prepared in advance for us to do." His Word gives us a much-needed reminder that each child is a special creation of our Lord and that He has a plan for each one. Your part in His design is to help these young saints get started today! Why wait?

Romans 12:6 points out the uniqueness of each child and his or her giftedness. Are we careful to celebrate the contributions of each student? Do some students feel that what they have to offer is insignificant or even unwanted?

A passage in 1 Corinthians 12 directs our thinking to the purpose of each child's gifts. While many people in our culture teach children to make the most of their talents for the advancement of their own careers, the acquisition of material possessions, and the guarantee of future security, verse 7 reminds us: "Now to each one the manifestation of the Spirit is given for the common good." Ephesians 4:16 echoes this concept of each child being trained to serve the Body of Christ: "The whole body, joined and held together by every supporting ligament, grows and builds itself up in love, as each part does its work." Each teacher and administrator is an instrument of God for training these parts of our Lord's Body—His Church.

Christian educators who are committed to teaching for the Master will want to be actively involved in helping each student discover his or her unique gifts. In their book *A Vision with a Task: Christian Schooling for Responsive Discipleship*, Gloria Stronks and Doug Blomberg refer to this activity of Christian school teachers as "unwrapping students' gifts" and explain that it must take place if Christian schools are going to be communities that produce students who are "responsive disciples" (1993, 16).

Through several vital activities, administrators and teachers can cooperate to make this a reality.

Once a school is committed to helping students unwrap their gifts, the Holy Spirit will give the administrators and teachers a new vision for schoolwide plans that will make an impact on individual students. Chapel leaders can use times of worship and Bible teaching to emphasize the importance of the Scriptures related to this issue. Curriculum planners should examine all aspects of the school's goals and objectives to identify ways to build these concepts into the curriculum at all grade levels. For example, students should examine the lives of men and women from diverse backgrounds who have overcome obstacles and been used by God in a variety of ways. As these studies take place, students can be challenged to investigate fields of study and careers that interest them.

Traditionally, Christian schools excel in extracurricular activities such as athletics and music. I was blessed to lead a faculty that had an ongoing commitment to find an activity for every student to explore areas of interest outside the classroom. Such exploration is especially important at the middle-school level. We established intramural teams without holding tryouts and actively encouraged participation. New performing arts groups, such as a mime troupe, were developed. Training for ministry and service was offered in areas of need such as sign language. God blessed us by allowing us to watch the blossoming of future church leaders during their formative years.

Classroom teachers have the best opportunity of all to stimulate the discovery of unique gifts by creating a classroom environment in which students know they are accepted and respected by both their teacher and their classmates. In such an atmosphere, students know they are appreciated for who they are and feel encouraged to attempt new experiences. In a classroom where the teacher is committed to unwrapping gifts, students feel comfortable taking new risks without fear of failure. Every adult can probably recall the fear of being ridiculed by classmates. All teachers should ask themselves, Do my students have the opportunity to try something new and fail without fearing the results?

All teachers should look for ways to encourage students, particularly when they struggle academically. As an English teacher, I tried to see how many different ways students could engage their own interests and abilities as we studied Shakespeare. The following are just a few of the projects I used: memorizing and reciting lines, planning stage directions, painting props, designing costumes, building a model of the Globe Theatre, reporting on medieval weapons, sketching examples of Tudor architecture, and discussing critical reviews of performances from different time periods. Through these experiences, students not only learned to enjoy the playwright and his works, but they also discovered something about their own abilities and learned to appreciate the unique talents of their classmates.

Following this approach to learning does not mean omitting uniform academic standards, nor does it imply a lessening of discipline requirements. However, an excessive emphasis on test scores or exceptional competition for grades can be extremely discouraging for students whose gifts do not lie in these areas.

The Lord has given each of us a special stewardship to bring out the best in our students, and the Holy Spirit promises to direct us. Perhaps God is calling you to start a gold rush in your school—there's treasure in those children!

Have You Articulated What Is Most Important?

Now that you have been challenged to reflect on your call, your training, and your philosophy, consider vehicles that will assist you in communicating your mission. Review the following symbols that are common in Christian schools today and consider adopting something similar at your school:

Using Symbolism to Express Your Philosophy		
Symbolism can be a powerful tool to communicate vital aspects of your school's philosophy.		
School Name	**Mascot and Scripture**	**Color and Meaning**
Southside Christian	Centurion—Ephesians 2:10, NASB	Garnet (changed by Christ's blood) Gold (living to produce eternal treasure)
Northside Christian	Knights—Ephesians 6:11	Blue (baptism) Gold (refining) White (purity)
Eastside Christian	Eagle—Isaiah 40:31	Purple (justification) Green (sanctification) White (glorification)

You Take the Helm

Select one of the schools listed on the previous page and reflect on the way Scripture and colors represent important spiritual values. Next, consider how you would communicate these concepts in the life of the school (hint: publications, public meetings).

Establishing Your School's Governance

Principle for Guiding Principals:

An effective administrator establishes healthy, productive working relationships with others involved in school governance in order to maintain a harmonious school climate.

The young administrator suddenly realized that things had gone terribly wrong. How else could he explain what he was observing and hearing: well-trained educators who appeared to have lost their confidence and mature Christians who had suppressed anger and frustration about his predecessor? As he listened carefully, he became aware that the previous administrator had broken their spirit, had isolated the teachers from one another, and had convinced the staff that the board was on his side. Meanwhile, this false shepherd had manipulated the board into following his self-centered plans. What remained upon his resignation was a fractured group of teachers and a school board that was out of touch with the organization it was supposedly caring for. The school's new leader turned to Scripture and the school's organizational documents for insight about the situation and the way he should proceed …

Numerous passages of Scripture can serve to inspire everyone involved with developing and maintaining the governance of a sound organization. Though Paul is specifically discussing worship in the well-known 1 Corinthians 14 passage, his words of exhortation can be extended to the management of all ministries: "God is not a God of disorder but of peace" (v. 33). "Everything should be done in a fitting and orderly way" (v. 40). The tedious tasks of establishing and implementing sound policies are vital for the healthy existence of any organization, but especially for Christian ministry—the target of Satan's schemes and individual agendas that derail meaningful work.

So why not just have one well-trained, gifted administrator who is responsible for the oversight of the school? Ecclesiastes 4:12 is a good place to start when answering this question. The Teacher says: "Though one may be overpowered, two can defend themselves. A cord of three strands is not quickly broken." Another helpful passage is in Proverbs 15:22. Solomon says: "Plans fail for lack of counsel, but with many advisers they succeed."

The instruction in Hebrews 13:17 is crucial for all those involved in Christian education, from the youngest student all the way to the most experienced administrator: "Obey your leaders and submit to their authority. They keep watch over you as men who must give an account. Obey them so that their work will be a joy, not a burden, for that would be of no advantage to you."

The theme that runs through each of these passages is the divine order that God established so that people can work and serve together harmoniously in complex organizations. Several principles are a part of this design. First, those who are more mature in their faith are charged with the responsibility to guide those who are less mature. Second, the Lord uses different men and women in unique ways to communicate insights into the most appropriate course of action in uncertain times.

Third, a team of faithful overseers is far stronger than one individual standing alone. Fourth, everyone involved in a Christian school must be accountable to other godly people who participate in the evaluation of every dimension of the organization, including the board's evaluation of itself and its members.

In addition to these biblical standards, there are legal requirements that exist for schools that wish to pursue incorporation. The primary advantages that incorporation offers are the ability to pursue tax-exempt status, known as 501(c)(3), with the Internal Revenue Service and the limiting of personal liability if the school is sued for any reason. Ralph Mawdsley (1995, 98), a professor of administration at Cleveland State University and former vice president of human resources at Liberty University, states that there are five minimum responsibilities for board members:

1. To attend meetings of the board and committees
2. To examine financial statements of the institutions
3. To acquire working knowledge of institutional policies
4. To make inquiries
5. To discharge responsibilities in a reasonable, prudent, and informed manner

Organizational Structure

Three Models of School Governance

At this point, we will examine various organizational structures or models that represent how lines of authority are established. James W. Deuink is an experienced administrator and author who has written widely in this area. He was an administrator for ten years and is dean of the School of Education at Bob Jones University. He has developed three general models, one of which will describe most schools. These are for an independent school, a church school, and a church-related school.

Independent school. Until the surge in the growth of the Christian school movement in the 1960s, most private schools were organized as independent parent-oriented schools—that is, they were conceived, developed, financed, and controlled primarily by groups of parents interested in the training of their children. Most such schools function independently of any other institution.

Almost without exception, these schools are organized as nonprofit educational institutions. As a result, they enjoy a number of benefits that work for their stability and growth. Since gifts to them are tax deductible, it is easy to develop the donor constituency that is essential for their development and survival. Furthermore, they are not required to pay corporate income taxes, real estate taxes, federal excise tax on gasoline, or state sales taxes in most states. These factors work together to present the most favorable income and expense picture possible.

Independent schools are operated by boards that are usually dominated by parents.

Figure 4.1

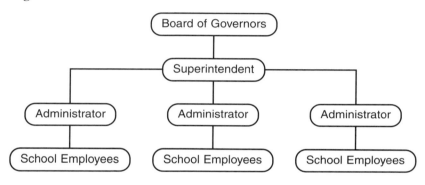

Church school. The same benefits of tax exemption that accrue to the independent school apply equally to the church school. Many schools are established because of a passionate vision of a church pastor or leader. In many cases, this visionary leader is led to inspire others in the congregation to see the benefit of housing the school in their church buildings. (The positive as well as the negative results of this approach will be discussed in chapter 10, "Finance and Facilities.") Research involving members of the Southern Baptist Association of Christian Schools states that 88 percent of those polled are located in local church facilities and 77 percent are not separately incorporated. One primary motivation for this form of governance is the strong concern that the policies, procedures, and practices of their school stay closely tied to the standards and values of the founding congregation. The oft-quoted expression associated with this concern is that "the tail will not wag the dog."

Table 4.1

> The Southern Baptist Association of Christian Schools (SBACS) collected the data below from a survey of pastors and administrators that was conducted at the annual meeting in 1997.
>
> Three characteristics concerning governance of member Southern Baptist schools emerged from the survey:

1. Member schools maintain close ties with a local church:
- 92 percent of the schools were founded by a single church.
- 88 percent meet in the buildings of the church that founded them.
- 77 percent are not incorporated separately but are included in the church's incorporation.

2. The governing body (board, trustees, committee) of the school is connected to a local church:
- 87 percent of the schools' governing bodies are selected by the churches' deacon boards.
- 92 percent of the schools have the church's pastor as ex officio member of the board or the pastor has some involvement.
- 85 percent of the schools' governing bodies are made up of church members only.

3. The governing bodies limit their involvement in school affairs to major/board issues:
- The oversight body most frequently is involved with policy formation and financial matters.
- These bodies less frequently are involved in teacher/pupil interviews, curriculum, textbook selection, and major discipline problems.

Implications

The survey results point to the significant role that pastors have in the founding of Christian schools. Because of their active involvement and the close relationship that these schools have with local churches, pastors need to network with other pastors to encourage each other. The leadership of the pastors is key to the continued growth and success of Southern Baptist schools.

The development of professional administrators is also vitally important. The pastors and church boards/committees cannot micromanage their growing schools, in addition to the pastor's leadership. "It's the *principal* of the thing."

A typical approach taken by a church that founds a school and keeps it under its authority would be to create a school committee in much the same way other committees in the church are created. Some churches have a special group called the nominating committee that is charged with the responsibility of staffing church committees. But some congregations leave that responsibility to the pastor and/or staff. The school committee will then do its work under the supervision of a church staff member. For example, a church with an extensive recreation program will establish a group of lay leaders who work with a church staff member to oversee the programs related to recreational ministries.

However, given the unique responsibilities that this committee will be challenged to shoulder, serious consideration should be given to the distinctions between a school committee and a church committee, and corresponding adjustments must be made. First, the typical annual rotation of committee members or its chair should be changed to allow for long terms of participation to ensure continuity of leadership. Second, the school's executive officer should be an ex officio member of the committee and should report directly to the church pastor. Having the school's day-to-day director report to another staff member other than the senior pastor is a governance structure that creates distance between the founding church's chief executive and the school's appointed leader. Their working relationship must be harmonious for a variety of reasons. A school that is well managed and that effectively ministers to the community could quickly enroll a student body that is larger than the church's active membership and could collect tuition receipts that exceed the church's budget.

The possibility of a sizeable school bank account leads to a third distinction between a school committee and other typical church committees. The monies collected from families for tuition and other fees in addition to contributions made by individuals specifically for school use must be carefully recorded. Though the church may perceive that it owns the school and all its assets, the director and the school committee must be able to report with absolute integrity that all the tuition money that was collected was used for the education of their children. It is generally understood that the school will set aside an appropriate amount for such line items as utilities, maintenance, and debt retirement. However, if all receipts were merely dumped into the same bucket as Sunday's collection, resulting in the commingling of funds, such close accounting would be impossible.

A fourth critical distinction needs to be stated. This school committee will be charged with the oversight of professional educators and must enact policies that reflect this recognition. For instance, the facilities committee will provide oversight of hourly employees who will probably not be receiving the same benefits as the school's college graduates. The nonteaching, nonpastoral employees of the church will likewise not accrue sick leave and professional leave in the same way, nor will there be the same level of concern for continuing education and the maintenance of professional certifications. The failure to consider these differences when developing policies would be extremely detrimental to staff morale and church/school relations.

Table 4.2

	Professional Employees	Hourly Employees
Work Agreement	Contract	At-will
Health Insurance	Same coverage	Same coverage
Retirement	Typical, including matching	Nontypical
Personal Leave	2 days/year	Vacation time
Sick Leave	Granted in contract	If granted, usually accrued per month
Vacation	Granted in contract	Earned for time served
Pay Increases	Basis for increases include education, length of service, cost of living allowance	Increments used tied to length of service

Figure 4.2 Church-Run School (Same Corporation)

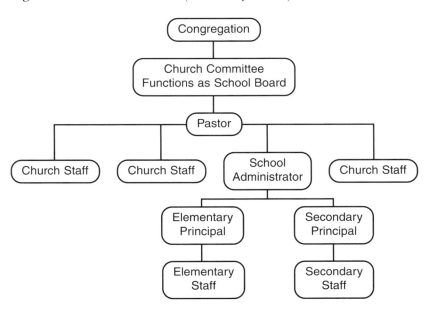

Church-related school. A few church schools have been organized as separate legal entities. In the years to come, we would probably be better off if all Christian schools were incorporated separately. James Deuink, author of *Management Principles for Christian Schools*, advises that it is best for all new schools to be organized as separate legal entities. Churches with existing schools should consider restructuring their schools to give them their own legal identity. This can be done without surrendering any control over them (1996, 41–43). Agreeing with Deuink, I would like to propose an organizational structure that allows the church and the school to stay inextricably intertwined while allowing for the complexities of an educational ministry that is unlike other church-run activities. At the outset, the congregation officially establishes a group of individuals to serve as the corporation, which will become the corporate head of a nonprofit 501(c)(3) corporation that is separate from the church's legal entity. The obvious question then would be, How can the pastor and other leaders ensure that the new ministry that the church has birthed will remain faithful to the founding congregation? That can be accomplished by selecting a group of church members who are willing to "wear two hats"—to love both their church and the school. An ideal concept is to ask an existing group such as the board of deacons or the trustees to serve in a dual capacity as the corporation of the school.

The corporation would serve in an advisory capacity as it oversees major tasks such as the election of a school board, the selection of the school's chief executive, and any changes to the bylaws. In most cases, the corporation would only need to meet semiannually to receive a report from the chair of the school board, to reelect existing board members or select new ones, and to ask any questions it may have about the major issues such as finances.

The business of overseeing the church's school would then be left to the school board, which functions as the policy governing entity of the school. In a manner of speaking, the school and its affairs are then one giant step removed from the affairs of the church. The genius of this approach is that it prevents a collection of well-meaning parents and faculty (all of whom could be church members) from showing up at a church business meeting and voting for their beloved teachers to receive a handsome pay increase! If such a motion were made, the moderator would be obligated to lovingly, but firmly, rule the motion out of order and refer the matter to the school board for consideration at its next meeting. Figure 4.3 illustrates the organizational structure for this model.

Figure 4.3 Church-Related School (The church and school are separately incorporated.)

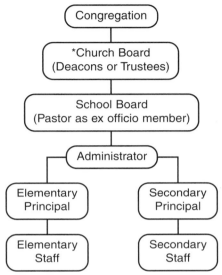

* Note: The congregation establishes the new corporation that in turn is responsible for the selection of the school board and the school's administrator.

Schools choosing to incorporate separately from the church will need to find out what the state's requirements are. The typical articles of incorporation will include the following:

Legal name of the school
Period of operation (usually perpetual)
Purpose for which it was organized
Definition of members (voting and nonvoting)
Makeup of the corporation or board
Debt obligations and personal liability
Distribution of profits: distribution of assets on termination of operation
Initial registered agent and office address
Procedure for amending the articles
Initial board of directors

Note: It is vital that those involved in forming a corporation understand that this list is only a generic, general set of examples. Legal requirements vary from state to state.

In addition, the directors or trustees will need to create the school's constitution and bylaws. These documents include the following:

The governance organization
Makeup of the board, description of its functions, list of officers, selection process
Job description and title of the executive officer
Additional administrative positions
General description of personal and professional qualifications of the teaching staff, along with hiring and dismissal procedures
Committees: creation, functioning, and termination of the board's committees
Meetings: the process for calling an official meeting and definition of quorum
Additional operating procedures (reference to the operating procedures manual)
Procedures for amending bylaws

You Take the Helm

Imagine that a church group has contacted you to assist them in establishing a Christian school, including creating the articles of incorporation. Create the articles of incorporation. ACSI's *School Articles of Incorporation and Bylaws* would be a helpful resource in creating these. Check with the secretary of state where you live and verify what needs to be included. Be sure to design an organizational model for the school's governance. If possible, ask an attorney to look over your work.

The Delicate Balance: The Role of the Board

John Schimmer, author of *Board Governance: Understanding the Roles and Responsibilities of Christian School Board Members*, states, "For generations citizens have struggled to distinguish between the authority of the board and the authority of the administration. When consulting with administrators and board members, I have found considerable consternation over authority and roles. Administrators believe that the board is either too involved in the day-to-day operations of the school or that it fails to give sufficient leadership, especially in policy development, fund-raising, and planning. Board members express frustration over lengthy board meetings and the lack of appropriate information and administrative responsiveness to parental concerns" (2004, 21).

Before we view several lists of traditional board responsibilities, it is helpful to consider the succinct phrasing of several experienced authors. David Hubbard, president of Fuller Seminary, describes the activities of board members as that of "governors, sponsors, ambassadors, and consultants" (Schimmer 2002, 21). Sandra Hughes, Berit Lakey, and Marla Bobowick, authors of *The Board Building Cycle*, summarize a board's primary functions as "setting the direction, ensuring resources, and providing oversight" (2000, 1). John and Miriam Carver, authors of *Reinventing Your Board*, state that the board "defines, delegates, and monitors" (1997, 2). Daniel Vander Ark, the former executive director of Christian School International, further reduces the job description to two activities: to govern and to sell. He expands on these concepts by adding that the board's responsibility is "preserving the heritage, auditing the present, and planning the future" (Schimmer 2004, 5).

In the *Nonprofit Board Answer Book*, Robert Andringa and Ted Engstrom present a powerful and profound metaphor that helps clarify the role of the board and its members. They say to think of each board member as having three hats (1997, 4):

1. *Governance hat:* Worn only when the full board meets, proper notice has been given, and a quorum is present.
2. *Implementation hat:* Worn only when the board gives one or more board members authority to implement a board policy.
3. *Volunteer hat:* Worn at all other times, when board members are involved with organizational activities as volunteers.

One Voice

Perhaps the most critical concept that must be communicated is the importance of the board as a group with members who individually speak as "one voice." This requires that the board meet together regularly and pray earnestly for the power of the Holy Spirit to bring a spirit of oneness among the directors as they set policy and assess the progress of the school. Having served for a number of years on the board of governors of a local school, I have found that I do not consider myself "on the board" unless I am actually at a meeting fulfilling some duty that the board requested of me. When I meet new people and discuss the school, I do not mention that I am on the board. In other cases, when asked a question about the board and its decisions, I state only information that has already been publicly communicated by the board chair or our superintendent. John Schimmer expresses the urgency of this concept in these statements: "The board governs the organization when the trustees assemble in a legally constituted board meeting to debate issues, vote on motions, draft policies, determine goals, and plan for the future. When governing the organization, the board speaks with *one voice*, the only governance voice heard outside the boardroom" (2002, 21).

Robert Andringa and Ted Engstrom claim: "The most misunderstood and abused principle of governance is the requirement for group action. The chief executive and staff cannot serve two (or 22) masters. The full board sets policy, not individual board members who feel strongly about something and voice their opinions to the chief executive. Board members must be taught this principle, and staff must be reminded of it. Otherwise, confusion and conflict reign and board effectiveness is diminished" (1997, 5). Andringa, president of the Council for Christian Colleges and Universities in Washington, DC, presented fourteen responsibilities of school boards. See table 4.3.

Table 4.3 (Andringa 1998)

Basic Responsibilities of School Boards
1. Determine mission and basic values
2. Maintain board standing policies on all aspects of governance
3. Select a chief executive and hold accountable to policies
4. Support the chief executive and assess his or her performance
5. Ensure effective organizational planning
6. Approve the major goals/desired results—strategic plan
7. Ensure financial solvency and integrity
8. Approve, monitor, and strengthen the school's programs and services
9. Help represent the school externally
10. Ensure legal and ethical integrity and maintain accountability
11. Encourage/nurture chief executive and staff
12. Serve as the "final court of appeals" for unresolved internal disputes
13. Recruit and orient new board members
14. Evaluate and improve itself and the governing board

Table 4.4 Board and Staff Roles Worksheet

For each issue or task, indicate with the appropriate letter where your board is now and where it should be:

A. The board initiates and decides on its own (chief executive may implement)

B. The chief executive formally recommends and the board decides

C. The chief executive decides and/or acts after a consultation with the board members during or outside of normal board or committee meetings

D. The chief executive and/or the staff act on their own within previous board policies

Issues and Tasks	Is Now	Should Be
1. Mission statement for organization		
2. Formal annual goals and objectives		
3. Recruitment of new board members		
4. Board and committee structure		
5. Policies regarding board role and activities		
6. Hiring and salaries of staff other than chief executive		
7. Changes in bylaws to keep current		
8. Annual income and expense budget		
9. Budget amendments as required		
10. Capital expenditures		
11. Staff compensation policies		
12. Other personnel polices and practices		
13. Investment policies		
14. Arrangements for external audit		
15. Fund-raising plan and policies		
16. Adoption of new programs and services		
17. Termination of current programs or services		
18. Staff organizational structure		
19. Organization's insurance program		
20. Board meeting agendas		
21. Other		

James Deuink states the duties of the board somewhat differently (1996, 47):

Duties of the Christian School Board
1. Hold title to any property owned by the corporation (In a church school, this function will be performed by the church board of trustees.)
2. Employ personnel (In many schools this responsibility is delegated to the school administrator by the board under employment guidelines established by the board.)
3. Enter into contracts
4. Develop policy and approve policy with the guidance of the school administrator
5. Supervise the management of the financial resources
6. Formulate the master plan for the development of the ministry with the guidance of the school administrator

Table 4.5

You Take the Helm

Identify key board/governance issues that you find in the following email:

> Dr. Coley, right now you are probably thinking, "not him again." After you read the following question and concern, you could write a book on me. You will probably want to.
>
> The question and concern is another school matter. The sharing of space issue I believe I have under control. This other problem rests with the school board. Again, my strengths do not rest with school administration.
>
> The school administrator of our church has been here about twenty years. There have been two other education pastors before me during this twenty-year period. They both had frustrations with this administrator and left because of difficulties with her. This information is what I have been told by many people. I am trying to resolve this conflict by working with the school board to create harmony between the school and church.
>
> The existing school board does not function as I think it should. Please let me know if the following is the correct structure or format the school board should be following.

The school administrator has selected and appointed her own board members. These same members have been on board for many years, and she wishes they could remain for a few more years. The school administrator does not have a parent-teacher organization, so she uses the school board to create the fund-raisers and other fun activities that the school holds. The business side of the board is operated by the administrator herself.

Is this wrong, or am I wrong? Do you have a resource that would provide the specific functions of a Christian school board? I am thinking, Where is her accountability? She has no governing authority over me. Who decides her own salary? Does she? Could I be missing something, or is this a corrupt system that I have been thrown into? Along with the resources that I hope you can provide, I need your prayers. I have a desire to see the church run effectively. It is my responsibility to make the education side reach the community for Christ. How can I do this with an administrator who has placed herself on a pedestal?

I do apologize for disturbing you with this problem, but I know you can provide the resources that I need to resolve this.

Sample Board Agenda

I. Devotion:
- A Scripture passage that applies to Christian education
- Prayer, including specific issues or events and special needs in the school family

II. Reading of Minutes:
- A list of those present should be included
- Action items with the name of the person responsible should be highlighted
- Assume these documents will be referred to in the future

III. Finance Report: Compare year-to-date with budget

IV. Old Business:
- Any items previously tabled
- Updates for ongoing projects
- Committee reports

V. New Business:
- Board matters such as board policy, election of officers, selection of new directors, evaluation of administrator
- School policy issues under the board's responsibility
- Future plans, events, expenditures that need to be communicated by the administrator to the board

VI. Closing: A season of prayer

Note: The agenda needs to be prepared by the administrator or the board chair and distributed in advance. Members should understand that they must submit items for discussion in advance. Do *not* blindside the chair or administrator.

You Take the Helm

How would you respond to this email from a first-year administrator?

Things are going well in general. I'm still extremely busy, but you already know that. As the only administrator, I stay quite busy with day-to-day things (discipline, teacher needs, parent concerns, etc.). At the same time, I have been trying to make strides on more strategic levels. We need more space immediately, but we are also trying to decide the best way to organize for the future (whether to be church-run, church-related, or interdenominational).

We are also refocusing at the foundational level as we prepare for the next school year. I proposed a philosophy of education statement that the school committee has adopted. They've gone sixteen years without a clear philosophy, so this is a critical step. This sets the stage for other policy changes to follow, namely, an admissions policy and procedure. Our student body is nearly 50 percent non-Christian/unchurched, and I think that is an insecure foundation to grow on.

There are countless things going on, but these are some of the highlights. I have a great staff. They pray for me regularly, and God has been gracious to answer their prayers. Talk to you soon.

Curriculum Leadership

Principles for Guiding Principals:

The effective administrator leads the school and community in a never-ending "curriculum dialogue" in an effort to meet all students' needs and reveal God's truth in the school's curriculum.

The effective administrator seeks to expand the spectrum of students who can be successfully ministered to by the faculty and the school community.

Accreditation! Everyone wants to talk accreditation with the new administrator. From previous experiences, she has a checklist of major categories that would be the major areas of emphasis. She knew the governance dimension needed some improvement, but the board had done an excellent job developing the school's primary statements and documents. The faculty was up-to-date on certification requirements, and the facilities were receiving some much-needed attention. Then she thought of curriculum ... Had this school developed its own? The leader remembered seeing rows of curriculum resource guides from the very best Christian publishers lined up on the resource-room shelves. But did writers from other states who have different experiences understand the needs of her children from this neighborhood? Had key instructional leaders in the past analyzed their program and considered the unique needs of this community in light of the school's commitments and philosophy of education? She certainly needed to find out.

The Helmsman

Imagine the following scene: It is a cool morning. You can smell the fallen leaves, feel a brisk breeze, and see the sun glistening on the dew. A coach is calling his thinly clad runners together for final instructions concerning the course they are about to run. They are advised about the many twists and turns involved in the circuit and the location of their destination. Soon the cross-country athletes disappear into the forest a few hundred yards away from the starting line. Their 3.1-mile journey (5 kilometers) will not be easy. They will not all stay together, but hopefully each member of the squad will complete the course. Coaches and volunteers along the way will offer encouragement, announce lapsed-time information, and supervise the runners to make sure each stays on the trail. Some will run in groups of two or three, others alone at a faster or slower pace. But no one is allowed to chart his or her path through the woods. The goal for each team is not to have the top finisher but to have all runners run their best times and finish the race. Such a picture is an apt metaphor for curriculum leadership today because of the complexity of the demands of the community (different terrains), the requirement for perseverance for all involved (the challenging distance), and the need for the participation of many (both runners and coaches, students and teachers).

Nearly all scholarly discussions about curriculum begin with a reference to the etymology of the word and its use at the Roman Colosseum. Its Latin root *currere* referred to the course or track—the curriculum—that the chariots raced around. It had a prescribed beginning, circuit, and finish line. However, I think the picture of a cross-country event is more fitting for a look at the word and its use in the twenty-first century, as opposed to the oval track found in most high school stadiums today. The cross-country comparison highlights what most instructional leaders have already discovered: today's plan or program for a school's learning experience is complex, varied, and difficult to define as opposed to the quarter-mile track that is smooth, consistent, and visible at a glance. And the skills needed to develop and supervise a school's curriculum are equally complex and demanding. Even the mere definition of *curriculum* is disputed in our day. Depending on one's school of thought or theoretical approach, an educator may view curriculum as something that can be clearly defined and organized or an educator may view it much more broadly to incorporate the host of unplanned learning experiences that students have at school. Peter Oliva goes so far as to argue that, like Bigfoot, Sasquatch, and the Loch Ness Monster, no one has ever actually captured "curriculum" (1997, 3). Or have they?

Every summer, many report with complete confidence that they know it's there. They can even tell you when it arrives. Can't you hear it? The distinctive sound of a delivery truck—beep, beep, beep—backing up. The ground shakes from the thud of a massive box as it falls off the tailgate onto the loading dock. If I'm not mistaken, I believe many administrators would call that a curriculum experience, one that has been purchased, packaged, and delivered from curriculum designers who are far away and unfamiliar with the unique mission and direction of their schools. Derek Keenan, vice president of academic affairs at the Association of Christian Schools International, provides a definition of *curriculum* that helps to clarify this confusion: "Curriculum is the planned instructional program that is to be delivered to students." Keenan argues that textbooks "can be regarded as a moderately useful tool for designing curriculum," but they "should not be seen as the source of everything taught in the classroom" (1998, 8). In *The Curriculum Connection: Building Biblical Principles into a Quality Academic Program*, Gregory Meeks points out, "However, many schools limit their curriculum development to the efforts of a textbook adoption committee, whose sole responsibility is to review and select commercially available textbooks to be used the following school year. It is important that the Christian school's philosophy, mission, and learner goals (sometimes known as schoolwide learning expectations) filter down and permeate the curriculum. The textbook-adoption-committee approach to curriculum development does little to ensure that your school teaches what it holds important" (2004).

With Keenan's definition of curriculum in mind, let's examine the course (curriculum), the coaches who design the layout (who plan the program), and the participation of volunteers and spectators (the larger community).

The Head Coach Points the Way

Instructional leadership begins in the heart and mind of the primary leader or leaders whom God raises up for each school. From my experiences, I have concluded that God gives this vision for each school to one individual in much the same way He gave the vision for the reconstruction of the wall around Jerusalem to Nehemiah. This vision or clear picture for God's design for a particular school usually comes to the administrator who is responsible for discovering, clarifying, and articulating this vision to all those involved in the school community. This initial task and responsibility is paramount because some members of the community could not find the finish line if they were standing on it. It is in the curriculum that the school's leader has the opportunity to infuse his or her vision into the bone marrow of the school.

Secondary leaders may include one or more board members, other administrators, and veteran teachers. However, because of the complexity of curriculum challenges today, one key leader is needed to point the way for a diverse community that, for instance, may or may not agree on the place of technology in the school's curriculum or the importance of a specific class in logic or apologetics.

Throughout the last fifty years, discussions about the administrator's leadership role have seen significant change, and an evolution of the administrator's pivotal role in instruction has brought about increasing significance in his or her responsibility. At the midpoint of the twentieth century, the administrator was viewed as a manager of staff who made sure specific tasks were carried out. In the 1970s, a trend for the administrator to become an instructional leader was fueled by the rise in the discussion of school effectiveness. In the 1980s, Shirley Hord and Gene Hall (1983) concluded that strong leadership by the administrator was instrumental in determining the extent of curriculum leadership. They found that those educational leaders who used an active initiating style were most effective in establishing effective implementation. Their research showed that effective administrators had the following attitudes and behaviors: (a) setting clear long-range policies and goals, (b) setting high expectations for students as well as articulating and monitoring those expectations, (c) seeking changes in schoolwide programs and policies, and (d) seeking input from staff, yet being capable of acting decisively (25). In the nineties and today, it appears that these perspectives fall short of what is needed. The new role of the administrator is that of community leader—an influence that extends past the walls of the classrooms under his or her care.

Assistant Coaches Along the Path

Unlike a track and field starter in a stadium, who can signal the beginning of a race and declare a winner at the end while viewing all runners throughout the race, today's school leader must be a "leader of leaders." In most schools, one person cannot possibly track each student's progress through the course of his or her years at the school. Needed throughout the school are skilled teachers who have been taught the overall direction of the school and who are not merely monitors of progress but who are inspired to reflect on the value and effectiveness of individual chunks of curriculum. These leaders must be challenged to initiate new approaches and needed objectives in the form of new units. This model was described by Hilda Taba in the 1960s (1962, 11). Taba, a renowned social studies educator and curriculum developer, argued that curriculum planning should begin with the classroom teacher at the unit level. She believed that teachers should design and teach new units as pilot projects. This approach is an inductive method to curriculum development, starting with the specifics and building up to a general design as opposed to the more traditional deductive approach of starting with the general design and working down to the specifics (Oliva 1997, 150). (Derek Keenan points out in his model that the logical place to begin in most schools is the writing of a scope and sequence for each course taught in the school.)

Figure 5.1 (Oliva 1997, 149)

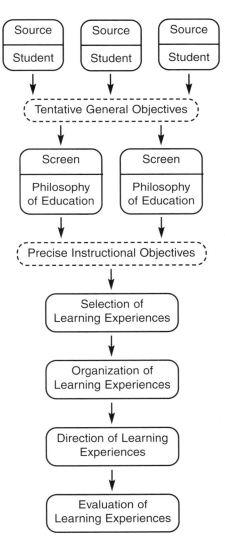

The phrase *site-based management*, from the 1980s, was used in large school systems. It acknowledged the need for planning and implementation to be done at the school level rather than at a central office where curriculum specialists were removed from both the students who have unique and varied needs and the teachers who knew firsthand what was and was not working. But do teachers have the burden of generating all of the various objectives that their students will achieve? Ralph Tyler, professor of education at the University of Chicago, believed that there are several "sources of curriculum" that influence its content and development (Ornstein and Hunkins 1998, 197). In his classic book *Basic Principles of Curriculum and Instruction*, Tyler suggests that curriculum may identify general objectives if planners examine data from three sources: the learners, contemporary life outside the school, and the subject matter. Information gathered from these sources is refined by filtering it through two screens: the educational and social philosophy of the school and the psychology of learning. Next in the process, the information is articulated in objectives that are more precise. The model goes on to describe the selection, organization, and evaluation of learning experiences (Tyler 1949). Peter Oliva depicts his understanding of Tyler's model in figure 5.1.

The use of Tyler's and Taba's models as references suggests what has been called the rational or scientific approach to curriculum planning. However, awareness of conflicting theories is crucial as we endeavor to pursue a biblical basis in every dimension of our school's curriculum. Even secular critics acknowledge the existence of postmodern designs or models for curriculum development that have their roots in the humanistic approaches developed by John Dewey in the last century (Oliva 1997, 188). Imagine this: the sponsor of a cross-country event calls all participants over at the beginning of the race. He informs the athletes that the starting point is in the general area where they have gathered, their destination is over on the other side of the park (which cannot be seen at this point, but just take his word for it), and the runners are free to pick any path they feel will get them there. This is the absurdity of curriculum planning apart from being challenged to "run with perseverance the race marked out for us. Let us fix our eyes on Jesus" (Hebrews 12:1–2). To return to the helmsman metaphor ... without channel markers and a set course, the ship will easily be blown off course. See table 5.1 for Meeks' Curriculum Guide Development Flow Chart. In this plan, the board is responsible for steps 1–3, after which a curriculum task force begins its work.

Table 5.1 Curriculum Guide Development Flow Chart (Meeks 2004, 3, 18)

The Board of Trustees/Directors Forms the Foundation	
The board of trustees, or directors, is responsible for steps 1–3 to develop a solid foundation.	
Step 1	Develop the philosophy statement.
Step 2	Develop the mission statement.
Step 3	Develop the educational, or learner, goals.
The Curriculum Development Task Force Builds the Framework	
Building on the trustees' foundation, the curriculum development task force follows steps 4–13 to develop the curriculum guide.	
Step 4	Develop a summary of the knowledge base. This summary represents accumulated evidence from research and practice. It substantiates effective teaching and learning in the subject, national curriculum projects, recommendations of experts, and high-quality commercial materials.
Step 5	Develop a vision of a curriculum of excellence. This statement identifies the ideal results of the work of the school or the teaching of a curriculum.
Step 6	Develop the hallmarks of excellence. These statements translate the vision into desired curriculum attributes for the subject. They often include "more" or "less" statements, e.g., higher-level thinking, less memorization of facts.
Step 7	Determine the curriculum framework. These statements identify the grade levels and ability ranges of the students for whom the curriculum is being developed. The statements address the following questions: • Is the curriculum required or elective? • What are the names of the subjects at the secondary level? • How much time is allocated to the subject at each grade level? • Is the curriculum designed to occupy all of the time allocated? • What is the view of knowledge and the learner represented in the curriculum? • To what extent will interdisciplinary integration be used? • Will the curriculum focus solely on mastery curriculum?

Continued

Table 5.1 *continued*

Step 8	Identify the strands of the curriculum. The strands are the recurring horizontal dimensions of the scope and sequence chart, e.g., in language arts: reading, writing, speaking, and listening; in mathematics: estimation, measurement, and so forth.
Step 9	Develop the scope and sequence chart. This chart lists the specific knowledge and skills designated for mastery at a given grade level.
Step 10	Develop the subject mastery goals and the organic goals. Subject mastery goals are knowledge and skills to be developed through instruction. On the basis of state frameworks, exemplary projects, and the recommendations of experts in the field, they are easily measured, e.g., subtract with regrouping using three-digit numbers. Organic goals are desired student attitudes and appreciations. They are not easily measured, e.g., enjoy reading.
Step 11	Identify curricular materials. These resources support the teacher's instruction, e.g., textbooks, videos, computer programs, and such.
Step 12	Determine the innovation configuration. This configuration describes how the program looks in actual practice in the classroom. Examples include which components of a program will be used, which are optional, and how much time will be spent on a given unit.
Step 13	Develop the curriculum guide. After you have completed steps 1–12, you are ready to work on the construction of each curriculum guide.

Scripture Permeates the Curriculum

Tyler describes the sources of curriculum that the school's objectives are derived from (1949, 3–25). Often, quoted lists of subject matter, student needs, and society's mandates omit the most important and foundational source of curriculum—Scripture. Everything in a Christian school must rest upon Scripture, and objectives coming from these other sources must be evaluated through Scripture. For instance, the popularity of a specific piece of literature in neighboring schools or in a traditional list of required reading does not necessitate its use if the themes, descriptions, or language in the work conflicts with the biblical mandate for holiness and purity. Another example might be the radical approach to the worship of nature finding its way into science curriculum as opposed to a biblical approach of responsible stewardship. Christian Overman, in his workshops on biblical integration, challenges teachers to connect each unit to at least one of several aspects of biblical thinking. He suggests that teachers ask, What does the unit teach us about God, humankind, creation, moral order, or purpose (Overman 2003, 22–33)? The presence of what is commonly referred to as "biblical integration" is one of the vital distinctions of our Christian school movement, and it is a characteristic that sets your school apart from all others in your geographic community. At the outset, let us simply describe this as the intentional weaving of God's Word into each dimension of school life. This definition that pushes the discussion beyond the classroom echoes the passion of Frank Gaebelein in his influential text *The Pattern of God's Truth: Problems of Integration in Christian Education.* Gaebelein strongly asserts:

> One of the commonest misconceptions of education is that which limits it to the four walls of the schoolroom or, to broaden the figure, to the acreage of the campus. In reality, however, education is a continuing process as broad as experience itself, and one in which all who have contact with youth share, either consciously or unconsciously. Therefore, it follows that a ministry not interested in education is only half a ministry, and that we who are called to be ambassadors for Christ cannot but be deeply concerned with something so vitally linked to our cause as Christian education. (2002, 7)

He goes on to state his definition of integration: "It is the living union of its subject matter, administration, and even of its personnel, with the eternal and infinite pattern of God's truth" (Gaebelein 2002, 9). Before we proceed, I want to clarify that not all educators think of integration in the same way. A distinguished research professor of education, Allan Glatthorn, lists a variety of ways to view curriculum integration (2000, 78–79):

Integrating While Retaining Separate Subjects
There are four ways to integrate the curriculum while maintaining the separate subjects.

1. *Correlation.* This term is used to ensure that the curricula of two related subjects (such as science and mathematics or social studies and English language arts) are developed so that their content supports each other. For example, students read colonial literature in English class while they are studying the colonial period in social studies.

2. *Skills across the curriculum.* The curriculum can be made more cohesive if developers ensure that skills such as reading,

writing, and study skills are reinforced across the curriculum, not confined to English language arts.

3. *Unified curricula.* This term designates the design of the curriculum for a given subject so that the divisions of that subject are minimized and its holistic nature is stressed. Whole language and unified science are examples of unified curricula.

4. *Informal integration.* In this model, the teacher brings in content from one subject while emphasizing the skills and concepts of another. Thus, an elementary teacher teaching a social studies unit on Mexico would informally provide examples of Mexican art and music.

Integrating Two or More Subjects

Most of the current discussion of integration is concerned with the need to combine content from two or more different subjects, such as English language arts, social studies, and science. Three major approaches are often used here.

1. *Subject-focused integration.* In this model, the developers begin with one subject (such as social studies) and then combine content from related subjects (such as English language arts and the arts).

2. *Theme-focused.* In this model, developers begin by identifying major themes that would be of interest and consequence to students. They then choose content from any subject that can support the theme. For example, a unit on *Conflict and Violence* might include content from social studies, English language arts, science, and the arts.

3. *Project-focused.* In this model, developers identify a complex project that would involve the students, such as developing a model community. In the course of completing such a project, students would need to master skills and concepts from social studies, science, mathematics, the arts, and English language arts.

Four Food Groups

Though thoroughly biblical in every aspect of his writing, Harro Van Brummelen (2002), the dean of education at Trinity Western University in Langley, British Columbia, and the author of *Steppingstones to Curriculum: A Biblical Path*, presents a very interesting view of four models of integration when considering the integration of content from different subject disciplines. His characterizations of curriculum integration fall into one of four types: turkey dinner, pizza, soup, or potluck dinner.

When integrating content in such a way that it resembles a turkey dinner, the teachers align curriculum content so that they deal with similar themes in different subject areas. The plate contains several foods that are separately identifiable but combine to form one meal.

The pizza model has a specific course or subject discipline as its crust, with extra toppings added to spice up the presentation and add extra meaning. When I was teaching English, some of my favorite teaching units involved the basic content of literature, but they also included art, music, and historical events from the author's contemporaries.

The soup type of integration involves the skillful blending of two or more disciplines into a project so that the individual disciplines are barely discernable, but the overall taste is the focus. Such projects take exceptional planning and large blocks of time. While students enjoy exceptional learning experiences of this type, the structure of individual course content is lost and may be lacking when students have to take achievement tests.

The fourth model in Van Brummelen's terminology is called potluck dinner. He uses this metaphor to describe the designing of thematic units by teachers in a coordinated effort as students move from class to class (2002, 91–94). For example, several teachers could plan an Elizabethan day and prepare special food, costumes, art, drama productions, and history videos.

Though some may pass over this final point and label it *semantics*, it is worth taking the time to think deeply about what is communicated when Christian educators use the term *integration* or its verb form *integrate* in connection with truth and God's Word. Are we saying that biblical concepts are being "added to" the larger whole of academic truth? Or perhaps it is the other way around—academic truth to the larger content of God's Word. Or maybe it is neither. On the basis of the presupposition that "all truth is God's truth," are we not leading students to investigate and discover the spiritual implications that are already part and parcel of the whole? Van Brummelen prefers the term *integral* as opposed to *integrated* because teachers can present material as holistic from the start, without differentiating and reintegrating. He explains, "The curriculum shows how our beliefs affect how we look at and use our learning.

Learning is always rooted in certain beliefs. As such, we do not combine faith and learning" (2002, 91). I choose to use the words *revelation* and *reveal*, for I believe that the true educator, in whom God's truth has been revealed, pulls back the curtain for His students to look into the wonders of God's mysteries.

Martha MacCullough (2001), the chair of the Department of Teacher Education at Philadelphia Biblical University, describes three models of biblical integration for Christian schools. First, the *interpersonal model* is based on the assumption that the teacher will intentionally look for teachable moments and will spontaneously weave in the Christian perspective. This approach was emphasized by Frank Gaebelein when he wrote, "The fact is inescapable; the worldview of the teacher, in so far as he is effective, gradually conditions the worldview of the pupil" (2002, 37). MacCullough maintains that this model is "necessary but not sufficient" for the Christian school (2001, 13–14). MacCullough describes her second model as the *parallel model*, which presents material in a type of dichotomy—teachers presenting course content as if there is secular knowledge and sacred knowledge. She points out that some may view these parallel tracks as faith and reason; others have referred to the tracks as general revelation and special revelation. This model is inadequate because it is misleading about the importance of spiritual values within course content and it does not assist students in their development of a biblical worldview.

MacCullough describes the third model that should be pursued by Christian educators as the *integrating core model*. In this model, one begins with a whole, the integrating core—a set of presuppositions (beliefs) about the world and life. One then moves to the new knowledge, skills, attitudes, and then back to a larger whole" (2001, 14). She argues that as this model is the basis of instruction, students may develop a sense of the whole in truth and learning.

In 1 Corinthians, Paul challenges our thinking and planning: "Everyone who competes in the games goes into strict training. They do it to get a crown that will not last; but we do it to get a crown that will last forever. Therefore I do not run like a man running aimlessly" (9:25–26). God's Word provides our administrators and students with a clear path and mile markers along the way.

> ## You Take the Helm
>
> Select a content topic that you are familiar with and develop one or more lesson plans that have an objective with a biblical truth embedded in the statement. Hint: Review Overman's list of possible choices for integration.

The Coaches and Volunteers Along the Course

Like the coaches and volunteers along the way who man special checkpoints to assure that the runners follow the prescribed course, teachers must evaluate student progress as they advance through the curriculum. Assessment is an exceptionally important part of instructional leadership and another important role for grade-level or department leaders. The informal procedures include each teacher's daily reflection on the progress of his or her students as they attempt unit objectives. If not daily, then periodically, teachers informally assess the effectiveness of instructional methods and the appropriateness of materials such as textbooks and other resources.

The formal process of carefully reviewing student achievement test scores by class or grade level usually yields important information about student performance relative to the school's curriculum, especially its scope and sequencing of specific units. Of course, test scores, both high and low, are influenced by many factors. However, item analysis of questions that were most often missed by each category of learners can highlight the need for change in the curriculum. Other assessments include information received from parents, community members, and alumni. Systematic feedback from graduates is crucial. Meeks presents an excellent rubric for curriculum review over a seven-year period in table 5.2.

Table 5.2 (Meeks 2004, 19)

Three-Year Cycle → Seven-Year Map ↓	Year 1: Plan	Year 2: Produce	Year 3: Implement
Year 1	Assessment		
Year 2	Social Studies/ Bible	Assessment	
Year 3	Science/Health/ PE	Social Studies/ Bible	Assessment
Year 4	Second Language	Science/Health/ PE	Social Studies/ Bible
Year 5	Fine and Practical Arts	Second Language	Science/Health/ PE
Year 6	Language Arts	Fine and Practical Arts	Second Language
Year 7	Math	Language Arts	Fine and Practical Arts
Development Cycle Begins Again		Math	Language Arts
			Math

The curriculum development cycle includes enough years to represent a full cycle for assessment and review of all subject areas. Once the cycle is completed, it starts again.

In *Steppingstones to Curriculum*, Harro Van Brummelen writes about curriculum leadership in this way:

> As I dream about the future, I see Christian schools that are truly Christ-centered communities of learning. The stakeholders in such communities learn through modeling Christlikeness, reflection, dialogue, inquiry, and action. These communities help students and teachers explore and experience what it means to be disciples of the Lord Jesus Christ and stewards of God's creation. (2002, 233)

The existence of such a spirit will lessen the importance of who initiates curriculum change or whether the model of curriculum development is top-down or vice versa. There are two realities—the formal process, which is linear if you will, in which a prescribed process takes place, and the informal influences in the community.

All stakeholders will be involved in what I call "curriculum dialogue." Those who have the formal authority to evaluate and codify change, the designated "instructional leaders," will in fact be in regular and genuine discussions with all sectors of the school's larger community—sharing, listening, learning, and reflecting. At a concert, in a committee meeting, on a field trip, at a game—if viewed properly, such moments of dialogue yield valuable insights into the effectiveness of the curriculum's impact on the lives and needs of students. Such opportunities also give the participants a chance to renew their overall commitments to what is important.

Meanwhile, the leader of leaders keeps everyone focused on the finish line and the biblical mile markers along the way. He or she must remember the words of Solomon: "Let your eyes look directly ahead and let your gaze be fixed straight in front of you. Watch the path of your feet and all your ways will be established" (Proverbs 4:25–26, NASB). The leader must see to it that no runners are lost along the way and that each achieves the goal of Christian education—a Christian worldview.

Exceptional Learners

An administrator does not have to be in his or her position very long before facing the challenge of deciding on the admissions application of a student with a learning disability. Such a determination is especially difficult when the family expresses enthusiastic support of the school's mission statement and a passionate desire to have their child in a Christian environment. A wise decision will be based on two areas of concern: the learner and the learning environment.

The Learner
The National Institute for Learning Disabilities (NILD) defines students with learning disabilities as students with average or above-average IQ who have a diagnosed learning disability but who can be placed in a mainstreamed classroom. The national average for the occurrence of learning disabilities is one child in twenty; up to one student in ten has a mild disability. The NILD requires a diagnosis by a licensed psychologist using the most recent edition of the Wechsler Intelligence Scale for Children (WISC). It is important to note that the learning disability, often occurring as a processing problem, may not show up until the child reaches third grade or even later. The WISC is designed to measure a child's intelligence as compared to performance in various areas. When a large difference occurs between aptitude and performance, then this is an area for further testing for a possible disability. Various areas of difficulty include the reception of information, the storage of information, or the

repeating of information. For example, dyslexia is the best-known learning disability; it includes the reversal of letters as a child reads or the reversal of letters or misspelling of the simplest of words when the student tries to write down what he or she has learned.

The Learning Environment

So the question remains, Can we accept or retain students who have received this diagnosis? Several follow-up questions naturally follow the broad issue. First, is the school leadership willing to lead the entire community to value and esteem students with learning differences? This will be evident in the way admission procedures are worded, the way schedules are designed, and the ways faculty members are trained to communicate with all students about the acceptance of those in the school who are bright but who learn differently. Many schools have named their special programs the Discover Program.

Next, are administrators willing to allocate the needed space for specialized classrooms to be created and appropriately outfitted? A typical classroom that is 20 feet by 25 feet could be subdivided into four smaller conference rooms where a trained teacher can meet one-on-one with a student. With the establishment of four rooms staffed by four teachers, the school could accommodate between 32 and 40 students.

The question about space leads to another issue. Will the administration budget the necessary monies for staffing and training in order to be successful? Without a grant or scholarship fund, the cost generally means that the family of the student enrolled in the program pays approximately twice the tuition amount in order to pay for the services of three hours of private therapy each week.

Finally, a significant hurdle is the full support of the faculty. Each teacher who has one or more students with a learning difference must be willing to make regular accommodations in the daily activities and assignments of these students. (It is recommended that an experienced, enthusiastic teacher have no more than two in any one class. A less experienced teacher may be successful with one in a group of twenty-five students. It is best not to assign a student to an inexperienced or unenthusiastic teacher.) For example, a student may struggle with 20 math problems and take an hour, while his classmates will complete the assignment in half the time. It is helpful in that case to assign only ten problems with varying degrees of difficulty. Modifications of classroom activities could be as simple as distributing lecture outlines for all students so that the learning-disabled (LD) student will be able to keep pace with the lecture. (See table 5.3 for a list of potential classroom modifications.)

Table 5.3 (Kienel, Gibbs, and Berry 1995, 379)

Potential Classroom Modifications
Listed below are a number of potential modifications teachers can make to assist such students [learning disabled]. Not all students will benefit from any single modification, and it is unreasonable to assume any one student would need a large number of the modifications. Again, teachers must evaluate each situation, while being careful to maintain the integrity of the classroom.

1. Provide preferential seating in the location that works best for a student. Be sure to give the student permission to move quietly to another seat when an activity requires closer attention.

2. Actively engage the student by frequently using his name, walking closer, pointing to his place in the book, marking directions or information as you talk.

3. Allow for delays in answering oral questions. Cue the student that the next question will be hers and provide time by responding to another student, erasing the board, then returning to her for the answer.

4. Allow the student to see your notes as you lecture, provide copies of notes, provide a marked teacher edition, provide a note-taker or a person to share class notes. An auditory learner will often do better by actively listening than trying to take notes independently. Later, the student can personalize the notes provided with information he remembers.

5. Ask parents or other students to read aloud and tape chapters so that the student can read and listen simultaneously. If possible, structure the listening process so that the student is listening for specific information. (A recording service is available free of charge for visually impaired and learning disabled students.)

6. Use several avenues of providing information in order to capitalize on strengths in visual or auditory channels. These students often benefit greatly from diagrams, charts, and other visual information.

7. When grading, consider a content grade and a form grade—or at least limited penalty for misspellings and similar errors.

8. When a student has really tried, consider providing extra credit for projects or special reports, or consider allowing optional assignments.

9. Reduce the length of assignments, but be sure that the essential material is covered. Circle the priority questions or assign problems from each section.

Continued

Table 5.3 *continued*

10. Provide lots of structure for assignments, especially long-term ones. Break them into several parts with checkpoints along the way.

11. Insist that the student keep a daily assignment notebook. Use a buddy system to make sure the assignments are written correctly. Ask parents to initial the completion of the assignments.

12. Provide study guides for exams with plenty of notes of the exam date. Structure the test with several avenues of receiving information, and make sure the test is organized well and is readable.

13. Consider allowing the student to record her answers or have additional time to work. Call attention to sections missed. Allow a student to give you an oral response when it appears she has misread a question.

Any Christian school with a program designed after the NILD program will have delightful anecdotes about students who made significant progress through the therapy sessions that each student attends twice a week for one and one-half hours per session. (In special cases, students may meet for three one-hour sessions.) The developers of the program emphasize that students do not receive tutoring for specific course work because that is comparable to giving a nonswimmer a life preserver. Instead, students receive therapy that is designed to strengthen deficient areas in the brain.

Let me tell you about one of the many success stories at our school. A teenager, whom I will call Josh, came to our high school after attending a special school where every student had a diagnosed learning disability. In our school, Josh would be enrolled in the NILD program and would be mainstreamed for his course work. One day I walked into a classroom where a few students were waiting for class to begin and discussing the room temperature while Josh was trying to explain possible points of breakdown in the electrical system that controlled the thermostat and the cooling unit in the classroom. His explanation included a schematic of the electrical system throughout the campus. Josh's dream was to become an electrical engineer, even though he was severely dyslexic and even his writing of his name looked like hen scratch on his best day! Did I tell you that Josh has an IQ of 140? Ten years later, the Lord brought Josh across my path when he visited my home as a prospective buyer. I was not surprised to hear that he had done well in college and that he was an electrical engineer!

During my fifteen years as an administrator, few decisions brought me more joy and satisfaction than the one that led to the creation of our Discovery Program. Few decisions led to the production of such meaningful fruit. I pray that you will seriously consider the additions and accommodations to your curriculum in order to expand the spectrum of students who can benefit from attending your school. A by-product will be the expansion of teaching skills that will make a positive impact on the learning of all students. During my time as the administrator of a community of learners, this was the most important decision that would influence the spiritual sensitivity of all students and faculty.

You Take the Helm

The new administrator has met with a third-grade teacher and the parents of a student whose performance was very poor during the first nine weeks of school. The previous year, their child's grades had slipped from all As to mostly Bs in the core subjects. Now, there have been many signs of difficulty, and the teacher does not know what to do. The parents have invested in the school for more than a decade. Two older siblings had earned a great reputation as they progressed into junior high and high school. How could the administrator encourage this anguished couple?

1. Respond to the case study by outlining how the headmaster should handle the conference.
2. What outside resources in your community are available?
3. What would you advise the classroom teacher to do after the conference?
4. Formulate a strategic plan to give direction to the board and the faculty as each prepares to respond to future needs.

III. The Helmsman as Builder:
Nehemiah 1-13

Community Builder and Transformational Leader

Principle for Guiding Principals:

The effective administrator demonstrates the characteristics of a transformational leader who builds a community by inspiring followers to become leaders.

What all administrators experience when preparing to lead a community …

> There it was again. He knew he felt it. He had never met an administrator who has not felt it. Each has experienced it at different times for a variety of reasons, but the hair-raising touch on the back of the neck is the same. Arid, sometimes pungent, this sensation occurs as the administrator faces a new crisis and the breath of the crowd at his back grows more intense as their heart rates accelerate in expectation of a showdown—a real-life, Dodge City, high-noon showdown between the school's leader and a difficult parent, a major donor, or a popular coach. Does he fall to the temptation to perform for his audience, who may or may not be driven by godly purposes? Those waiting behind him, like a mob anticipating a lynching, were there to test his mettle. Questions

ripped at his mind: Have I prepared them for times of crisis? Am I even spiritually prepared? Will God's school withstand the aftershocks of any action I take?

If you are called to lead a school and are convinced that the administrator must build a community, consider carefully the behavior of Nehemiah as God used him in a time of national crisis. If you behave as he did, you will be an administrator who builds a community.

As previously discussed in chapter 2, the administrator of a Christian school must be more than a skillful manager, instructional supervisor, or curriculum developer. The effective administrator must become the leader of a community that is drawn together by its love for the kingdom and its love for learning. This chapter presents biblical qualities of leadership found in Nehemiah that have been echoed in educational literature about administration. Students of educational leadership are challenged by God's Word to emulate the extraordinary characteristics in this ordinary man who was found faithful as a cupbearer, called to serve as general contractor, and finally elevated to the position of governor. Look for eight essential leadership skills as you examine the challenges that faced Nehemiah. Do your faculty members recognize these skills in your leadership style? Is God using you to build a community that is bound by its commitment to Christ and its pursuit of truth?

Characteristic One: The Building Block of Prayer

In Nehemiah 1, Nehemiah receives word that Jerusalem's walls are in shambles. The stones are in ruins, and the gates have been consumed by fire. God's people are disgraced as they live among the rubble and fall victim to passing caravans of thieves and looters. Nehemiah turns immediately to the Lord and demonstrates the behavior of a godly leader: "When I heard these things, I sat down and wept. For some days I mourned and fasted and prayed before the God of heaven" (1:4).

An entire generation of Christian school administrators who are now actively leading schools that regularly face difficult challenges were not brought up to respond to a crisis in this manner. Instead, their knee-jerk reaction is to respond in the manner of larger-than-life hero John Wayne. In countless situations, "The Duke" saddled up as quickly as possible and in the next scene, moviegoers saw a horse and rider enveloped in a cloud of smoke. He was a man of action! He was a man of passion and courage who responded unflinchingly in times of trouble.

However, Nehemiah demonstrates "a more excellent way." He was a "leader from the knees up" (Swindoll 1978, 30). God's man for this occasion brought his heartbreak and despair before God's throne and waited for his King to work on the heart of Nehemiah's earthly king, Artaxerxes. After months of steadfast prayer and fasting, the cupbearer's answer came: he was given permission to depart and was blessed with letters from the king for safe passage and the necessary supplies.

Frequently, school administrators cave in to the pressure from the crowd to act quickly and decisively. Yes, some emergencies require immediate attention and demand lightning-quick reflexes. However, as a former administrator, I can cite far too many instances when I responded quickly rather than prayerfully.

Characteristic Two: The Building Block of Vision

Once in Jerusalem, the former cupbearer did not call a press conference, sponsor a parade, or recruit a public relations firm. What Nehemiah did might be considered a prayer walk today. He spent time quietly touring the city that he had been taught to revere but had never visited. After a late-night tour of the perimeter to examine the full extent of the damage and the work that lay ahead, he was prepared to meet with the city's leaders. Countless citizens and visitors to the city had seen the dilapidated wall, but God gave one man a special vision for its reconstruction. After several days, he called the community leaders together and rallied God's people to the special task: " 'You see the trouble we are in: Jerusalem lies in ruins, and its gates have been burned with fire. Come, let us rebuild the wall of Jerusalem, and we will no longer be in disgrace….' They replied, 'Let us start rebuilding' " (Nehemiah 2:17–18).

Nehemiah clearly and passionately described the current state of affairs and succinctly presented the challenge before them. It is crucial to note that Scripture explains the source of this vision as God, not Nehemiah's imagination or personal ambition. Prior to the announcement, the author wrote, "I had not told anyone what my God had put in my heart to do for Jerusalem" (Nehemiah 2:12). The narrative also says, "I also told them about the gracious hand of my God upon me" (Nehemiah 2:18).

Those who are laying the foundation of a new school or who have been called to lead an existing school are challenged to consider these verses carefully. During a period of prayer and research, God painted a unique picture in Nehemiah's mind. George Barna, well-known demographic researcher and Christian author, defines *vision* as "foresight with insight based on hindsight. It is an informed bridge from the present to the future" (1992, 28). The Lord used those days of prayer and fasting to inspire Nehemiah with a vision for the reconstruction of the once impressive wall. During the days immediately preceding his announcement of this vision, God's leader collected valuable information about the present condition of the wall to enable him to effectively lead his work crew toward its future goal.

Barna, in his work *The Power of Vision*, describes the leader's responsibility to impart this God-given vision to others:

> Vision is a picture held in your mind's eye of the way things could or should be in the days ahead. Vision connotes a visual reality, a portrait of conditions that do not exist currently. This picture is internalized and personal. It is not somebody else's view of the future, but one that uniquely belongs to you. Eventually, you will have to paint that mental portrait for others if you wish the vision to materialize in your church. Just as you have used your imagination to create this view of the future, you will have to lead others to catch the same vision so that they, too, might share in its implementation and impact. Thus, having a clear picture in mind is essential. A fuzzy perspective is not vision. (1992, 29)

When I was an administrator, I carried a vivid picture in my mind of a fully developed Christian school program for grades kindergarten through twelve. I strongly believed that my calling was to describe this image to everyone involved in the community that I ministered in for fifteen years. I was absolutely convinced that a significant aspect of the vision becoming reality is an administrator's passion for reproducing that picture in the minds and hearts of others involved at every level of the school. The Lord used me to lead our school in two renovations and two major building programs as our community responded to the needs of our students. As we added facilities, expanded the faculty, and increased course offerings and activities, we were always focused on pursuing the mission that God called us to. This mission or purpose took shape in the vision that I communicated to our board, our church, and our school community. As these groups were inspired to take part in the pursuit of "what we can become," they participated in focusing the vision through strategic planning and writing specific objectives. The result was a large suburban campus ministering to over 700 students and graduates who were successful in college studies, many of whom are in full-time ministry today.

> ## You Take the Helm
>
> Has God entrusted you with a vision for a Christian ministry or
> Christian home? Do those who serve with you share your picture of
> the future? Discuss specific steps an administrator can take to transfer
> his vision into the minds of those who serve with him.

Transformational Leadership

The leadership behavior that Nehemiah demonstrates in Nehemiah 2 has
been described by researchers as the ability to identify and articulate a
vision. This and five other leadership characteristics have been described
as the qualities of a transformational leader.

Transformational leadership has been defined and examined in detail by
James MacGregor Burns (1978). He describes transforming leadership as
occurring when the leader recognizes and exploits an existing need or
demand of a potential follower. In addition, the leader looks for potential
motives in followers, seeks to satisfy their higher needs, and attempts to
engage the full person of the follower. As a result, both the leader and
follower in this relationship experience mutual stimulation and elevation
that may convert followers into leaders and may transform leaders into
moral agents. By the concept *moral leadership*, Burns means "that leaders
and those they lead have a relationship not only of power but of mutual
needs, aspirations, and values" (4).

As referred to in the previous quote, the concept of power is crucial in the
leader-follower relationship. Burns views this relationship between two or
more people as tapping motivational bases in one another and bringing
varying resources to bear in the process. He also makes an important
distinction between those who are mere "power wielders" and those who
are "leaders." Understanding this distinction helps bring the concept of
transformational leadership into clearer focus. Burns explains: "Power
over other persons is exercised when potential power wielders, motivated
to achieve certain goals of their own, marshal in their power base
resources that enable them to influence the behavior of respondents by
activating motives of respondents relevant to those resources and those
goals" (1978, 18).

This exercise of power takes place in order to realize the purpose of the
power wielder, regardless of whether these are also the goals of those who
respond. Leighton Ford, a Christian author who has written on this
subject, warns:

Transformational leadership is, however, a double-edge sword. When we look for leaders who can transform, we need to be aware that people can be transformed *down* in destructive ways as well as *up* to lift their level of achievement. Mother Teresa was a transformational leader, elevating the aspirations of people. So was Jim Jones, only he led nine hundred followers into a downward spiral, a blind obedience which ended in mass suicide at a jungle camp in Guyana. The same dynamics which can lead people to better things can also be used by leaders in ways that bring great social disorder. (1991, 22)

Like power, leadership has as its main function achieving certain purposes. All leaders are actual or potential power holders. They induce followers to act for certain goals that represent the values and the motivations—the wants and needs, the aspirations and expectations—of both leaders and followers. "The genius of leadership lies in the manner in which leaders see and act on their own and their followers' values and motivations. Leadership, unlike naked power-wielding, is thus inseparable from followers' needs and goals" (Burns 1978, 19).

Another important distinction that Burns draws is between transactional leadership and transformational leadership. Transactional leadership occurs "when one person takes the initiative in making contact with others for the purpose of an exchange of valued things" (1978, 19). These things could be monetary, political, or psychological in nature. The two bargainers involved in this process share a common purpose at least within the process, but the relationship does not go beyond this. Though a leadership act takes place and some goal is achieved, there is no enduring purpose that binds leader and follower together. Leighton Ford makes these distinctions (1991, 22):

- Transactional leaders work within the situation; transformational leaders *change* the situation.
- Transactional leaders accept what can be talked about; transformational leaders *change* what can be talked about.
- Transactional leaders accept the rules and values; transformational leaders *change* them.
- Transactional leaders talk about payoffs; transformational leaders talk about *goals*.
- Transactional leaders bargain; transformational leaders *symbolize*.

Burns carefully examines the complexities of transactional relationships. One such dimension is that of small group leadership. Drawing from an account of a group of boys called "the Norton Street boys" in the slums of Boston in the 1930s, Burns describes the structure, interrelationships, and leadership of a group of boys who appear to be "an amorphous collection of young drifters" (1978, 287). The tough pugilist who was the group's leader demanded loyalty and cooperation from the others. In exchange, he offered them protection from any outsider.

In a much larger context, Burns discusses consensus building through legislative leadership. He believes that much of the time lawmaking is based on exchanges rather than motivated by transforming leadership. Burns explains:

> The classic seat of transactional leadership is the "free" legislature ... Typically the chamber becomes a trading arena in which members' individual interests and goals are harmonized through age-old techniques of bargaining, reciprocity, and payoff. The trading system is not necessarily self-sustaining. Modal values of fairness, tolerance, and trust guide legislative action. Leadership is necessary for the initiating, monitoring, and assured completing of transactions, for settling disputes and for storing up political credits and debits for later settlement. (1978, 344)

The skillful bargaining of President Lyndon Johnson earned Burns' designation as "the consummate transactional leader of legislation" (1978, 345).

Transformational leadership, on the other hand, occurs when "one or more people engage with others in such a way that leaders and followers raise one another to higher levels of motivation and morality" (Burns 1978, 20). Using Gandhi as a modern example, Burns describes how transforming leadership reaches this level of being moral. It does so when the level of human conduct and ethical aspiration of both the follower and leader are raised because of this experience. It transforms both. He concludes this point by stating: "Finally, and most important by far, leaders address themselves to followers' wants, needs, and other motivations, as well as to their own, and thus they serve as an independent force in changing the makeup of the followers' motive base through gratifying their motives" (20).

The Gospel of John provides students of leadership with a powerful illustration of transformational leadership in the account of Christ's encounter with the Samaritan woman. What began as a simple request for a drink of water ended in a life-changing experience that transcends the earthly, temporal concerns of the secular theorists. Jesus touched in her a greater need than her desire for a cool drink when He stated, "If you knew the gift of God and who it is that asks you for a drink, you would have asked him and he would have given you living water" (John 4:10). Indeed, this is the greatest need of every heart, and Jesus led her to understand the only way to satisfy this need. She was transformed into a follower as she said, "Sir, give me this water so that I won't get thirsty and have to keep coming here to draw water" (John 4:15).

The thrilling transformation continues as the new follower becomes a leader. In the rest of the narrative, the reader learns that the Samaritan woman becomes a leader of others. Verse 28 points out that she left her water jar behind as she headed back to her community. What had been of primary importance was now set aside as a new motivation took over. Based on the powerful testimony of one woman with a poor reputation, others came to Jesus; even they themselves soon believed. Just as Jesus inspired this woman to lead others to Him, God can use willing servants today to lead a Christian school community to the Savior.

Characteristic Three: The Building Block of Developing Unity

After clearly articulating the God-given vision to rebuild the wall, Nehemiah had the superhuman task of developing a workforce consisting of untrained laborers from every segment of society. Nehemiah 3 presents an amazing list of a diverse community that rallied to the project: priests, government officials, temple servants, perfume-makers, daughters of noblemen, goldsmiths, and merchants of all types. One technique that Nehemiah used to create unity among his volunteers was to establish a method of rallying his followers together in times of danger: "Then I said to the nobles, the officials and the rest of the people, 'The work is extensive and spread out, and we are widely separated from each other along the wall. Wherever you hear the sound of the trumpet, join us there. Our God will fight for us!' " (Nehemiah 4:19–20).

Skillful leaders understand that without creating ways of helping followers feel connected, they can lose focus, become scattered, and grow discouraged. Nehemiah establishes a method of communication. Perhaps the trumpet can be considered a symbol for the group—something that draws people physically and emotionally to stay inspired to uphold the group's vision. Sports teams and military units draw heavily on references to mascots or other objects that represent their causes.

In the transformational leadership literature, this quality is referred to as the ability to foster the acceptance of group goals. For an administrator, this is behavior on the part of the leader aimed at promoting cooperation among teachers and assisting them in working together toward a common goal.

The work of Bernard M. Bass (1985) was based on the conceptual framework of Burns, and Bass sought to operationalize and quantify Burns' work. His research using business executives and military officers led to an instrument entitled the Multifactor Leadership Questionnaire. This Likert-style questionnaire asks respondents to rate their supervisor by determining to what extent he or she exhibits certain behaviors. Bass classified these behaviors into one of five categories or factors. Two factors—contingent reward and management by exception—characterize transactional leaders, and the three other factors—charisma, initiating support, and intellectual stimulation—characterize transformational leaders.

Bass views the presence of these processes differently than the Burns continuum viewpoint. Bass believes that some leaders are generally more transformational than others, but most possess or employ some mixture of the two. However, Bass and his associates concluded that transformational factors are preferable. Where leaders were rated as strongly transformational, Bass found that employee job satisfaction was higher, group performance was more effective, and subordinates put in extra time more readily.

Literature currently contains few examples of researchers applying the works of Burns and Bass to educational administration, especially as it pertains to private education. Nancy R. Hoover is the only researcher to have administered Bass' Multifactor Leadership Questionnaire to private school headmasters. She examined the leadership characteristics of private independent schools in the South and found that the administrators' scores were comparable to their counterparts in business and the military. That is, school administrators were rated as transformational at the same frequency as the factors occurred in other sectors. These results were corroborated in the research I did when I examined administrators in independent Catholic and evangelical Christian schools in Maryland. Administrators were rated as transformational at the same frequency as those in Hoover's research (Coley 1993, 119).

Thomas Sergiovanni has done several case studies involving transformational leadership and school restructuring. He found that the presence of transformational factors was highly significant where schools were successfully responding to change efforts and restructuring. He discovered that transformational leadership enhanced the growth of professionalism, collegiality, and the development of school norms and values (1992b, 42).

Like Bass, Sergiovanni views the concepts of transactional and transformational leadership as being embedded in each other and that skillful administrators employ both as the occasion requires. His four stages—bartering, building, bonding, and banking—reflect his belief that the relationship between leader and followers must be developed and maintained. However, sometimes a leader may be successful by returning to the initial stage of bartering if the need arises (1991, 31).

Kenneth A. Leithwood and his associates are the only researchers in the field of education to build on Bass' work by altering his questionnaire to fit an educational setting. While studying educational reform and school restructuring in districts in Ontario, Canada, Leithwood reduced the number of items in Bass' questionnaire to a 33-item leadership survey. Some of the wording in the items was changed, and the list of transformational factors was expanded from three to six. Leithwood thought that this would more accurately describe the behaviors of school administrators. Where school restructuring was successful, Leithwood's survey revealed the positive effects of transformational educational leadership and that these leaders are pursuing three basic goals (1992):

1. Helping staff members develop and maintain a collaborative, professional school culture
2. Fostering teacher development
3. Helping teachers solve problems together more effectively

(See table 6.1 at the conclusion of this chapter for a summary of the literature that discusses transformational leadership.)

You Take the Helm

Consider examples of leaders you have known personally who were gifted at galvanizing people to share a common vision. What techniques did they use to create unity in the group or organization?

Characteristic Four: The Building Block of High Expectations

No leadership characteristic is mentioned and discussed more often in current management and administration literature than the importance of establishing high expectations. Bass defines the quality as the expectation of high performance. Administrators with this quality have behaviors that demonstrate the leader's expectation for excellence and quality from the teachers.

Few employers of any school should have any serious complaints about their workload when they consider the high expectations of Nehemiah for this makeshift crew of builders. The narrative explains: "So we continued the work with half the men holding spears, from the first light of dawn till the stars came out. At that time I also said to the people, 'Have every man and his helper stay inside Jerusalem at night, so they can serve us as guards by night and workmen by day' " (Nehemiah 4:21–22). Nehemiah challenged his followers to stay at their work site, to work all day, and to take turns standing guard at night. These were high expectations! Why did they respond as they did? Nehemiah's followers stuck with this enormous task because they shared their leader's vision and felt the deep satisfaction that comes in following a man of God who challenges his community to work sacrificially on a project of *significance.*

Characteristic Five: The Building Block of Individual Support

While the work on the wall was in progress, the people approached their leader with several major distractions that were interfering with their ability to focus on the project that they had committed to. In Nehemiah 4, the Jews reported their dread of being attacked by those who opposed the construction of the wall. (Note: In verse 12, the narrative states that this was reported ten times!) In Nehemiah 5, there was "a great outcry" because some Jews could not feed their families in time of famine; some had to mortgage their land and homes to survive and pay the king's tax. In some cases, Jews were forcing the children of other Jews into bondage because of this economic crisis. How did Nehemiah respond? He certainly could have taken the approach of a Marine drill sergeant and ordered everyone back to work with a buck-up attitude. On the other hand, he could have ignored their difficulties altogether and pretended to be unaware. Instead, this compassionate leader provided individualized support. Administrators who share this characteristic with Nehemiah are able to demonstrate respect for teachers as individuals and communicate sincere concern for their personal feelings and needs.

It must be noted that Nehemiah did not merely listen sympathetically to a group of outraged employees. Nor did he react in a dispassionate manner that may have conveyed a lack of understanding of their distress. Nehemiah 4:14 (NASB) says he "saw their fear" and responded with reassuring words of encouragement. Nehemiah 5:6 describes Nehemiah's reaction after he learned of the usury: "When I heard their outcry and these charges, I was very angry." After careful consideration, he called together all those who were responsible and rebuked them. "They kept quiet, because they could find nothing to say" (Nehemiah 5:8). The showdown ended with an agreement by the offending Jews to repay their brothers. God's strong leader used another symbolic act: "I also shook out the folds of my robe and said, 'In this way may God shake out of his house and possessions every man who does not keep this promise. So may such a man be shaken out and emptied!' " (Nehemiah 5:13).

First, using valuable time, energy, and resources to assist individuals in personal difficulties is Christlike. Second, such expressions of individual support may not only restore a professional's ability to complete his or her tasks, but it may result in fresh enthusiasm for his or her work and the school where the professional serves. I served with a faculty member whose sister was dying of cancer in their hometown, which was two hours away in another state. It was obvious to those who knew him well that he may have been physically present at school, but he was mentally and emotionally with his family. One day I pulled him aside and said, "You've served this school very well for ten years. I want you to take next week off with pay and go home to spend time with your sister. Stay as long as you need to." After ten days, the teacher returned and was a stronger, more focused instructor and coach. When his sister went to be with the Lord a few weeks later, he had that time with her to remember.

You Take the Helm

What are some common issues that interfere with a teacher's ability to give his or her best energy to provide individual support?

Characteristic Six: The Building Block of Modeling

So far in this discussion, I have pointed out that Nehemiah was able to share an inspired vision, unify his followers, challenge them with high expectations, and comfort them with individual support. However, readers who are new to the narrative may wonder if the leader was willing to get his hands dirty and calloused by personally committing to this grueling work. Bass calls this characteristic "providing an appropriate model," which means the leader shows behavior that sets an example for teachers to follow, behavior that is consistent with the values that the leader espouses.

And did Nehemiah ever! The narrative in Nehemiah 4 explains that Nehemiah and his brothers labored alongside the other volunteers and took their turns at standing guard. What a spirit of commitment; they did not change their clothes except to bathe! When it was mealtime, Nehemiah refused to partake of the lavish banquets made available to city officials of his status. Instead, he arranged to serve many of the other citizens of Jerusalem who were participating in the reclamation project. Scripture tells us that he refused to purchase land during this period, even though he was privileged to do so. Perhaps this was an opportunity for a type of "insider trading," which would grant him the freedom to set aside choice land or living quarters near the most scenic places around the city's new wall. Nevertheless, Nehemiah provided crucial leadership in setting the right example by refusing to enjoy many of the perquisites of his position.

Administrators of Christian schools have a daily, even hourly, opportunity to provide an appropriate model for their staff and the school's student body. Numerous Scriptures exhort administrators not to lose sight of this vital responsibility:

> A student is not above his teacher, but everyone who is fully trained will be like his teacher. (Luke 6:40)

> You became imitators of us and of the Lord; in spite of severe suffering, you welcomed the message with the joy given by the Holy Spirit. (1 Thessalonians 1:6)

Jesus set the ultimate example when He gave Himself completely on the Cross for all humankind. Shortly before the Crucifixion, He discussed greatness and leadership with His disciples. He explained, "The greatest among you should be like the youngest, and the one who rules like the one who serves" (Luke 22:26). The wisdom of His words is discussed by Sergiovanni in his text *Moral Leadership: Getting to the Heart of School Improvement:* "Servant leadership is the means by which leaders can get the necessary legitimacy to lead. Servant leadership provides legitimacy partly because one of the responsibilities of leadership is to give a sense of direction, to establish an overarching purpose" (1992a, 125). However, for the administrator to be successful at having this purpose accepted, others must trust him or her: "For trust to be forthcoming, the led must have confidence in the leader's competence and values. Further, people's confidence is strengthened by their belief that the leader makes judgments on the basis of competence and values, rather than self-interest" (125).

During my years in school administration, influenced by the models of my own administrators and empowered by Christ, I tried to emulate this attitude of servanthood. As time allowed, I stayed in the cafeteria after lunch on many days and helped the custodian fold and roll the tables out of the way to prepare the room for afternoon activities. I attempted to be present during the tedious times of morning and afternoon carpool lines to encourage other faculty members who were assigned the task. Other opportunities to emulate this attitude included chaperoning field trips, helping prepare for a band concert, or visiting a student who had been hospitalized.

You Take the Helm

Discuss the following quote by Sergiovanni: "Servant leadership is more easily provided if the leader understands that serving others is more important but that the most important thing is to serve the values and ideas that help shape the school as a covenantal community. In this sense, all the members of a community share the burden of servant leadership" (1992a, 125).

Characteristic Seven: The Building Block of the Word

The discussion in this chapter examines the leadership qualities of Nehemiah and points out the occurrence of these qualities in the literature on transformational leadership and specifically educational administration. A significant building block in the development of a Christian community is the foundation of God's Word. In order of significance, it should be placed first, but it occurs in this chapter at this point because of the presentation of the Book of the Law of Moses by Ezra in Nehemiah 8:1–3:

> All the people assembled as one man in the square before the Water Gate. They told Ezra the scribe to bring out the Book of the Law of Moses, which the Lord had commanded for Israel.
>
> So on the first day of the seventh month Ezra the priest brought the Law before the assembly, which was made up of men and women and all who were able to understand. He read it aloud from daybreak till noon as he faced the square before the Water Gate in the presence of men, women and others who could understand. And all the people listened attentively to the Book of the Law.

Nehemiah describes a captivating scene where the city "assembled as one man." Would that this might be said of each Christian school as the administrator stands before the student body during chapel, the faculty at morning devotionals, and the parents and extended community at orientation and graduation. It is important to note their reaction to God's Word and this special opportunity for hearing it. Verse 3 points out that the reading took place from early morning (first light) until midday. Verses 5 and 6 describe their posture—standing, lifting their hands, and bowing with their faces to the ground. Their commitment to the Lord and His Word was reflected in their passion to stay and hear it read for a long period, and they were inspired to worship their King in different postures.

As previously stated, no individual corporate experience can bring about growth and understanding (verse 8) like that of worship, and so it is for Christian schools. It is important to encourage teachers and school leaders to grow academically and professionally. In this sense, the transformational leader provides for intellectual stimulation, educational opportunities that challenge teachers to reexamine some of their assumptions about their work and to rethink how it can be performed. Sergiovanni explains: "Within communities of learners it is assumed that schools have the capacity to improve themselves; that, under the right conditions, adults and students alike learn, and learning by one contributes to the learning of others" (1992a, 125). Chapter 12 of this text will explore in detail a variety of models for staff development that challenge teachers to take control of their own professional development.

Another researcher in this chapter's discussion on transformational leadership has emphasized the important influence the administrator has in the area of staff development. During the early 1990s, Kenneth Leithwood and his associates examined several aspects of transformational leadership through research projects in secondary schools in Canada. Leithwood summarized their findings (1992). These will be outlined here, and then the individual studies will be examined. He argues that "the term *instructional leadership* focuses administrators' attention on 'first-order' changes" (9). These changes include the improvement of instruction activities and the monitoring of students' and teachers' work. However, second-order changes are needed in the many restructuring efforts that are being initiated in many school districts. These include such important goals as developing a shared vision, improving communication, and creating participative decision-making processes.

Kenneth Leithwood and Doris Jantzi (1991) observed school administrators maintaining a collaborative culture in their case study of twelve improving schools. Leaders encouraged faculty participation in goal setting and helped reduce feelings of isolation by establishing time for joint planning. Another study, by Kenneth Leithwood and Rosanne Steinbach (1991), revealed activities and approaches used by transformational leaders to foster teacher development. They found that "teachers' motivation for development is enhanced when they adopt a set of internalized goals for professional growth" (Leithwood 1992, 10). Teachers are inspired by internalizing a set of goals for professional growth, receiving feedback from colleagues about these goals, and having a role in school improvement within an environment that encourages professional growth. In a third study (Leithwood and Steinbach 1991), principals were observed in meetings demonstrating their confidence and respect for teachers' input as they avoided preconceived notions, listened to others' ideas, and did not impose their own perspective. They summarized their findings by stating: "In sum, we judge the evidence regarding the effects of transformational educational leadership to be quite limited but uniformly positive; clearly, giving more attention to such leadership in the future is warranted" (Leithwood 1992, 12).

> **You Take the Helm**
>
> In what ways can teachers be involved in the spiritual growth of the faculty and student body? How can they participate in their own academic/professional growth?

Characteristic Eight: The Building Block of Celebration

The final building technique illustrated in Nehemiah that is used by an administrator to strengthen and encourage community is the concept of celebration. After the completion of the wall in a staggering fifty-two days and after the reading from the law of God, the general contractor turned civic leader was led by God to encourage the people to enjoy a time of celebration:

> Then Nehemiah the governor, Ezra the priest and scribe, and the Levites who were instructing the people said to them all, "This day is sacred to the Lord your God. Do not mourn or weep." For all the people had been weeping as they listened to the words of the Law.
>
> Nehemiah said, "Go and enjoy choice food and sweet drinks, and send some to those who have nothing prepared. This day is sacred to our Lord. Do not grieve, for the joy of the Lord is your strength."
>
> The Levites calmed all the people, saying, "Be still, for this is a sacred day. Do not grieve."

> Then all the people went away to eat and drink, to send portions of food and to celebrate with great joy, because they now understood the words that had been made known to them. (Nehemiah 8:9–12)

Leaders from all cultures and civilizations have recognized the powerful influence of a celebration to bring community members together. As men and women enjoy special food and drink in a festive atmosphere, the value and importance of the reason for celebrating are cemented in the participants' minds. Ticker-tape parades have been held to honor the accomplishments of war heroes, astronauts, and athletic teams. Unfortunately, nearly all celebrations are designed to lift up human accomplishments rather than to glorify God.

In Nehemiah 8, those who had participated in worship were instructed by their new governor to turn their attention to cheering rather than mourning, "for the joy of the Lord is your strength" (Nehemiah 8:10). See table 6.2 for a summary of the eight building blocks of building a Christian community.

Administrators are called to build a Christian community that is founded on Christ and His Word. This chapter has carefully examined leadership behaviors exemplified by Nehemiah. God's man for that day galvanized the support of a cadre of volunteers who previously had little in common except their citizenship in a city that was in much need of a transformational leader. The result was the unified effort of government workers, merchants, perfume-makers, priests, and temple servants who combined their efforts to accomplish a task in fifty-two days, a feat that many considered impossible. As administrators of schools that bear the name of Christ, we must examine our leadership behaviors for the characteristics discussed here. Who can garner the energy and support of teachers, students, church laity, and neighborhood leaders to build a community that loves Christ and learning? God is still calling His servants to be transformational leaders of communities today.

Table 6.1

Transformational Leadership Overview of Literature		
Theorist	**Background/Contribution**	**Publication**
James MacGregor Burns	• Political Scientist/ Historian • Defined and developed conceptual framework	*Leadership* (1978)
Bernard Bass	• In business management • Quantified the measurement of six characteristics	*Leadership and Performance Beyond Expectations* (1985)
Kenneth Leithwood	• Educator • First to study the presence of six characteristics in school leaders (Canada)	Numerous Articles on Transformational Leadership and School Restructuring
Thomas J. Sergiovanni	• Educator • Furthered Leithwood's work in U.S. schools	*Moral Leadership: Getting to the Heart of School Improvement* (1992)
Leighton Ford	• In Christian leadership • Application of concepts to Christian ministry	*Transforming Leadership: Jesus' Way of Creating Vision, Shaping Values and Empowering Change* (1991)
Phillip V. Lewis	• In church leadership and management • Application of concepts to church laymen	*Transformational Leadership: A New Model for Total Church Involvement* (1996)

Table 6.2 (Adapted from notes prepared by Dr. D. S. Sherrill, superintendent of North Raleigh Christian Academy in Raleigh, North Carolina. Printed with permission.)

Inspiring a Community of Believers	
Transformational Leadership: The leader looks for potential motives in followers, seeks to satisfy higher needs, and engages the full person of the followers. The result is a relationship of mutual stimulation and elevation that converts followers into leaders (Bass 1985). The transformational leader motivates followers to envision more than the status quo by raising awareness of different values and challenging them to transcend personal self-interest.	

Nehemiah—A Model for Building Principals Transformational Leadership	
Building Blocks—Nehemiah	**Educational Theory—Bass**
1 Prayer (1:4) Nehemiah spent months in prayer. Pray consistently. Pressure on a man of action can cause a man to act too quickly. Be "a leader from the knees up."	
2 Vision (2:11–18) God placed a vision upon Nehemiah's heart. What has God put on your heart?	**Identify and Articulate a Vision** The behavior of the leader is aimed at identifying new opportunities for his or her school. The leader develops and articulates his or her vision of the future and inspires others.
3 Unity (4:19–20, 5:12–13) Nehemiah instituted activities and symbols that gathered people together.	**Foster the Acceptance of Group Goals** The behavior of the leader is aimed at promoting cooperation among teachers and assisting them in working together toward a common goal.
4 High Expectations (4:21–23) Nehemiah set the bar high and stretched his followers.	**Expect High Performance** The leader's behavior demonstrates his or her expectations for excellence, quality, and/or high performance of the teachers.
5 Individual Support (5:1–7) Nehemiah heeded outcries of workers and dissension in the ranks. He defended workers.	**Provide Individualized Support** The leader's behavior indicates respect for teachers and concern about their personal feelings and needs.

Continued

Table 6.2 *continued*

	Building Blocks—Nehemiah	Educational Theory—Bass
6	**Role Model** (5:14–18) Nehemiah kept the same status of the people by eating the same food as they do and by not purchasing land.	**Provide an Appropriate Model** Setting an example for teachers to follow, the leader behaves in a way that is consistent with the values he or she espouses.
7	**Power of the Word** (8:1–3) Nehemiah wanted the people to hear the Word from Ezra. Gathering "as one man" to hear it, the people showed unity and the influence of the Word.	**Provide Intellectual Stimulation** The leader behaves in a way that challenges teachers to reexamine some of their assumptions about their work and to rethink how they can perform it.
8	**Celebration** (8:9–12)	
"You also, as living stones, are being built up a spiritual house, a holy priesthood, to offer up spiritual sacrifices acceptable to God through Jesus Christ." (1 Peter 2:5, NKJV)		

Six Forces of Leadership
and Leadership by Outrage

Principles for Guiding Principals:

The effective administrator creates a climate of motivation for the faculty by making use of the six forces of leadership.

The effective administrator inspires others to become moral leaders of the school by demonstrating "leadership by outrage" when the community's core values are violated.

The road had become much clearer now. The administrator had a fix on the horizon, though it was so far away and some of the details were still fuzzy. His immediate steps, however, were crystal clear, and he was ready to get everyone moving. If he could just get the picture that God had put into his head into the heads of the others, he was convinced that they would then follow him to that horizon. Or would they? Was there anything about him that would inspire others to work toward a common goal for the good of the community, despite their own individual needs? These nagging doubts left him wondering and praying.

Many prospective administrators are quickly excited about concepts of leadership and are passionate about inspiring others to join them in the pursuit of a special vision. However, young leaders ask me, "How do I get others to follow me?" An even more basic question is, "How do I get others to do what I want them to do?" On one level, there is the dynamic of the leader understanding the deepest needs or desires of the followers. At this point, we are considering basic concepts of motivation.

Most authors agree that one person cannot make another person do something that he or she does not want to do, that motivation is an internal decision. The root word is *motive*, a need or desire that causes someone to act. The etymology of the word *motive* comes from the French word *motif*, which means "moving." So when administrators consider ways to get people up and moving, they must reflect on what inner needs or desires the individuals possess that make them want to take action. The complexity of the unique responses within a faculty makes this process both difficult and mysterious. The incredible blessing that leaders of kingdom ministries have in their favor is the presence of the Holy Spirit, who is tutoring their minds to understand those they are called to lead. Also, leaders can call on the Holy Spirit to direct the decisions, attitudes, and energies of those they lead. Certainly, God in us transforms our needs and desires—in other words, that which motivates us.

A student once challenged my statement that one person cannot motivate another. He played on Clemson University's 1983 national championship football team. Remembering his coach's legendary speeches, the student presented his argument. He maintained that when Coach Ford challenged the players in the locker room before a game, they were willing to run out to the interstate highway and take on an eighteen-wheeler. I calmly made my case to the graduate-school student who towered over me, "Coach Ford simply called on the desire that each player already brought to the team. He knew you wanted to win football games."

In *Good to Great*, Jim Collins and his researchers discover that the corporate leaders of companies that were transformed from average performing companies to extraordinary companies have the ability to get the right people involved in their organizations.

> The executives who ignited the transformations from good to great did not first figure out where to drive the bus and then get people to take it there. No, they *first* got the right people on this bus (and the wrong people off the bus) and *then* figured out where to drive it. They said, in essence, "Look, I don't really know where we should take this bus. But I know this much: If we get the right people on the bus, the right people in the right seats, and the wrong people off the bus, then we'll figure out how to take it someplace great." (Collins 2001, 41)

Much of the early discussion on leadership describes what has become known as the "trait theory" approach. For centuries, those who have had the prevailing notion that physical characteristics make a successful leader have assumed that followers conform to the wishes of a leader because of some outstanding trait, or traits, that the leader possesses. King Saul is a popular example of the trait theory of leadership. Scripture tells us that he was a handsome man, head and shoulders above other men. In "Leadership Characteristics That Facilitate School Change," Sylvia Mendez-Morse presents an excellent review of research investigating individual traits such as intelligence, birth order, and socioeconomic status. She concluded from the literature that "the attempts to isolate specific individual traits led to the conclusion that no single characteristic can distinguish leaders from non-leaders" (1992).

Beginning in the 1970s, leadership discussions shifted away from the trait theory to examinations of the "situation" as the determinant factor. According to the concept of situational leadership, a person can be a follower or a leader depending on circumstances. Though the situational leadership revealed the complexity of leadership, it failed to provide insight into which *leadership skills* would be more effective in certain situations. During this same time period, theorists such as Robert Blake and Lance Mouton developed a two-dimensional structure they called the Managerial Grid, which examines the balance between focusing on the project (termed "initiating structures") and focusing on the people (termed "consideration").

For further research on the background of leadership theory, review the following:

• Blake and Mouton
    Blake, Robert, and Jane S. Mouton. 1985. *The managerial grid III: The key to leadership excellence*. Houston: Gulf Publishing.

• Fiedler's Contingency Model
    Fiedler, Fred E. 1971. *Leadership*. New York: General Learning Press, University Program Module Series.

• The Ohio State Leadership Studies
    Halpin, Andrew W., and B. J. Winter. 1957. A factorial study of the leader behavior descriptions. In *Leader behavior: It's description and measurement*. Columbus, Ohio: Bureau of Business Research.

• Hersey and Blanchard and Situational Leadership
    Hersey, Paul, Kenneth Blanchard, and Dewey Johnson. 2000. *Management of organizational behavior: Utilizing human resources*, 8th ed. Englewood Cliffs, NJ: Prentice-Hall.

Continued

continued

- Path-Goal Theory of Leadership
    House, Robert J. 1971. A path—goal theory of leader effectiveness. *Administrative Science Quarterly*, 16:321–38.

- The Michigan Studies
    Likert, Rensis. 1961. *New patterns of management.* New York: McGraw-Hill.

Five Forces of Leadership

How can the administrator create a climate of motivation? By what force will the staff be moved to join in with pushing the school forward to its goals? Thomas Sergiovanni has outlined "five forces of leadership" that he says are important for the school to move in a positive direction toward effectiveness and to avoid being pushed backward. The first three—technical, human, and educational—are foundational forces that must be provided to ensure that the school will function effectively. The fourth and fifth forces—symbolic and cultural—are "stretcher" forces that help schools rise to levels of extraordinary commitment and performance (Sergiovanni 1995, 84).

The Technical Force

Administrators derive power from their ability to develop efficient structures in the organization and operation of the school. Sergiovanni has termed this role as that of "management engineer ... who provides planning, organizing, coordination, and scheduling to the school and [who is] skilled at manipulating strategies and situations to ensure optimum effectiveness" (1995, 85). Obviously, the lack of these skills creates a stressful, frustrating environment that leads to teacher demotivation. For instance, frequent interruptions of the daily schedule, even with early warning, will discourage even the most dedicated teacher from laying out well-defined, long-range lesson plans. On the other hand, a leader who establishes a smooth operating schedule and a means to quickly manage daily problems will establish a work environment where teachers are secure and confident. Illustrations of such frequent events in Christian schools usually include the chapel schedule, fire drills, athletic team dismissal, collection of assignments for absentees, and the accounting of student attendance. The accurate accounting of the school's finances and the clear reporting of the status of the budget to the school's constituents have significant potential for positive or negative leadership force.

The Human Force

The second force available to administrators is the power that comes from skillfully harnessing the human resources present in the school and the community. In this leadership role, the administrator is a "human engineer ... who provides support, encouragement, and growth opportunities for teachers and others" (Sergiovanni 1995, 85). Imagine an organization or ministry such as a school, where human relationships and interaction are intense and meaningful. It is inconceivable that a school would function properly without this leadership force. As an administrator of a staff that matured over several years, I identified several key instructional leaders who were growing stale or who could reach that state in a short time. I recruited these teachers to enter a new phase of their careers by becoming instructional leaders and mentors for the other faculty members in their departments. I provided them with special training to learn how to effectively observe their peers and then gave them the time and resources they needed to accomplish the tasks. Over the next five years, each of these teachers became successful leaders and enjoyed a new sense of purpose and energy in serving the Lord and others at the school.

Warren Bennis, in *Managing People Is Like Herding Cats* (one of his many books on leadership), discusses untapped human capital. One of numerous illustrations comes from Louis B. Mayer, the former head of MGM Studios, who is said to have understood that the only capital that really counts is human capital. Bennis quotes Mayer, "The inventory goes home at night." He knew that his filmmaking company would have been nothing without the creative energies of the writers, directors, and actors (1999, 43). Can this be said of our schools, where the faculty is the single most influential ingredient in the school community?

The Educational Force

The third force available to administrators is the power that comes from having expertise in education and schooling. At this point, the administrator is viewed as a "clinical practitioner ... who is adept at diagnosing educational problems; counseling teachers; providing for supervision, evaluation, and staff development; and developing curriculum" (Sergiovanni 1995, 86). Throughout the school day, an administrator has the opportunity to empower the faculty and exert influence in one-on-one problem-solving conferences, in curriculum planning meetings, and in classrooms in which he or she conducts demonstration lessons.

In my experience, the educational force is a crucial force that is sorely lacking in our movement. Many leaders are unfamiliar with child development characteristics, recent developments in curriculum issues, new techniques in classroom instruction, and the critical need for instruction in technology for students and faculty alike. No more vivid example of this exists in my experience than with the influence my first principal had on my career. During my early weeks of teaching and coaching in an intermediate school (seventh and eighth grades), I struggled to understand the needs and attitudes of the students in a community that was foreign to me. (My strong Southern accent was particularly entertaining to the kids!) I would drop by the principal's office and start pouring out about a management problem or some classroom conflict. Immediately, my mentor would switch into role-play mode and perfectly mimic the lingo of my students and complete the hypothetical dialogue by describing exactly how I should respond and react. His advice never failed, and for that reason, I was always ready to follow his leadership.

Sergiovanni summarizes the discussion at this point before moving to the final two forces:

> Technical, human, and educational forces of leadership—brought together in an effort to promote and maintain quality schooling—provide the critical mass needed for basic school competence. A shortage in any of the three forces upsets this critical mass, and less effective schooling is likely to occur. Studies of excellence in organizations suggest that despite the link between technical, human, and educational aspects of leadership and basic competence, the presence of the three does not guarantee excellence. Excellent organizations, schools among them, are characterized by other leadership qualities represented by symbolic and cultural forces of leadership. (Sergiovanni 1995, 87)

The Symbolic Force
The fourth force of leadership comes from the leader's ability to focus the attention of others on matters of importance to the school. In this role, the administrator acts as "the chief ... who [emphasizes] the modeling of important goals and behaviors and signals to others what is important and valuable in the school." These activities can include "touring the school; visiting classrooms; seeking out and spending visible time with students; downplaying management concerns in favor of educational concerns; presiding over ceremonies, rituals, and other important occasions; and providing a unified vision of the school through proper use of words and actions" (Sergiovanni 1995, 87). There are several key opportunities in the life of your school to exercise symbolic force. Unfortunately, I have visited numerous campuses where the administrators have failed to discipline themselves to capitalize on these.

A vice principal once invited me to be the chapel speaker at his school. The administrator opened the worship service with a series of comments about a current event from the previous day and then inexplicably left the worship center, not to return.

With the national emphasis on safe school environments, I think that it behooves administrators to be present at the arrival and dismissal of students as often as is possible. I asked not to have any appointments especially at the close of school so that I could be a visible presence as students were picked up in the car-pool line. I made sure I was there if the weather was stormy, setting the example for the rest of the staff and providing my experience to help the traffic flow as smoothly as possible.

The Cultural Force
The fifth force available to administrators is the power of leadership that comes from building a unique school culture. The literature of a successful school discusses the importance of this dimension in building a culture that promotes and sustains a school's distinctives and values. In this role, the administrator is acting as "the high priest who is seeking to define, strengthen, and articulate those enduring values, beliefs, and cultural strands that give the school its unique identity over time." Some of the leadership activities that the administrator might engage in as a high priest include "articulating school purposes and mission; socializing new members to the school; telling stories and maintaining or reinforcing myths, traditions, and beliefs; explaining 'the way things operate around here'; developing and displaying a system of symbols; and rewarding those who reflect this culture" (Sergiovanni 1995, 88). One of the earliest opportunities to demonstrate this role and to exert this force of leadership is on opening day with the staff each school year. This day was the highlight of my work year, the day I had planned for since the previous one twelve months earlier. I asked the Lord for just the right Scripture that would exhort the faculty. I saved teaching and student products to present as samples of work that we believed our students should be producing. And I always included humorous and touching stories from the past that illustrated the presence of God in the life of our school.

If you are involved in establishing a new school, it is vital that you begin now to create a sense of tradition and high expectation, no matter how small the student body. At our school's first graduation, with a class of only eleven graduates, I scripted a formal processional, a uniformed movement for each student to follow when it was his or her turn to receive a diploma, and a synchronized turning of the eleven tassels. My wife, the organist for the gathering of less than 200, found my routines somewhat stuffy. Ten years later, however, when our graduating class had over fifty students and our attendance exceeded 1,000, she confessed to me, "Now I get it."

You Take the Helm

Review the forces of leadership as summarized in table 7.1. For each of the five, describe an activity, which has not already been presented, that the school leader can perform. Can you identify and describe a leader from your past who has exhibited most, if not all, of these behaviors?

Table 7.1

Force	Role	Management of ...
technical	management engineer	structures and events
human	human engineer	psychological factors
educational	clinical practitioner	curriculum and instruction
symbolic	chief	expectation and commitments
cultural	high priest	the confidence in the school

Gene Garrick, author of one of the early books on Christian school administration, shared the following insights:

> The administrator has the chief responsibility to teach the philosophy and its implications to the school family. He is the professional, the one who is expected to do the most thinking and have the greatest knowledge.
>
> It is vital to the long-range success of the school that every member of the educational team understand and be committed to the school's philosophy of education. This will make the difference between a genuinely Christian school and one in name only.
>
> The first requisite is that the administrator learn to articulate the philosophy. "Reading maketh a full man…, and writing an exact man," said Sir Francis Bacon. First, write it so that another educator can comprehend it in philosophical terms. Produce the

philosophy in popular, readable form for in-house publications such as the newsletter for parents, school brochure or church bulletin.

At every opportunity, speak on the Christian philosophy of education. Do not always give it that title, however, or people may not respond. Develop one or more messages from Scripture which set forth the basic concepts and use them widely. (1984, 18–19)

The Spiritual Force

Prominently missing from this chapter's discussion on the forces of leadership as developed by Sergiovanni is that which is most significant in a Christian school—the spiritual force. In this role, the administrator serves as God's under-shepherd to the flock that has been assigned to him or her and carries out this responsibility through the power and the presence of the Holy Spirit. If you have never been under the authority of a godly man or woman who exudes the glow and confidence that results from a close walk with the Lord, then this dimension will remain unclear until you identify such a leader. There is such a man on the campus where I teach. When his name is mentioned, the universal response is, Reverend Motley is a godly man. A conversation with this man is a delight, because you walk away knowing that you have been with someone who has spent time with the Lord that day.

The power of the Holy Spirit is immeasurable as an administrator interacts with students and faculty throughout the day. During many conferences, I prayed not only before the conference began, but silently as it progressed. On some occasions, the Spirit would tutor my mind: "Say nothing; merely listen." Often those sessions ended with my visitor praising me for great insight or sensitivity, when in fact, I had not said a word. In other situations, perhaps during a time of discipline, including deciding on some appropriate punishment, the Holy Spirit can lead you to a determination that will make all the difference in the life of the student, though he or she may not know it at the time. Frequently, I believed He was directing me as I created some new alternative to help solve a difficult situation. Following such a conference, I would think to myself, "Thank you, Lord. I know that this idea today has not come from any textbook or class that I have taken."

Leadership by Outrage

After an administrator's leadership has been recognized through one or more of the "forces" discussed previously, he or she can use another technique to protect and advance the values that have been established in the school community. This approach flows naturally from within the leader because of a passion for these core values and the purposes that the community has embraced. Sergiovanni has termed the forceful expression of this passion as leadership by outrage: "Leadership by outrage is a symbolic act that communicates importance and meaning and that touches people in ways not possible when leadership is viewed only as something objective and calculated. Leaders use outrage to highlight issues of purpose defined by the school's shared covenant and this outrage adds considerable value to their leadership practice." To clarify, these moments of toughness and course correction are expressed by leaders because standards that have been agreed on have been violated, not because the leaders have been inconvenienced in some way. Sergiovanni adds, "They are outraged when they see these values ignored or violated. The values of the common core represent nonnegotiables that comprise cultural strands that define a way of life in the school" (Sergiovanni 1995, 138). When administrators demonstrate their serious commitment in a passionate way, others will want to follow the administrators' lead and this expression of outrage becomes an obligation of everyone on the faculty and beyond. The leaders will seek to kindle this commitment in others.

Christ gave us a perfect example of leadership by outrage when He cleansed the temple of the money changers and other merchants. Certainly no believer would argue that our Lord acted hastily or capriciously. He did not shout, "Everyone, be quiet! I'm trying to teach!" He acted forcefully and passionately about the blatant violations against His Father's house. Caution must be taken at this point. I cannot think of a situation in which I would condone throwing chairs or turning over tables. But the point remains that violations of strongly held values must be spoken about in passionate terms. Nehemiah once again provides us with outstanding leadership illustrations in chapter 13. While Governor Nehemiah is out of town in Babylon (v. 6), Eliashib the priest had provided Tobiah, a relative of the priest and archenemy of Nehemiah, a room in the temple that was supposed to be used for grain offerings and storage of implements of worship. Here's how God's man responded: "Some time later I asked his permission and came back to Jerusalem. Here I learned about the evil thing Eliashib had done in providing Tobiah a room in the courts of the house of God. I was greatly displeased and threw all Tobiah's household goods out of the room. I gave orders to purify the rooms, and then I put back into them the equipment of the house of God, with the grain offerings and the incense" (Nehemiah 13:6–9). Note the forceful language of the passage—*evil, greatly displeased, threw,* and *gave orders.*

A second illustration follows immediately when Nehemiah discovers that the food allotments due the Levites had not been given out and, consequently, they and the singers who performed in the temple had left their temple posts and gone out to work in the field. The leader expressed outrage: "I *rebuked* the officials and asked them, 'Why is the house of God neglected?' Then I called them together and stationed them at their posts" (Nehemiah 13:11, italics added). Once again, his language was strong and he took corrective action.

Seemingly, with ever-increasing passion, Nehemiah responds to a third confrontation in the next passage. Some of the men of Judah were violating the Sabbath by working and trading: "In those days I saw men in Judah treading winepresses on the Sabbath and bringing in grain and loading it on donkeys, together with wine, grapes, figs and all other kinds of loads. And they were bringing all this into Jerusalem on the Sabbath. Therefore I *warned* them against selling food on that day" (Nehemiah 13:15, italics added).

Note here that Nehemiah does not flinch, nor does he delay. He deals with the problem as it occurs. But it did not end there: "Men from Tyre who lived in Jerusalem were bringing in fish and all kinds of merchandise and selling them in Jerusalem on the Sabbath to the people of Judah. I *rebuked* the nobles of Judah and said to them, 'What is this *wicked* thing you are doing—*desecrating* the Sabbath day? Didn't your forefathers do the same things, so that our God brought *all this calamity* upon us and upon this city? *Now you are stirring up more wrath against Israel by desecrating the Sabbath*' " (Nehemiah 13:16–18, italics added).

In this passage, the leader connects their current sin to the evil of their fathers and reminds them of the heavy penalty that the nation had paid for their rebellion. Once again, Nehemiah does not stop short but follows through to make sure his instructions are followed: "When evening shadows fell on the gates of Jerusalem before the Sabbath, I *ordered* the doors to be shut and not opened until the Sabbath was over. I stationed some of my own men at the gates so that no load could be brought in on the Sabbath day" (Nehemiah 13:19, italics added). Even then, not everyone knew he was serious. Some traders and merchants dared to spend the night outside the city gate. And the governor didn't blink: "But I *warned* them and said, 'Why do you spend the night by the wall? If you do this again, I will lay hands on you.' From that time on they no longer came on the Sabbath" (13:21, italics added).

At this point, I will mention that I encourage administrators to tell an unruly person, when necessary, that they are prepared to call the police and have the person removed if he or she cannot behave properly. But Nehemiah had one more challenge to deal with—the violation of God's instructions about marriage: "Moreover, in those days I saw men of Judah who had married women from Ashdod, Ammon and Moab. Half of their children spoke the language of Ashdod or the language of one of the other peoples, and did not know how to speak the language of Judah" (Nehemiah 13:23–24). Can you imagine his shock when he not only discovered that his men had married alien wives but that the language of their children was not Hebrew! He saved his greatest passion for this violation of God's instructions: "*I rebuked them and called curses down on them. I beat some of the men and pulled out their hair. I made them take an oath in God's name* and said: 'You are not to give your daughters in marriage to their sons, nor are you to take their daughters in marriage for your sons or for yourselves' " (13:25, italics added).

Did Nehemiah go too far this time? Scripture does not comment on his decision to put his hands on those who had violated the teachings of Moses. We quickly recognize that such behavior today would result in the arrest of an administrator who grabs or assaults someone. Having said that, there was no doubt in anyone's mind about what Nehemiah's standards were or about his conviction to deal with those who went against God's covenant.

In summary, the effective administrator must clearly communicate what the community holds dear, be vigilant to watch for the continuation of these values, and be prepared to speak and act boldly when these standards are violated.

In their best seller, *The Leadership Challenge*, James Kouzes and Barry Posner (2002, 14–19) report on the five personal qualities that they found in the executives of organizations in which extraordinary things are being done. Through case analyses and questionnaires, they examined the dynamic process of leadership and uncovered the following practices:

Model the way. The leaders' stories that the authors heard reveal that the executive first must have a clear sense of his or her own values and guiding principles. However, the researchers observed that the leader must do more than articulate these ideas; the leader must actively demonstrate them in his or her lifestyle and work ethic. I was fortunate to see this behavior in the administrators that the Lord brought into my life, especially one I knew for only a few hours. Principal Angie Fortunato was like Vince Lombardi, the former coach of the Green Bay Packers, in his passion, energy, and commitment, but he was a servant leader as well. After being hired as a new teacher in a high school in Howard County, Maryland, I showed up for some last-minute work on the Saturday before school was to start. Much to my surprise, Angie walked into my classroom that morning and asked if I needed anything. I responded that I was ready to go except that I did not have an eraser or a stapler. He chatted briefly and left, saying that he would put them in my teacher's box in the main office. Moments later, he returned with them in hand and wished me a smooth start. I left a few minutes after this exchange and would not learn until school opened that this servant leader had died of a massive heart attack within an hour of bringing me what I needed. I was perhaps the last person to see Angie alive. The faculty grieved for their leader for weeks, and his actions as a model will never be forgotten. During my fifteen years of serving as an administrator, I sought to live out his passion for service each day of my career.

Inspire a shared vision. Kouzes and Posner write, "Leaders have a desire to make something happen, to change the way things are, to create something that no one else has ever created before. In some ways, leaders live their lives backward. They see pictures in their mind's eye of what the results will look like even before they've started their project, much as an architect draws a blueprint or an engineer builds a model. Their clear image of the future pulls them forward" (2002, 15). Remember the vision of the Promised Land that Joshua and Caleb described? They could taste it; the picture was so real! Unfortunately, their vision of God's best was not shared by the others, and these two saints would have to delay carrying out the plan God had placed in their hearts. On the topic of vision, Ollie Gibbs reflects, "Vision is the ability to see God at work, in spite of the obstacles. To put this in a school context, vision is education with eternity in view" (1999, 29).

Challenge the process. Do you see yourself as a pioneer? Leaders are just that. They see a development where others see just a forest. But do not be confused by thinking that this applies only to roads and buildings. Kouzes and Posner discovered that innovations, risk taking, and creative thinking were taking place in the minds of the leaders they talked to.

An important word of caution is in order at this point. All too often, new administrators will wreak havoc in an established school, if for no other reason than to put their mark on the structures and procedures of their new environment. I have encountered leaders who will symbolically set off an atomic bomb, let the dust settle, and see who is still around to do things their way. Do I need to say that this behavior is not Christlike? Yes, such behavior occurs every day in the world, but we are called to be an example for the world to follow, not the other way around.

Enable others to act. The authors recorded during their interviews that they developed a simple test to determine if someone was in the process of becoming a leader. That test was the frequency of the use of the word *we* (Kouzes and Posner 2002, 18). Tom Landry, the famous coach of the Dallas Cowboys, said of leadership, "It is the ability to get others to do that which they may not want to, to become all they have dreamed they could be." During his historic leadership of that football team and organization, both were known as an exceptional example of teamwork and cooperation.

What would your passion to see others develop into leaders look like if it were to be placed inside of a vehicle? I have met administrators who are satisfied to do ministry in a subcompact as long as they get to oversee every activity that is taking place in the school. And the first time someone shows initiative, he or she is asked to sit in the back or get out.

Effective leaders, however, wish to have a busload of independent-thinking, enthusiastic staff members who are ready to participate in a team effort to do ministry.

Encourage the heart. One of the great opportunities in administration is to seize every chance to cheer others on. Effective administrators are frequently moving around the building, stopping by classes, and observing both teachers and students. In those times, you can identify a teacher assisting a student one-on-one, answering the questions of struggling students, or challenging students to perform at their best. Take a moment and write a brief note to be placed in the teacher's mailbox. As a teacher and administrator, I tried to discipline myself to call at least one parent a week to report the good performance of a student I had observed. And the school and faculty need celebrations on a larger scale to praise God for what He is doing in and through students and adults at the school.

At Southeastern Seminary in Wake Forest, North Carolina, the president of the school gave the final message of the school year each spring and had a special time of dedication for the many families who would be leaving for the mission field. During this ceremony, Dr. Patterson would call these men and women forward for an altar call, along with all the professors who would be praying with them. It was always an extremely heartfelt experience as he would weep at the thought of the dedication of these young couples who were committed to following Christ, even at the risk of the lives of their young children.

Management and Leadership in a School Setting

The research of Gerald Ubben, Larry Hughes, and Cynthia Norris in *The Principal: Creative Leadership for Effective Schools* will help a school administrator place the broad discussion of leadership roles, qualities, and skills in a school environment. Before identifying what they term the five functions of administration, they first clarify the two dimensions of leadership and management. In general, they believe that the demands of orderliness in a school organization require the presence of good management skills, while the challenges and struggles that accompany any school community demand leadership skills to work toward satisfactory change. They make this distinction:

> Management is status quo oriented and assumes a highly stable environment. There is an assumption made that the standards or norms that have been previously established are appropriate ones and the task is to see that conditions are aligned with the established goals. If things are not operating effectively, it is the

job of the manager to see that corrective action is taken to bring things back into balance. Management operates from a problem-solving perspective with little attention given to questioning the appropriateness of established norms.... The notion of leadership is much different. Leaders build on the status quo, to be sure, but go well beyond it. As Foster stated, "Leaders always have one face turned toward change" (1984, 13). There is a constant reexamination of current conditions and a formulation of new possibilities. Leadership is a problem-finding as well as a problem-solving approach. It is a dynamic process that challenges the organization to higher levels of consciousness and growth. (Ubben, Hughes, and Norris 2001, 18)

Within the context of this differentiation, the authors state that the principalship comprises five functions, four "inside" and one "outside" (Ubben, Hughes, and Norris 2001, 12): staffing and instructional development (see chapter 8), curriculum development (see chapter 5), student services, and resource procurement including budgeting and facilities (see chapter 10). They term these "inside" functions. The "outside" function is public relations (see chapter 6).

You Take the Helm

Consider the five functions as outlined in *The Principal: Creative Leadership for Effective Schools* and identify one management activity and one leadership activity for each function:

Administrative Function	Management Activity	Leadership Activity
staff and instructional development		
curriculum development		
student services		
resource procurement		
public relations		

Leadership Roles in the Life Span of an Organization

In its simplest form, the distinction between leadership and management (see the preceding discussion of Ubben, Hughes, and Norris) can be seen as the contrast between present orientation and future orientation. The roles of management involve the efficient ordering of the present as presented in Gulick's POSDCoRB (planning, organizing, staffing, directing, coordinating, reporting, and budgeting), which I discussed in chapter 2. The roles of leadership involve having the courage to change the present for a preferable future. Both involve significant influence in a ministry or organization. To artificially separate all roles or activities into "management" or "leader" piles is to miss the complexity of interaction between humans involved in dynamic organizations. However, in the cultural life span of most ministries and learning communities, there are critical roles that are needed for their continued success. The leadership roles grid in figure 7.1 identifies the vital roles that must be present in order for a school to survive present challenges and prepare for future growth.

The leadership roles grid presents four personas or roles that are demanded over time, usually ten to twenty years, depending on the longevity of the original leadership and how rapidly the organization grows. The administrator will be called on to function primarily in one of these roles, depending on the age of the institution. Drawing on the research of Ubben, with slight modifications, the administrator must execute the five functions of *governance, finance, personnel, community,* and *instruction,* no matter which role he or she is carrying out. However, the activities (see table 7.2) associated with these functions will vary, depending on the role that the administrator is fulfilling at the time. The five functions are as follows:

Pioneer
The leader is called on to explore new territory for the creation, relocation, or expansion of the school. The leader's activities are characterized by breaking new ground and testing creative solutions to the challenges that face the ministry.

Mayor
The leader is called on to bring the first stages of order to the new ministry by articulating a more focused vision and clarifying the core values of the community. During this time, traditions are established and the constituents begin to rally around those things that are most important to them.

Town Manager
The leader is called on to bring further clarity to the core values of the community by making practices and policies that are a part of the daily

activities routine. Consensus building and teamwork characterize the leader's activities.

Judge

The leader is called on to take decisive action as the vision is managed and maintained. In order to protect the vision and values of the community, the leader must make changes, including the removal of those who threaten the continuation of the mission of the organization.

Figure 7.1 Leadership Roles Grid

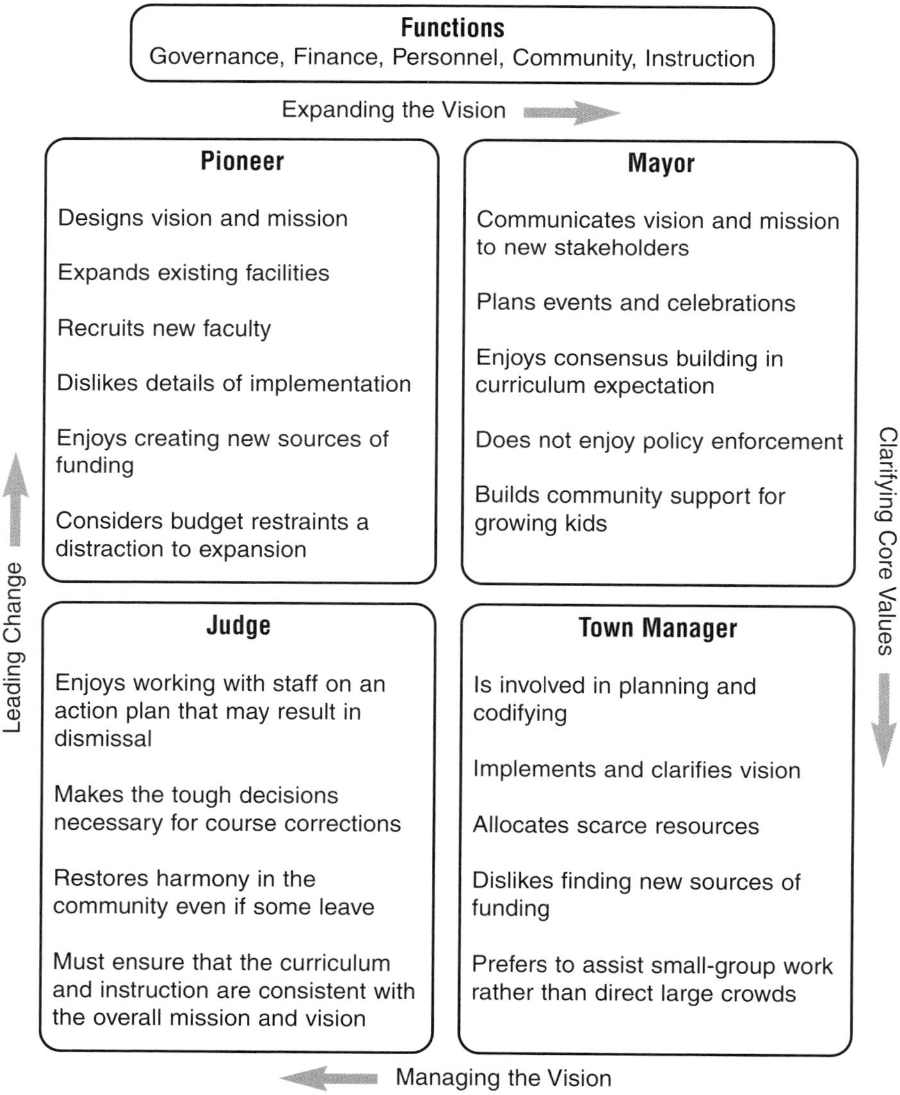

Functions
Governance, Finance, Personnel, Community, Instruction

Expanding the Vision ➡

Leading Change ⬆

Clarifying Core Values ⬇

Pioneer

Designs vision and mission

Expands existing facilities

Recruits new faculty

Dislikes details of implementation

Enjoys creating new sources of funding

Considers budget restraints a distraction to expansion

Mayor

Communicates vision and mission to new stakeholders

Plans events and celebrations

Enjoys consensus building in curriculum expectation

Does not enjoy policy enforcement

Builds community support for growing kids

Judge

Enjoys working with staff on an action plan that may result in dismissal

Makes the tough decisions necessary for course corrections

Restores harmony in the community even if some leave

Must ensure that the curriculum and instruction are consistent with the overall mission and vision

Town Manager

Is involved in planning and codifying

Implements and clarifies vision

Allocates scarce resources

Dislikes finding new sources of funding

Prefers to assist small-group work rather than direct large crowds

⬅ Managing the Vision

Table 7.2

Leadership Role Preference

Record your preference for the following roles in a school setting by writing "True" beside each statement that describes your preference.

_____ 1. I enjoy communicating vision and mission to new stakeholders.

_____ 2. I do not enjoy finding new sources of funding.

_____ 3. I prefer to assist small-group work rather than direct large crowds.

_____ 4. I enjoy designing the vision and mission statements from scratch.

_____ 5. I dislike the details of implementation.

_____ 6. I enjoy making the tough decisions necessary for course corrections in the direction of the school.

_____ 7. I enjoy recruiting new faculty who are unfamiliar with the school.

_____ 8. I enjoy implementing and clarifying the vision in concrete ways.

_____ 9. I do not enjoy policy enforcement of personnel matters.

_____ 10. I enjoy making sure that the curriculum and instruction are in alignment with the overall mission and vision of the school.

_____ 11. I dislike the budget restraints that are a distraction to expansion.

_____ 12. I enjoy planning events and celebrations.

_____ 13. I enjoy looking for ways to expand beyond the existing facilities for a growing program.

_____ 14. I enjoy planning and codifying curriculum in preparation for accreditation.

_____ 15. I enjoy restoring harmony in the community even if it means that some may leave.

_____ 16. I enjoy building consensus in order to execute the curriculum.

_____ 17. I enjoy building community support for developing kids' talents.

_____ 18. I enjoy working with a staff member on an action plan that may result in dismissal.

_____ 19. I enjoy allocating scarce resources to various projects.

_____ 20. I enjoy creating new sources of funding from sources unfamiliar to our program.

Leadership Role Preference Score Sheet		
On your response sheet, circle the numbers in each column that you've marked "True."		
Pioneer	4, 5, 7, 11, 13, 20	Total: _____
Mayor	1, 9, 12, 16, 17	Total: _____
Town Manager	2, 3, 8, 14, 19	Total: _____
Judge	6, 10, 15, 18	Total: _____
After totaling each row of numbers, record the labels below for your highest and second highest scores. These represent the roles for which you have the strongest preference.		

You Take the Helm

Read the following letter that arrived at the home of a child (we will call him Ben) who was dismissed from a Christian school. Evaluate the administrator's leadership style on the basis of his approach to this family.

> It saddens me to realize that the time we have spent working with you and Ben during this school year has for the most part been a total waste. We have listened and attempted to respond, keeping Ben's best interests in mind. We have in fact spent more time with you than we have with any other parent at the school.
>
> In a last effort to salvage this year for Ben, we bowed to your request that we send Mark away. You insisted that Mark was the cause of Ben's problems and that things would be better without Mark at school. This, of course, did not help solve Ben's problems.
>
> The truth of the matter is that you are doing Ben a terrible disservice. You continue to talk with my faculty members and

other parents regarding Ben's problems. Yet, you refuse to take any of their advice. This makes life worse for Ben because he feels that in order to please you he must tell you unpleasant things.

The latest problem involves a private party for which we have no responsibility. I have instructed all of my employees not to listen to any complaints you have resulting from this party. Since the eighth-grade trip seems to be a huge problem for your family, I have instructed Mr. Ashby to remove Ben's name from the list of those traveling on that trip. We are enclosing your money for the trip. Hopefully, this will help Ben to understand that his social behavior, his inability to follow simple instructions that are meant to help him, and your constant interference are severely limiting his ability to have acceptable interaction with his peers. Ben's refusal to listen to and follow suggestions is his problem. You need to let him "own" his problems and not continue to enable him in his lack of social skills. You, on the other hand, must stop the phone calls to my faculty and staff.

I have instructed my faculty and staff not to respond to you in the future. This is a problem that you need to solve as a family. There is nothing further we can do to help you. I suggest that you get Ben some counseling before he goes to high school. If you do not, all of his problems will follow him wherever he goes.

Ben has much potential. He is trying desperately to grow up. However, he will not be able to develop that potential until you allow him to grow up on his own terms and in his own way. I hope you will think about this and see this as a positive step for Ben.

IV. The Helmsman as Builder of the Body: Ephesians 4:11-16

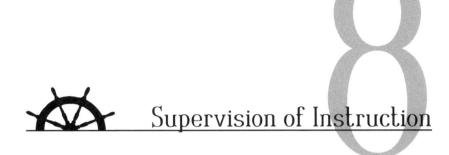

Supervision of Instruction

Principle for Guiding Principals:

The effective administrator equips the faculty to grow professionally by developing a positive, trusting relationship with each teacher and by carrying out meaningful supervisory activities.

"Are you aware of what's going on in the seventh-grade math class?" the parent on the phone asked. Mary, the administrator, had to admit to herself that she was not, but she was reluctant to be that transparent with the caller. She had been by informally on a weekly basis to peer into each classroom, but she was unaware of any problem in Miss King's room. Apparently, there were discipline problems that caused the teacher and students to waste time on management issues. In addition, the young teacher had instituted too many rules that were resulting in frequent interruptions for such things as trash and sharpening pencils, which students could have been taught to manage themselves. Mary reassured the anxious parent, thanked her for the call, and promised to get back with her. After checking her calendar, she grabbed a clipboard and a legal pad and headed for the middle-school wing. As she walked, she reviewed in her mind what she had told the staff she would be looking for during her classroom visits. Unfortunately, she had not

The Helmsman

recorded these expectations on a form that she could use for such an occasion. She wondered if she would have the right answers.

My first teaching job was in Williamsburg, Virginia, at a school located on the beautiful Colonial Parkway. Nestled among the lovely dogwoods and magnolias along this picturesque drive was the Yorktown Naval Weapons Station, where U.S. ships delivered and loaded various secret munitions. The parkway ends at Yorktown, the site of the final engagement of the Revolutionary War. Situated at the mouth of the York River, the town has a prominent bridge that connects the mainland to a peninsula across the river. The bridge is unusual because it does not open like a drawbridge, but two sections of the bridge rotate on giant columns to create an opening for large ships to pass through.

After returning home from school one afternoon, I observed a major traffic backup in this small community and learned that the unthinkable had occurred—one of the naval destroyers had collided with the bridge and had knocked off one section from the mechanism that allowed it to close. Unfortunately, many commuters from the other side of the bridge had to drive nearly 100 miles up to Richmond and back again to get to and from work for weeks while the bridge was being repaired. The military's decision was not made public at the time, but everyone assumed that the captain of the ship lost his commission. His crew, because of poor training or lax supervision, had failed to carry out their assigned tasks.

I share this story to illustrate the most significant responsibility that the helmsman has after correctly setting the course of the ship. That responsibility is to train the crew and to monitor their performance. The helmsman is ultimately responsible for how effectively each crew member carries out his or her assigned tasks. It is at this point that the leader has the greatest influence on the organization's success in reaching its prescribed destination. The helmsman may not be able to carry out the specifics of each crew member's job, but the helmsman must understand the relationship each member's performance has to the whole and be able to provide the necessary training and resources to help each one be successful. How this training and monitoring is carried out is vital to the health and vitality of the entire community. In the above illustration, the bridge was eventually repaired and life returned to normal for all those inconvenienced by the accident. However, in the execution of daily instructional duties in a Christian school, the school's crew is responsible for the destiny of far greater cargo—the souls of God's children.

As I have had the privilege to speak at a number of Christian school conventions, I have experienced that the seminars I teach on the topic of supervision of instruction are filled each time. The administrators are hungry for insights into how to more effectively carry out this portion of their leadership. I have also learned from these administrators' comments and testimonies that the reality of their daily activities chokes out their best intentions to participate in the most important function of the school—classroom instruction. This chapter will present a biblical foundation for supervision, practical techniques for the implementation of basic models, and a recommended calendar of activities to guide an administrator through an entire school year. I challenge you to consider these concepts carefully, because I believe no single leadership role will make more of an impact on the achievement of the school's mission than supervision of instruction. However, no single role is more neglected in school administration today.

The Helmsman as Equipper and Builder of the Body: Ephesians 4:11–16

The apostle Paul challenged the church leaders at Ephesus to build the Body of Christ as they equipped each member to perform some ministry for the advancement of the kingdom. This exhortation applies to leaders of kingdom schools today: "To prepare God's people for works of service, so that the body of Christ may be built up until we all reach unity in the faith and in the knowledge of the Son of God and become mature, attaining to the whole measure of the fullness of Christ" (Ephesians 4:12–13).

The Greek word that gives us our word *prepare* can also be translated as "equip." This word in Paul's day was used to describe the activity of mending nets. (We find this same word used in Matthew 4:21 to describe the work of James and John when Jesus called them to join Him.) Paul presents the leaders with the responsibility to adequately equip God's people so they can actively and effectively participate in serving. The result is powerful—the Body is unified and mature, and it is able to strive for the fullness of Christ.

The Helmsman as Shepherd

In Proverbs 27:23, Scripture provides administrators with another exhortation: "Know well the condition of your flocks, And pay attention to your herds" (NASB). The shepherds in Solomon's day were expected to be diligent, compassionate, and caring while supervising the flock. A literal translation for the word *condition* is "face." To respond in this way requires the overseer to spend the necessary time to focus on each person under his or her care to understand each person's unique needs, personal struggles, and maturity level. I have always found that the most challenging aspect of leading people is the mysterious process of discovering what motivates or demotivates them. To do so, the administrator indeed must "pay attention" to identify what inspires each staff member to do more than is required.

The parable of the good shepherd spoken by Jesus presents a beautiful picture of the relationship that results when a supervisor is attentive and caring: "But he who enters by the door is a shepherd of the sheep. To him the doorkeeper opens, and the sheep hear his voice, and he calls his own sheep by name and leads them out. When he puts forth all his own, he goes ahead of them, and the sheep follow him because they know his voice. A stranger they simply will not follow, but will flee from him, because they do not know the voice of strangers" (John 10:2–5, NASB). This picture of Jesus as the Good Shepherd whom believers respond to reveals the heart of a leader who has spent the time with His flock that is necessary to be known by them. The result is that the sheep respond to His voice and follow. It is well known that shepherds lead sheep; they do not drive them. It is also well known that if shepherds spend time with their sheep, they will smell like them.

Byrle Kynerd, the superintendent of Briarwood Christian School in Birmingham, Alabama, reflects on the importance of building personal relationships: "People are of supreme value to God. They are the only part of creation made in His image and the only part that is immortal. Cultivating personal relationships should be a priority for administrators. An environment that prioritizes and values relationships develops a special community. This community has a service focus designed to help people meet one another's needs and to provide outreach to unbelievers" (2002, 127).

The Helmsman as Steward

A third picture from Scripture is that of steward—one to whom God has entrusted a special responsibility. In his letter to the Ephesians, Paul wrote of the life-changing assignment the Lord gave to him: "If indeed you have heard of the stewardship of God's grace which was given to me for you" (Ephesians 3:2, NASB).

At this point, the helmsman takes on a new role as part of God's design. Figuratively speaking, the helmsman goes down to the lowest deck of rowers, picks up a paddle, and becomes an "under-rower," the Greek word

Paul chose to describe his stewardship to his Savior. Have you looked at your responsibility to Christ in this way? Do you view your position as one of lowliness when you consider God's abundance toward you? Do you value each person God has placed in your care as a part of your stewardship that you will be accountable for? Viewing your administration and supervision in this way will inspire you to make the most of the time and talents each staff member can contribute to the kingdom.

Let's summarize the biblical pictures of supervision:

Equipper and Builder of the Body
The supervisor believes that God has gifted each staff member with special talents that need to be developed. *Growth* is the key word in the relationship; instructional supervision provides the staff member with the opportunity to learn and grow.

Good Shepherd
The supervisor believes that he or she is God's "under-shepherd" while overseeing the sheep in his or her care. *Trust* is the key word in the relationship. The sheep respond to the suggestions and directions of the leader because there has been a spirit of trust established through the care and concern that has been shown to each sheep.

Steward
The supervisor believes that he or she has been given a responsibility from the Lord to care for the needs of the staff. *Service* is the key word in the relationship. The steward serves both the Master and those entrusted to him or her.

Definition of Supervision

Morris Cogan, Robert Goldhammer, and other educators at Harvard University began to develop the basic concepts of supervision as part of their preparation of student teachers in the late 1950s. Since then, a variety of definitions have been put forth to explain the role most educators call "the supervision of instruction." Here are a few:

• "Supervision may be defined as all the activities of the school team including such matters as all the methods of teaching; teacher morale and motivation; in-service training; biblical integration of the curriculum; and the evaluation of instruction carried on within the framework of the Christian philosophy of education, to the glory of God" (Fortosis 1984, 100).

- Carl Glickman, another researcher and author in the field of supervision, defines supervision as "assistance for the improvement of instruction" (Glickman, Gordan, and Ross-Gordon 1997, 8).

- Gordon B. Brown, author of *Guiding Faculty to Excellence*, claims: "Supervision will be conceived as activities performed directly with teachers for the purpose of improving their delivery of classroom instruction and, consequently, student learning" (2002, 3).

As we proceed in our discussion of supervision, key terms must be identified and their relationship to the overall process must be clarified. Building on Brown's definition above, supervision involves a number of activities as the part of a process that usually begins prior to the first day of school and continues in an ongoing cycle with specific benchmarks occurring throughout the year. These include the following:

Classroom observation: The collection and analysis of data during instructional time, with the main purpose of providing data (developed in a later discussion on clinical supervision).

Observation instrument: A prescribed format that is used by the observer for the collection of data. Ideally, the faculty member assists in the creation of the instrument. At the very least, the teacher should be given a copy of the instrument and understand the categories, specific items, and terms of measurement.

Formative evaluation: The ongoing descriptive assessment of a teacher's performance for the purpose of improving the teacher's instructional effectiveness and overall performance. Key words are *formative* and *ongoing* as opposed to *summative*.

Summative evaluation: The periodic objective assessment by the administrator of a teacher's overall performance for the purpose of making personnel decisions. The key word is *summative* because the evaluation occurs near the end of the school year and is a summary of the data collected throughout the year. (For a more in-depth study, see www.ascd.org.)

Staff development: The formal and informal arrangement of activities designed to assist teachers in professional growth.

The Purpose of Supervision

Sergiovanni presents three reasons or purposes for establishing supervision in your school (1995, 216–17):

1. *Quality control.* The principal is responsible for monitoring teaching and learning in her or his school and does so by visiting classrooms, touring the school, talking with people, and visiting with students.
2. *Professional development.* Helping teachers to grow and to develop in their understanding of teaching and classroom life, in improving basic teaching skills, and in expanding their knowledge and use of teaching repertoires is the second purpose of supervision.
3. *Teacher motivation.* Often overlooked, but important nonetheless, is a third purpose of supervision—building and nurturing motivation and commitment to teaching, to the school's overall purposes, and to the school's defining educational platform.

History of Supervision of Instruction

In *Administration of the Christian School,* Anthony Fortosis provides a brief history of supervision of instruction (1984, 100–101):

Colonial Time to Civil War Period
Laymen did the supervising of these early schools, and they were concerned about accountability physically, academically and spiritually. The concern was not only that children be taught their "letters" but that the doctrines of Christianity might be inculcated in them.

Post Civil War to 1930s
During this period, educational professionals did most of the supervising. They inspected the schools with a rather autocratic approach, putting little emphasis on helping the teacher improve professionally. This supervision was thus labeled "snoopervision." The writer remembers being an elementary student in a public school classroom where his teachers were visibly frightened by the austere presence of a school superintendent who hovered silently in the back of the room for a few tense minutes and departed to the intense relief of the teachers.

1930s to the Present
This period has progressed from direct classroom observation to assess teacher weaknesses to more sophisticated methods involving what has been termed clinical supervision, a cooperative effort involving supervisor and teachers who work together to bring assistance to the teacher toward improving

instruction via various means, including in-service activities, curriculum development, etc.

Clinical Supervision

The clinical supervision model is the most fundamental strategy for an administrator to use to interact with a teacher in order to obtain a baseline of information that will be used to determine the teacher's performance. This process includes a variety of steps in addition to the well-known point of emphasis—the classroom observation.

Clinical supervision is a powerful model for professional development for two reasons: It works, and it provides a conceptual framework that can be transferred to other models of supervision and evaluation also directed to professional development. Pioneered by Morris Cogan, clinical supervision refers to a specific cycle or pattern of working with teachers (1973, 9). The essential ingredients of clinical supervision include the establishment of a healthy general supervisory climate, a mutual support system called "colleagueship," and a cycle of supervision comprising conferences, observation of teachers at work, and pattern analysis.

Before we examine the specific steps involved in the model, it is important to examine five basic assumptions presented by Sergiovanni and Starratt that must be a part of the administrator's thinking before it is implemented (1993, 225–26):

1. *That supervision is a process for which both supervisors and teachers are responsible.* Professional growth is a significant outcome of this process, and such growth is not possible without both the administrator and the teacher being committed to seeing it take place. The teacher is not a passive participant in a drill that is carried out by an administrator.

2. *That the focus of supervision is on teacher strengths.* Once again, I state, "It is not snoopervision!" The focus is on strengths rather than catching someone doing something wrong. In addition, areas for improvement are, nonetheless, an important part of the process.

3. *That given the right conditions, teachers are willing and able to improve.* Leaders must not be distracted or disheartened by the poor performance or attitudes of a few. In general, in an atmosphere where excellence is emphasized, one must view

teachers through a positive lens and believe that individuals want to develop new skills.

4. *That teachers have large reservoirs of talent, often unused.* Repeatedly throughout my career in administration and in graduate school teaching, it has been thrilling to watch educators blossom as they learn new techniques and methodologies.

5. *That teachers derive satisfaction from challenging work.* The dynamic is much different when we approach the process in this manner—that teachers will have a positive attitude and experience when challenged to do more as opposed to being negative and resistant.

Several of these assumptions are supported by the parable of the talents (Matthew 25:14–30). When the steward returned to evaluate the performance of the servants, those who were found faithful were given more. This perspective adds a spiritual dimension to professional growth; those teachers who are willing to serve the Lord with the gift, or gifts, that He has given them will be blessed with growth in those areas and the promise of new talents added on.

Clinical supervision is a partnership in inquiry whereby the person assuming the role of supervisor functions more as an individual with experience and insight (or, in the case of equals, with a better vantage point in analyzing another colleague's teaching) than as an expert who determines what is right and wrong. The clinical supervisor derives his or her authority from being able to collect and provide information desired by the teacher and from being able to help that teacher to use this information in the most effective way. This authority is functional, as compared with formal authority derived from one's hierarchical position. Morris Cogan (1973, 10–12) identifies eight phases in the cycle of supervision, and I have expounded on them:

Phase 1 requires establishing the teacher-supervisor relationship. The significance of the trust factor begins at this initial step. Does the faculty member sense that you have a positive, compassionate attitude about each teacher? Do you exude an enthusiastic approach to the relationship and process? Prayer shared with the teacher is a powerful force to help build the relationship.

Phase 2 requires intensive planning of lessons and units with the teacher. These sessions are crucial for the administrator to become informed about the teacher's management techniques, favorite methodologies, and overall understanding of the schoolwide goals. These conferences also provide the administrator with a great deal of valuable information to assist with parent conferences and curriculum planning.

Phase 3 requires planning of the classroom observation strategy by the teacher and supervisor. Again, this planning puts the teacher at ease because the dimensions of the activities that the observer will focus on are clear. The administrator will know what will be presented and can be focused so that valuable time is not wasted while the observer tries to get oriented.

Phase 4 requires the supervisor to observe in-class instruction. Numerous alternatives to assist with recording notes are recommended later in this chapter. It is vital that the observer not participate in the instructional activities on the day of the observation. However, it is highly desirable for the administrator to return on other occasions to do a model lesson or to team teach with the teacher.

Phase 5 requires careful analysis of the teacher-learning process. The supervisor should carefully consider what needs to be communicated in writing. If possible, same day feedback is a great way to reward a teacher for an effective lesson or to stimulate change while the experiences are fresh. I believe that the teacher should receive this written document prior to the post–observation conference so that the teacher can thoughtfully consider appropriate responses. Remember that you are trying to build trust and stimulate growth.

Phase 6 requires planning the conference strategy. Only the most seasoned administrator can skip this step, especially if there are difficult issues to be discussed.

Phase 7 is the conference. I always lead with a simple, open-ended question to get the conversation going after a brief time of prayer. I simply ask, "How do you think the class period went?" Talk through the write-ups and allow time for questions.

Phase 8 requires the resumption of planning. Later in this chapter, I will emphasize the need for staff development activities that are designed to meet the needs of faculty members.

All new administrators will look at an eight-phase process and probably abandon it before they get started. Experienced administrators, on the other hand, will mentally start to combine steps as they review Cogan's eight phases. I would recommend the following three-stage process:

Stage 1: Combine Cogan's phases 1, 2, and 3. Schedule a follow-up conference if adequate time for planning has not been allotted.

Stage 2: Combine Cogan's phases 4, 5, and 6. Special analysis and planning will be required in instances where the supervisor observed difficulties.

Stage 3: Combine Cogan's phases 7 and 8. Consider a follow-up conference if more observations are in order or if additional time is needed to plan staff development activities.

Alternative Models

As experienced teachers demonstrate professional competencies, develop specific interests, and "outgrow" the benefit of a routinized cycle of supervision, then it is time for the teacher and administrator to consider an alternative method of supervision. This is not to say that an individual teacher has nothing to learn about basic issues such as management, discipline, and methodologies. However, most experienced supervisors will tell you that once a veteran teacher has been evaluated several times with the same instrument and rubric, growth tends to plateau.

In *Supervision*, Thomas Sergiovanni and coauthor Robert Starratt argue that teachers must play key roles in deciding which of the options are best suited to them (1993, 216). Also, supervision should be viewed as a process that is equally accessible to teachers and administrators. These experienced researchers emphasize the need for a variety of options. They warn, "There is a danger that continuous use of the clinical approach can result in ritualism as each step is followed. Clinical supervision may be too much supervision for some teachers in that not all teachers need such an intensive look" (287). However, it is extremely important that an administrator be able to incorporate other models of supervision beyond the clinical model. It is my experience that most teachers will progress in three to five years to the point that items on a supervisory checklist are no longer challenging or no longer providing an incentive for change.

Allan Glatthorn (1984), Thomas Sergiovanni (1995), and Gordon Brown (2002) discuss several exciting alternatives that should be considered because teachers' needs and dispositions, as well as learning styles, vary. Glatthorn refers to this process as "cooperative professional development"—a collegial process in which teachers agree to work together for their own professional development (1984, 39). This supervisory relationship can be explained as a moderately formalized process by which two or more teachers agree to work together for their own professional growth, usually by observing each other's classroom, giving each other feedback about the observations, and discussing shared professional concerns. In some schools, teachers might organize themselves into teams of two or three. Sergiovanni calls this "collegial supervision."

Five possible activities for collegial supervision follow:

- Professional dialogue
- Curriculum development
- Peer supervision
- Peer coaching (workshops on new methods)
- Action research (study of problems and possible solutions)

Self-directed supervision is another alternative designed to allow teachers to work alone by assuming responsibility for their own professional development. This approach gives teachers the freedom to do the following:

- *Develop a yearly plan with targets or goals based on an assessment of their own needs.* This plan should be shared with a supervisor.
- *Have room for flexibility in the development of this approach.* The supervisor is responsible for seeing that the plan is realistic and attainable.
- *Have periodic discussions, as the year progresses, to review progress.* At the year-end meeting, the teacher provides evidence (a portfolio) of progress.
- *Set new targets for future self-directed supervisory cycles.*

The self-directed supervisory model has several advantages. It is beneficial for teachers who prefer to work alone or teachers whose schedules make it difficult to coordinate with others. It also allows for the efficient use of time, funds, and energy.

The *informal model* of supervision, as described by Sergiovanni, is based on casual encounters that occur between supervisors and teachers and is characterized by frequent informal visits to the teacher's classroom, conversations about the teacher's work, and other informal activities. Typically, no appointments are made and classroom visits are not announced. Successful informal supervision requires that certain expectations be accepted by teachers. Otherwise, it will likely be viewed as a system of informal surveillance.

The *inquiry-based model* of supervision in the form of action research is an option that can represent an individual initiative or a collaborative effort as pairs or teams of teachers work together to solve problems. In *action research*, the emphasis is on the problem-solving nature of the supervisory experience. One or more teachers work with a supervisor to define a problem and develop a strategy for its resolution and share findings and conclusions (Sergiovanni 1995, 230–34). The basic steps follow:

1. Identify the problem.
2. Develop hypotheses about causes and solutions.
3. Test one or more hypotheses.
4. Collect data.
5. Evaluate and draw conclusions.

Brown refers to the use of various alternative models as "differentiated supervision" (2002, 41). He describes a three-tier rubric that can assist an administrator in matching appropriate levels of supervisory activities to the professional needs of individual teachers.

Table 8.1 Brown's Three Professional Levels

Beginning professional: The beginning professional should receive direct, intensive supervision as a support mechanism to ensure success as an educator. These supervisory activities may include

- Mentoring by a veteran teacher
- Two cycles of three classroom visits and conferences with a supervisor, one each semester
- Occasional one-hour interventions by the supervisor or mentor as needed

Intermediate professional: By contrast, the intermediate professional requires only moderately intensive supervision. This teacher has demonstrated a growing level of teaching excellence and is occasionally able to initiate self-evaluation and make recommendations for her own improvement. The supervisory activities for this teacher may include

- Peer coaching with another equally ranked teacher
- One cycle per year of two or three classroom visits and conferences with a supervisor
- One-hour interventions by a peer or supervisor as needed

Resource professional: The resource professional may require no formal observations. This person is a proven professional who has the expertise and initiative to self-correct. As a result, supervisory activities for this teacher may include

- Peer coaching with another equally ranked teacher
- One-hour interventions by a peer or supervisor as needed
- Personal setting of improvement goals, monitoring of progress, and conferencing with a supervisor twice a year to report status of professional growth

Peer Coaching

Peer coaching is a means through which teachers can receive constructive evaluations without fear of supervisory judgment. Peer coaching involves implementing the two-way model. To be successful, those involved need advanced training in conducting observations. Resource support such as providing substitutes to cover classes on occasion is also necessary. The administrator must assist the teachers in establishing frequency of the observations, conferences, and write-ups.

The one-way model calls for veteran teachers to serve as mentors for beginning teachers. The special advantage of the mentor approach is that one teacher is the recognized expert and the other the novice. Peer coaching that implements the one-way model eliminates some of the social uncertainty created when two equals compete over how much "help" they give to their partners.

What Are You Looking For?

The central question on the mind of each administrator is, What am I looking for when I observe a teacher? Certainly, the answer must be established in writing prior to the observation, as previously discussed. At minimum, the contents of the observer's rubric should be explained thoroughly in the teacher handbook and be reviewed prior to the opening of the school year. Ideally, the faculty members should be allowed to participate in developing the structure and content of the supervisor's rubric. In *Guiding Faculty to Excellence*, Gordon Brown lists three excellent choices for possible rating scales (2002, 180):

> *Comparative ratings.* These ratings require supervisors to compare individual teachers with a certain population of teachers. The rating values often used are *Excellent, Above Average*, or *Good; Average, Below Average*, or *Fair; Poor;* and *Unsatisfactory.* A comparative scale does not indicate whether the teacher's performance is acceptable or unacceptable in a particular school, and thus it provides no clear basis for determining the teacher's total worth to the school's ministry.

> *Frequency ratings.* Frequency ratings call for descriptions of teacher performance that assign a quantitative rating to each behavior. These schemes provide such classifications as *Always, Usually, Seldom,* or *Never,* or similar ones. Another form is *Consistently, Occasionally,* and *Seldom.*

Criterion-referenced ratings. These ratings compare teacher performance against a standard of excellence that all teachers should strive for and can achieve. This type of scheme usually includes words like *Acceptable* or *Competent, Satisfactory, Needs Improvement, Unacceptable,* and *Unsatisfactory.* These words suggest that performance criteria for teachers are not dependent on comparisons between them. Potentially, every teacher can achieve excellence. Teachers must be evaluated against standards of performance expected by the school.

I believe that every faculty, whether the school is relatively new or generations old, needs to have periodic dialogue about what goes on in a successful classroom. Questions need to be asked: What is effective teaching? What do we believe teachers can do to see that learning takes place? Here is a list of practical topics that could be discussed and included in the school's rubric for classroom observation:

What is our teaching/learning philosophy?
- Memorization
- Drill and practice
- Higher-level thinking skills
- Cooperative learning
- Teacher's awareness of learning styles
- Student's awareness of his or her own style

What is our philosophy about students becoming independent learners?
- Use of computer technology
- Inclusion of research skills

What is our philosophy of discipline?
- Use of warnings or reprimands
- Expectations of respect and cooperation
- Expectations for self-management (such as sharpening pencils and trips to bathroom)

What is our philosophy of assessment?

Do assessment techniques reflect an awareness of Gardner's Multiple Intelligences?

Research on "Effective Teaching"

Prior to retiring from the University of Maryland, Gil Austin, an internationally known statistician, joined with his colleagues to see if they could identify characteristics of effective teaching in classrooms and schools where students performed especially well when compared with the teachers and classrooms in those schools where the scores were significantly below average. (Both groups were *outliers* when compared with a line of regression.) Their research findings were based on elementary schools in Maryland, but multiple studies spun off this project, and collectively the results are known as "the effective schools literature."

The research has provided documentation that certain teacher behaviors, such as the ones listed below, are related to student gains on both criterion- and norm-referenced tests:

- Establish classroom rules that allow pupils to attend to personal and procedural needs without having to check with the teacher.
- Communicate expectations of high achievement.
- Start off each class by reviewing homework and by reviewing material covered in the previous few classes.
- Make the objectives of the new instructional episode clear to the students.
- Directly teach the content or skill that will be measured on the test.
- After teaching the new material, assess student comprehension through questions and practice.
- Provide for uninterrupted successful practice that is monitored by the teacher moving around the classroom.
- Maintain direct engagement by the student on the academic task. Engaged academic time is a critical variable for student achievement.
- Assign homework to increase student familiarity with the material.
- Hold review sessions weekly and monthly.

Most of the studies that led to these findings were concentrating on the reaching of basic skills in reading and arithmetic in the earlier grades of elementary school. This research on effective teaching does not account sufficiently for other variables that may affect student achievement.

Lecturing is favored over discussion in achievement and retention of subject matter, but student-centered discussion is favored over teacher-centered discussion for building understanding of subject matter and promoting positive attitudes toward learning. It appears that the lower the level of learning (facts, simple recall), the more appropriate are direct methods of instruction.

Informal or more open teaching strategies seem superior to structured approaches in promoting creativity, self-concept enhancement, positive attitudes toward school, curiosity, self-determination, independence, and cooperation.
(Walberg, Schiller, and Haertel 1979)

These characteristics have found their way into many observation and summative evaluation instruments. You and your faculty should consider these findings as well as those discussed in the additional resources listed at the end of the book.

You Take the Helm

As the supervisor of four different teachers, you need to respond to each of the scenarios below in ways that reveal your awareness of Gordon Brown's concept of differentiated supervision. Discuss your responses to the questions with your colleagues.

Scenario One

Miss Laney is a recent graduate of one of the state's best teacher education programs. The state university required that she have frequent field experiences at local schools along with videotaped mini-lessons in her college methods course. Miss Laney is trained in the use of technology for the classroom and is committed to seeing each student in her class progress, regardless of the student's background or special needs. However, because she is new to Christian schooling, she is unfamiliar with the curriculum, the expectations of her principal and the other faculty members, and the overall values of the community in which God has called her to teach. In addition, she struggles with explaining to her students how her Christian faith is related to the content of the class. During the infrequent observations by the administration, she finds herself concentrating so heavily on getting the content correct that her follow-through on classroom management procedures is inconsistent. Twice during the first semester, she had to return phone calls from parents who questioned her discipline techniques that were not a part of school policy.

• In what areas of teaching does Miss Laney need help?
• What supervisory procedures would be effective?

Scenario Two

Mr. Stack has been teaching for seven years, including two years in the Christian school where he is now employed. He is well liked by parents, students, and teachers. His file contains evaluations that reflect high praise in nearly every category that was examined by his supervisors. The exceptions seem to be the orderliness of his room, the appearance of his bulletin boards, and his promptness in completing forms requested by the school and administration. He has attended summer workshops involving the preparation of advanced placement courses in his school and has successfully implemented an Advanced Placement United States History course. He very much wants to raise the overall academic standards of the school, and specifically he would like to inspire students who are traditionally average in their performance to sign up for advanced placement classes and do well. Mr. Stack hopes to develop a new course entitled Advanced Placement European History.

- Would it be beneficial for Mr. Stack to continue to be supervised according to a clinical supervision model?
- What other model might be more effective?

Scenario Three
Mrs. Roberts has been teaching primary grades for twenty years. For the past five years, she has been teaching first grade at her current school. She is a very dependable professional who is well organized in all aspects of her responsibilities—attendance reports, parent conferences, and extra duties, such as lunchroom supervision and parking lot duty. She has a dynamic faith that comes through in her lesson content and her relationship with her students. She knows the curriculum very well and even helped write portions of it. Mrs. Roberts' students performed well on standardized tests and seem to respond well to her use of direct instruction techniques that she uses every day. She has frequent discussions with administration and the other primary teachers about improving various aspects of the curriculum, and she has been especially concerned about the requirements for handwriting throughout the primary grades.

- Which alternative model would be best suited for Mrs. Roberts?
- In what ways could she contribute to the life of the school outside her classroom?

Scenario Four
Mr. Galleys has taught a variety of secondary grades and subjects but prefers teaching middle school Bible. He is very comfortable with the unique characteristics of students in grades 6–8, and he has shared his management procedures with other younger teachers. All students

develop a better understanding of the Bible in his classes, especially the average to below-average ones. Mr. Galleys has a special interest in taking mission trips, and he has started work on a graduate degree at a nearby seminary. No other teachers teach the same classes that he does, and he has little in common with the adjunctive teachers who teach the high school classes. After the last observation, he expressed a lack of interest in the various categories included in the observation checklist. From time to time, he has inquired about available resources for writing his own Bible lessons rather than purchasing the materials from Christian publishing companies.

- Which alternative supervisory model seems best suited for Mr. Galleys and his teaching assignment?
- Could his interest in writing lessons for his classes be useful in evaluating his performance?

Schedule for Success

Are you a victim of "tyranny of the urgent"? The word *tyranny* comes from a Latin term that means "tyrant." This is also the root word in the name of the most famous and feared dinosaur—*Tyrannosaurus rex* (literally, the king tyrant lizard). That might be a fitting metaphor for most administrators as they try to manage their schedules while being pursued by a tyrant lizard! Most administrators readily agree that being in classrooms, observing teachers, and discussing students' progress are vitally important. However, the sad truth is that very few leaders actually budget time that is needed to execute an appropriate level of supervision for every teacher who is assigned to them.

Let's consider carefully the scheduling concept I call the 20 percent rule. I propose that each administrator intentionally schedule 20 percent of his or her time to be involved in some aspect of supervision of instruction. Of course there will be exceptions, but the challenge is to use eight hours per week or approximately one out of five days in the implementation of plans that are laid out prior to the beginning of the school year. In many cases, this may not be enough time, but it is a great beginning point. Table 8.2 outlines a typical week in which an administrator could schedule eight hours of contact with teachers who are involved with various models of supervision.

Table 8.2

Monday	Tuesday	Wednesday	Thursday	Friday
10:00–11:00 Pre-conference with teacher A	10:00–11:00 Conference with teacher C who is designing action research	9:00–10:00 Observe teacher A	10:00–11:00 Post-conference with teacher A	Open for appointments that were rescheduled
1:00–2:00 Pre-conference with teacher B		1:30–2:30 Observe teacher B	1:00–2:00 Post-conference with teacher B	
			3:00–4:00 Conference with teachers D & E, who are involved in peer review	

Table 8.3

Teacher Supervision Calendar of Activities	
First Quarter Goals	Before school: Each teacher has a copy of the observation instrument and evaluation instrument. The principal has reviewed these with the faculty, and time was set aside for questions and discussion. The principal observes every teacher on an informal basis.
September	Begin a pattern of brief visits to each teacher's classroom. Written feedback is optional.
October	Meet with new staff individually at a rate of one or two per week for the clinical supervision process (3–6 hours per week).

Continued

Table **8.3** *continued*

Second Quarter Goals	Before Christmas: Is each staff member satisfactory? If not, have you met with, observed, and planned with each who is not? Each new teacher has one observation write-up in his or her file.
November	Carry out the clinical supervision model with any teacher who is not included in the first quarter. Also, meet with veteran teachers who will use an individual improvement/growth plan.
December	Follow up.
Third Quarter Goals	All teachers have at least one observation write-up in their file, except for those using a model that is not clinical. Have a follow-up conference for any teacher in jeopardy of being dismissed or being placed on probation. Have a conference with each teacher and observe each one during the quarter, except veterans who are working on the individual model.
January– March	Continue to use clinical supervision with one or two teachers per week.
Fourth Quarter Goals	Each teacher has a complete evaluation in his or her file.
April	Have an evaluation conference with each teacher at a rate of three or four per week (approximately 6–8 hours including preparation).
May	Catch up. Evaluate teachers using unique models. Terminate any teacher whose contract is not renewed.
Summer	Plan staff development and individual activities that are based on needs of staff. Begin training veteran teachers to assist you in the observation process.

When the Job Isn't Being Done

Unfortunately, some teachers experience extreme difficulties in their classroom performance, and an effective administrator must be prepared to assist a teacher who is struggling. The list of suggestions in table 8.3 is by no means exhaustive, nor is it intended to be presented in an order that suggests increasing severity. These activities are intended to stimulate prayer, communication, and growth and must be considered with great care.

You Take the Helm

Review the list of activities in table 8.4 and consider a brief scenario in which you think that the activity is an appropriate intervention. If you believe that one or more is an inappropriate technique to use with a professional teacher, be prepared to explain why you would not consider it a viable option.

Table 8.4

Prior to Dismissal: Options for Discipline of Employees

1. Verbal warning—note in the administrator's file
2. Written warning—signed by the employee
3. Suspension with pay
4. Suspension without pay
5. Probation—with clearly defined objectives and a periodic evaluation
6. Counseling—suggest 50/50 payment
7. Training or a workshop
8. Research and writing
9. Biblical study and writing
10. Poor evaluation
11. Freezing or lowering of salary
12. Accountability team

Once the painful decision has been made to dismiss a faculty member, the supervisor must *carefully document* that proper procedures have been followed, according to the teacher handbook, the teacher contract, and any corresponding board policy. Remember Paul's exhortation in Ephesians 4:15 about speaking the truth in love. Most sources state that a minimum of three conferences is needed from the time that problems surface to adequately communicate the need for change, to monitor progress, and to dismiss a teacher. However, I would recommend at least two additional conferences in which to review progress. The administrator must systematically document his or her communication with the teacher and ask the faculty member to sign these documents, stating that they have been received.

Three Approaches to Growing Your Staff: In-Service, Staff Development, or Renewal

Traditionally, staff improvement has been sought by providing formal and informal in-service programs and activities and by providing an array of staff development opportunities for teachers. Supervisors are placed in the driver's seat, taking responsibility for the whats, hows, and whens of improvement as they plan and provide in-service and staff development programs.

In *Teacher Renewal: Professional Issues, Personal Choices,* Frances Bolin, Judith Falk, and their colleagues suggest that though in-service programs and staff development may be legitimate and important in their own right, neither are expansive enough and penetrating enough to fully tap the potential for teachers to grow personally and professionally. They write the following:

> What would happen if we set aside the questions of how to improve the teacher and looked instead at what we can do to encourage the teacher? Asking how to encourage the teacher places the work of improvement in the hands of the teacher. It presupposes that the teacher desires to grow, to be self-defining, and to engage in teaching as a vital part of life, rather than as unrelated employment. This leads to looking at teaching as a commitment or calling, a vocation ... that is not adequately contained in the term *profession* as it has come to be used. When supervision shifts away from providing improvement experiences and opportunities to encouraging teachers, in-service and staff development give way to renewal. (1987, 11)

The assumption behind holding in-service workshops and meetings is that teaching is a job. These sessions focus on the development of job-related skills that can be accomplished through training and practice. But staff development is a higher-level approach that designates teaching as a profession. Staff development events focus on the development of professional expertise that is accomplished through problem solving and inquiry. Most school leaders today, however, are searching for plans that result in renewal, which assumes that teaching is a vocation. These individualized experiences focus on the development of the personal and professional self that is accomplished through reflection and reevaluation (Sergiovanni 1995, 209).

All three approaches continue to be viable options for administrators in Christian schools. Each fall there is the obvious need for in-service training to review the mission and philosophy of the school and introduce program changes. First-aid training would be an example of a job-related skill that all teachers need. Beyond these sessions, teachers need to be involved in the development of professional inquiry activities such as improvement in biblical integration in the school's curriculum. At the highest level, teachers are involved with personal and professional growth that contributes to the building of the school and its larger community.

Table 8.5 (Estacion, McMahon, and Quint 2004, 27–28)

The First-Things-First Classroom Observation Study
(as adapted from materials provided by Dr. Phyllis Blumenfeld, University of Michigan)

Strategies Associated with Teaching for Understanding

1. Teacher models ways to think about, organize, and remember information.
   a) Teacher models thinking strategies, such as outlining or summarizing, or shows students how to outline.
   b) Teacher demonstrates use of a mnemonic and makes suggestions for ways students can use mnemonics for future learning/remembering.
   c) Teacher models using a visual organizer (i.e., the setting up of information in charts, tables, diagrams, maps, Venn diagrams, etc.) or tells students how to use a visual organizer(s) or discusses the rationale for organizing information in this way.
   d) Teacher illustrates concepts (e.g., using colors, shapes, manipulable objects to demonstrate a math concept).
      (1) Uses multiple representations of ideas
      (2) Uses multiple examples that convey the points in several ways

2. Teacher explains ideas by connecting them to students' own experience and prior learning.
   a) Teacher draws on his or her own experiences and students' lives or experiences, relating them to the current academic topic.
      (1) Relates to teacher's own experiences
      (2) Relates to students' own experiences
      (3) Relates to current events
      (4) Relates to media representations
   b) Teacher reminds class of previous lessons, concepts, and activities and relates these to current work in a way that goes beyond remembering facts but rather, broadens or extends what was previously learned.

3. Teacher talks about reasoning.
   a) Teacher provides a "why" or "how" explanation, rather than simply telling students the right answers.
   b) Teacher develops the reasoning behind right or wrong answers.
   c) Teacher explains and elaborates to move students beyond a wrong answer.
   d) Teacher talks about how to think through problem.

Continued

Table 8.5 *continued*

4. Teacher teaches students strategies for planning, revising, and evaluating.
   a) Teacher models for students how to plan, through techniques such as brainstorming, outlining, etc., or teacher tells students how to use these techniques.
   b) Teacher helps students examine, revise, and reflect on their own work, showing them strategies for doing this.
   c) Teacher and students create a rubric together to be used in evaluating work.

5. Teacher structures an activity or lesson.
   a) Teacher breaks down more complex and ambiguous tasks into steps or shows students how to do this for themselves later.
   b) Teacher sets up an activity or lesson by providing steps of the process.
   c) Teacher suggests several different ways to break down the task.
   d) Teacher provides checkpoints, so students stay on track.
   e) Teacher models how she/he is structuring a lesson/activity so that students are exposed to the steps the teacher went through.

Table 8.6 (Estacion, McMahon, and Quint 2004, 29–30)

The First-Things-First Classroom Observation Study
(as adapted from materials provided by Dr. Phyllis Blumenfeld, University of Michigan)

Strategies Associated with Pressing for Understanding

1. Teacher encourages students to come up with their own ways to think about, organize, and remember information.
   a) Teacher encourages students to come up with, to use, and to evaluate a variety of options for thinking about, remembering, and organizing information. (Examples may include writing, diagramming, use of mnemonics, visual organizers such as mind maps. The key is that it is not enough for the students to be doing this. The teacher must be asking "how" and "why" questions about their choices, e.g., "Why do you think this might be the most effective way to organize this "information?")
   b) Teacher asks "how" and "why" questions about what the students are doing and asks about the pros and cons of their methods of organizing information.

2. Teacher encourages students to explain ideas through linking, showing the meaning they have constructed.
   a) Again, the key ingredient of pressing for understanding is asking the "why" or "how" questions ("How does your example relate to what we're studying here?").
   b) Teacher asks students for examples of the current content/topic in their own experiences, in current events, in the media and asks them to explain why or how the examples relate to the topic.
   c) Teacher asks students to relate the current content/topic to previous lessons, concepts, or academic activities and to explain how or why these are related.

3. Teacher encourages students to reason with "how" and "why" questions.
   a) Teacher asks students how and why questions (e.g., "How did you get that answer?" or "Explain why you think that.")
   Note: This is more than asking a student to repeat a procedural rule. Students would be asked to provide reasons behind the rules they are applying to demonstrate their understanding of the rule.

Continued

Table 8.6 *continued*

4. Teacher encourages students to talk about planning, revising, and evaluating.
   a) Teacher asks students to talk about planning, revising, or evaluating their work, and to explain how or why they planned, revised, evaluated as they did.
   b) Teacher encourages students to explain pros/cons of the options they considered.
   c) Teacher asks students to plan and think about ways to evaluate what they did and to develop a rationale for choosing the ways they plan to use.

5. Teacher asks students to structure an activity or lesson.
   a) Teacher asks students to explain, in their own words, a complex procedure they have performed and to explain why they did what they did.
   b) Teacher asks students to go over their work, explaining it verbally or in writing, while the teacher is checking for understanding.
   c) When students give various answers, the teacher asks them to talk about the differences and similarities of the answers.

Leadership Development

9

Principle for Guiding Principals:

The effective administrator intentionally mentors faculty members so that they may become effective leaders themselves.

Over the years, he had become exceptional at multitasking and making it look effortless. On occasion, he double booked and even triple booked events and meetings, thinking that everyone would understand and even appreciate how hard he was working. Sometimes he thought of himself as being like an entertainer he once watched who juggled a chain saw, a burning torch, and a bowling pin, while taking bites of an apple that was also in the mix. However, there were major dimensions of the school— curriculum development, classroom supervision, and budget analysis— that never received the much-needed attention that each deserved because he was attending to necessary but less important matters. If he would just take the time to prayerfully consider men and women on his staff who were spiritually ready for new … But wait—how could he possibly train them to do things his way?

The Helmsman

The term we now use for leaders in mentoring relationships came about in ancient Greece because of a father's love and concern for his son. Before Ulysses, the warrior, set sail for the Trojan War, he recruited a trusted friend, an older man he had known since childhood, to watch over the training of his son, Telemachus. The trusted friend's name was Mentor. The impact of that arrangement would not be evident until Ulysses returned some twenty years later and the three would stand together to fight off the angry band of suitors that had gathered in their home in pursuit of his lovely wife, Penelope. When called on, Telemachus was prepared to perform as a man at his father's side.

In light of this legend, my story is much less dramatic and somewhat ironic. My son was God's instrument to teach me about leadership development. My battlefield was my backyard, and my foe was the tall grass that rose up against my family every week. How ironic that I thought I was teaching my son, when it was he who trained me. My training began when Scott was four years old and asked if he could help with the yard work. I purchased a toy lawn mower that made bubbles when it was pushed, but his interest quickly waned when he discovered that he was not actually cutting any grass when he followed along beside me. The next week, he came over to get between the engine and me and reached up for the handle. "I want to help, Dad," my son announced. We proceeded to try to guide the mower together, stumbling along in ninety-five-degree heat. It was slow going, but I did not want to extinguish his desire to learn. After a few more trips down and back, he tired of the project and left to play.

The next summer, his reach was higher and his limbs were stronger. This time he announced that he was ready to do it by himself. After grabbing the handle of the mower, which was now just slightly over his head, he gave his dad a push with one hand and started across the yard. Yes, he was holding on while the engine pulled the big mower, but unfortunately, not much grass was being cut because the front wheels were not touching the ground. I watched as the boy and machine traversed the yard a few times, and I calmed his mother's fears about her son losing a foot during this exercise. Once again, he tired and needed to rest after a few passes. His first solo flight was not a success by anyone's standards—I had to retrace his steps over the uneven spots. However, he kept coming back, and at age seven, he took over one hot afternoon and cut a good portion of the grass while I stood in the shade and watched. With the exception of a little bit of weaving (he could barely see over the top of the handle), the blades were cut straight, all four wheels touched the ground, and the job was well done. The next summer, he cut half the yard while I drank lemonade and watched the baseball game with one eye and my new assistant with the other. (His mom kept a closer watch out the kitchen window.) At age nine, five years into the process, my son cut the entire backyard while I did other chores.

When Scott turned eleven, I spent two hundred dollars on a small, self-propelled mower—the best two hundred dollars I ever spent. We made an agreement. He would cut our yard, front and back, whenever it needed to be cut, without expecting any money from his parents. In return, I would pay for the mower and the gas and he could cut the neighbors' lawns and pocket all the money that he earned. Soon he was mowing three lawns in addition to ours, and I no longer had to concern myself with cutting grass. I left home for a business trip when Scott was fourteen and he said I did not have to worry about the lawn—he would take care of it. When I returned, he had cut it in a new diagonal design after raising the base to allow for a taller cut so the grass would not burn in the summer heat. At age sixteen, he fussed at me one afternoon when he returned home from baseball practice and saw me behind the mower. He claimed, "Dad, that's my job."

What had happened over the period of twelve years? You might be cheering and laughing as you conclude that I got out of performing a never-ending task that is despised by most. But actually, I gave up an activity that I enjoy and shared it with my son, because he wanted to participate in something meaningful with his dad. After a period of supervision and coaching, my son took complete responsibility and ownership of the project and learned to accomplish the task more quickly and effectively than I could do it.

In *Mastering Church Management*, Leith Anderson, Don Cousins, and Arthur DeKruyter cite Ken Blanchard's writing about training leaders as they describe the need for working with each person as an individual (1990, 141). They endorse Blanchard's model called "situational leadership," but they prefer to rename it "personalized leadership." They say that they want to keep their focus on leading people, not just handling situations. They use Blanchard's model to outline four critical steps in developing leaders:

1. *Direction.* The first stage involves the careful training of the inexperienced mentee. Basically, the leader is actually doing the ministry through the trainee. This process can take the form of regular meetings to discuss step-by-step activities, the demonstration of necessary steps by the teacher, or the side-by-side execution of the tasks. As is discussed by the authors and Blanchard, the extent of the supervision depends on variables such as the level of maturity and experience the mentee brings to the relationship, the critical nature of the projects that need to be completed, and the length of time the student requires to gain confidence and skill in the new area of training.

2. *Coaching.* The next step takes place when the mentee's confidence and competence grows. At this point, the leader steps off the court and begins to observe the performance, making specific corrections as necessary. The student makes suggestions and the two work together; the project is a joint venture. The coach's primary responsibilities are affirmation and redirection.

3. *Support.* The first two steps may take as long as a year, depending on the progress of the follower and the sophistication of the new task. At this point, he or she is ready for the third step in the relationship. A significant milestone occurs as the leader turns over more responsibility to the follower; the follower begins to set the agenda and prioritizes what needs to be done. He or she knows what needs to be accomplished and primarily needs to know that the mentor is there to provide emotional support, encouragement, affirmation, and correction, if necessary. The coach now becomes a cheerleader.

4. *Delegation.* The final step is turning over the project or activity to the new leader. Even though reporting continues and the mentor maintains interest in the mentee, the task now belongs to the latter. Unfortunately, the act of turning over a ministry or responsibility all too often happens first before any guiding and training are done. The usual result, in this case, is a "train wreck" that brings about the dismissal of an employee who began with great enthusiasm for the task but was given no training or guidance. Another difficulty can occur at this point. The mentor can be unwilling to let go of the activity that the follower was trained for, and he or she can insist on continuing to micromanage the project and the trainee. The result from this behavior can be that the follower will not feel trusted or adequate to do the job and may mean that, though well trained, he or she will leave the organization in pursuit of a yard of his or her own to cut and to take care of.

I was blessed early on in my seminary teaching experience to meet a young youth minister, named Jamie, who was full of enthusiasm for doing ministry and was ready to learn as much as he could. He took careful notes in class, participated in discussion, and scored very high on every evaluation. When Jamie completed most of his course work, I asked him to be my grader, which meant he would assist me in evaluating other students' work and he might even lecture on occasion as the need arose. After two semesters of training, I challenged him to create a lecture from scratch on a topic that he was interested in. I watched with great interest as he lectured with creativity and precision on a challenging topic. Two years after Jamie graduated, a family emergency required that I leave town within a few hours, leaving very little time to prepare for the class that I would miss the next day. What did I do? I called Jamie, and he agreed to spruce up and update his lecture and drive 200 miles to substitute for me the next day. My students were in great hands.

Leaders of kingdom schools have an infinite number of opportunities in the course of growing a school to grow new leaders. For example, a young college graduate named Dave began his teaching career at my school. In addition to his classroom responsibilities, Dave wanted to use his athletic abilities in coaching. During his first two years, he showed exceptional abilities in leading teams and working with adults. When he expressed interest in the administrative activities that go on behind the scenes of an athletic program, I began directing him to complete tasks such as organizing game schedules, transportation, and officials. The next year he became athletic director and began learning from me how to develop a budget for a multisport program. He would be planning all the equipment needs for over a dozen different sports played by boys and girls at various ages. After five years, Dave was completing all the schedules and the budget on his own and became the commissioner of the Christian school league in which our school was involved. Soon Dave was working with me to recommend major expenditures such as team buses, and he worked with an architect to help design our new gymnasium. I did not know the process was complete until the spring of his tenth year of teaching. The culminating activity for our sports program at that time every year was a sports banquet involving hundreds of students and parents. That night, I entered the banquet without having been involved in any of the planning—the menu, trophies, decorations, nothing. All the things that used to take me weeks to do had been done without my participation at any level. I had to make only one decision prior to my arrival—chicken or beef for my dinner. And I did only one thing that evening—I returned thanks for the food. I was able to just sit and watch.

It is important at this point to briefly explore a few reasons why some leaders say they do not actively involve themselves in the preparation of other leaders:

1. *It takes too much time.* It is tough to argue with this statement if you view everything from the perspective of what is most efficient today. But when you fix your gaze on a longer period of time, it is easier to see the wisdom of making an investment for the future—the new leader, the organization, and your own resources of time and energy. Let's face it: many leaders are unfortunately just not willing to make a long-term commitment or a long-term investment.

2. *It won't be done my way.* There are two responses to this objection. If you take the time to do the proper guidance, your trainee will understand what the outcome is when the task is done properly. Following the four

steps outlined in the preceding discussion will mean evaluating the person's progress and performance before turning him or her loose to operate alone. Secondly, who said that there is only one right way to complete the project? Any valuable coworker must be given some freedom to demonstrate his or her creativity and individual style.

3. *The mentee may fail.* William Shakespeare allowed Lady Macbeth to respond to this objection when her husband balked at killing King Duncan:

> MACBETH: If we should fail?
> LADY MACBETH: We fail? But screw your courage
> To the sticking place,
> And we'll not fail.
> (1974)

Leadership development takes courage because it is not an exact science and there are always unknowns. This is where trusting the Lord is vital, provided you are in His perfect will, unlike the aforementioned Macbeth. The alternative means not preparing anyone to help you in ministry and not providing learning experiences, including failing, for an entire generation of leaders in your school or organization.

4. *I don't know how to train another person to do my roles in the school.* First, learn to simply talk in a conversational style about how certain tasks are done. Then, let prospective leaders watch you or shadow you as you work through specific issues. Provide these followers with journal articles or Internet sources that discuss the project. Also, encourage your mentee to consult other professionals or to take course work that explores the needed skills.

5. *My staff member will think I am just dumping menial tasks on him or her.* If you are just dumping menial tasks on him or her, then rethink the assignment and choose something more meaningful. The task that a person trains for needs to have the following special qualities in order for the person to be motivated to learn it and do it well:

Challenging. People grow when they are stretched to develop new skills. More importantly, they expand in their faith as they encounter hurdles that cannot be overcome in their own strength. Consider the blunt, unattractive truth of the following recruitment notice for the Pony Express that was printed in a California newspaper in the 1800s:

> WANTED: Young, skinny, wiry fellows not over 18.
> Must be expert riders willing to risk daily.
> Orphans preferred.

The simple fact is this: the Pony Express never experienced a shortage of riders!

Significant. People are motivated to accomplish tasks that they view as significant in kingdom work. If just anyone can do the work, then let someone else do it. Administrators who are effective recruiters emphasize the importance of the project, describe it in terms of its eternal significance, and connect it to the overall goals of the school. Here is another recruitment advertisement allegedly from a London newspaper:

> Men wanted for hazardous journey: small wages, bitter cold, long months of complete darkness, constant danger, safe return doubtful. Honor and recognition in case of success.

Countless men responded to Ernest Shackleton's ad for men to accompany him to the Arctic Circle. They were looking for significance.

Personalized. People need to be challenged to learn new tasks that they are uniquely qualified for. When discussing a new opportunity with someone you are mentoring, point out the mentee's gifts or abilities that make him or her capable of performing at a new level and that will encourage the mentee to consider how God wants to use those gifts in this situation. Knowing Peter's strength of personality and courage, Jesus singled out one disciple and made a very bold statement: "On this rock I will build My church" (Matthew 16:18).

Leighton Ford clearly articulates the concept of personalization in his ministry. He explains it this way:

> God's description of His servant as "a polished arrow" (Isaiah 49:2) also became a formative part of my thinking. Young leaders are to be polished like arrowheads. These arrowheads are not to be mass-produced, but hand shaped through personalized attention.

> The arrow also becomes a symbol of leadership development. We want to help young leaders sharpen their vision—like the point of the arrow—and to understand clearly God's call to them. As Jesus in many ways would ask His disciples, "What do you see?" I developed the habit of asking every young potential leader, "What is your vision?" If the person was not sure, I would say, "If you did have one, what would it be?"

> The base of the arrow also has significance: shaping their values. As Jesus would ask His disciples, "Where is your heart?" we need

to see that the leader's vision is carried forward only with solid Christlike values.

Finally, we are called to help young leaders by sharing their ventures. Like the shaft that helps the arrow fly forward, we need to encourage young leaders to act on the visions God gives. Jesus was constantly pushing His disciples beyond their depth and comfort zone, saying, "Where is your faith?" He also made them venture out. So our task is not to recruit young leaders for our cause and visions, but to stand with them and behind them—to invest "spiritual risk capital," so to speak, and give them a chance to go for the ventures God has put into their hearts.

Sharpening vision. Shaping values. Sharing ventures. This sums up the leadership development process. (1991)

6. *But I love doing the work myself.* Peter Drucker, the author of numerous books on business management, argued that leaders have what he calls "their unique contribution" to the organization. This task or responsibility is where the leader leaves his or her imprint on the culture of the organization. This task or activity need not be delegated or given away to a subordinate. In ministry, the unique contribution of a pastor might be doing pulpit ministry or officiating at such events as weddings and funerals. For a youth minister, it might be teaching the weekly Bible study or planning the annual youth retreat. For a school administrator, the significant roles of leading faculty meetings or evaluating staff may be examples of an administrator's opportunity to make a unique contribution.

But I want to encourage you to consider sharing these opportunities with others in order to provide them with special events to stretch their faith and for you to demonstrate your trust in their abilities. For example, observing classroom instruction is something that I have always enjoyed, and it was a critical opportunity for me to connect with each teacher under my supervision. However, at a certain time, I found it difficult to schedule all the conferences and observations for all the high school teachers. At the same time, I discovered some veteran teachers who were becoming a little stale in their approach to teaching. I concluded that these teachers needed a new challenge.

After recruiting one veteran teacher from each department (English, social studies, math, science, and physical education), I met with each one individually to discuss his or her working relationship with coworkers. In most cases, the new department head knew the younger teachers well and only had one or two colleagues to interact with. Then we met as a group, which we named our Instructional Council, and began discussing what new skills each needed to effectively supervise and coach the other members of the department. We reviewed the steps involved in clinical supervision (see chapter 8), which each had already experienced because of the observations I had done in their classrooms. The results were five new instructional leaders who developed new skills along with closer working relationships with their fellow teachers.

One of the greatest authors of our day, Kenn Gangel, along with April Moreton, has this to say about the benefits of mentoring, tempered by the realities of carrying out the process successfully:

> A good leader constantly works herself out of a job—training and mentoring others so that when she moves on to her next position or role, the school continues to thrive without her. But don't forget that mentoring has its downside for leaders. Investing in another and delegating tasks is time-consuming and risky. Many leaders find they do not have the time to think through a mentoring relationship, or they consider it less than beneficial for those they mentor. Some misunderstand their role as mentors and simply delegate mundane tasks without thought or purpose. When that happens, mentoring no longer benefits the protégé. Mentoring takes a great deal of energy on the part of the mentor but, if performed correctly, benefits both parties greatly. (2002, 44)

In *Leadership by the Book: Tools to Transform Your Workplace*, Ken Blanchard, Bill Hybels, and Phil Hodges simplify the development process as they explain how you can take potential winners and make them winners (1999, 152–54):

> As a servant leader, if you want to help potential winners perform well in a particular task regardless of whether you're around or not—there are five steps:

> 1. Tell them what to do.
> 2. Show them what to do.
> 3. Let them try what you want them to do.
> 4. Observe their performance.
> 5. Praise their progress or redirect.

Related to step four is a warning from the authors about the importance of observing day-to-day progress versus being what they call "seagull" managers: "Seagull managers aren't around until there is a problem. Then they fly in, make a lot of noise, dump on everybody, and then fly out!" They concluded, "This is certainly not a servant leadership approach" (1999, 146).

John Maxwell, in *Developing the Leaders Around You*, structures the process in these five steps (1995, 99–101):

> Step I: Model—the trainee watches the entire process.
>
> Step II: Mentor—the trainee receives instruction while participating in the process.
>
> Step III: Monitor—the trainee performs the task and the leader watches and corrects as needed.
>
> Step IV: Motivate—the leader removes himself once the trainee knows how to perform the task, but is there for encouragement.
>
> Step V: Multiply—the new leader is free to begin to develop other trainees.

Jesus, as in all things, is our supreme example in leadership development. During the early days of His ministry, it is clear that He modeled for His disciples how to heal hurting people—spiritually, emotionally, and physically. Matthew 9:35 summarizes His ministry in this way: "Jesus went through all the towns and villages, teaching in their synagogues, preaching the good news of the kingdom and healing every disease and sickness." Matthew explains in the next passage Jesus' charge to His disciples in which He presented the significance of the task and the vision for what they were to accomplish: "When he saw the crowds, he had compassion on them, because they were harassed and helpless, like sheep without a shepherd" (9:36). But how were they to accomplish these impossible feats? In their own strength, they knew this would be impossible. Matthew 10:1 explains that Jesus *empowered* them when He "gave them authority to drive out evil spirits and to heal every disease and sickness." Does our Lord still empower His servants today to fulfill the special tasks He has called each one to do? I believe He does, and I know He can use you to direct and inspire others to ask Him for the power that only He supplies.

He also instructed them (Matthew 10:5). Often, well-meaning leaders present employees with exceptional opportunities without giving them the specialized instruction that should accompany power and authority. Such leaders skip the first three stages of leadership development and jump immediately to the delegation stage without specifying boundaries of authority. The result is most often poor performance or even disaster. All too often, this occurs in situations in which the leader has a vague notion of what an effective performance will look like but has no idea about the steps for implementation or the potential land mines he will encounter along the way. Frequently, the more energy and initiative the trainee exercises, the farther out-of-bounds he goes. Jesus carefully provided this coaching and these boundaries.

On another occasion, Jesus sent out seventy-two others, as recorded in Luke 10. In the previous chapter in that Gospel, Luke explains that Jesus resolutely set out for Jerusalem (9:51). Perhaps with the completion of His ministry in mind, Jesus designed a teaching lab for seventy-two followers who were, no doubt, a part of the crowd that had been observing His ministry and listening to His teaching. He coached them on the basics of what to say, where to go, and how to present themselves. He even gave them instruction on handling rejection. Then He turned them loose!

What an experience! They came back fired up! "The seventy-two returned with joy and said, 'Lord, even the demons submit to us in your name' " (Luke 10:17). We must ask ourselves if it is possible for our followers to get this excited about their assignments. He trained them, He allowed them to do ministry, and then He praised them for their efforts. The training episode concludes with the Master Teacher thanking His Heavenly Father: "At that time Jesus, full of joy through the Holy Spirit, said, 'I praise you, Father, Lord of heaven and earth, because you have hidden these things from the wise and learned, and revealed them to little children. Yes, Father, for this was your good pleasure' " (Luke 10:21).

But this was not graduation or the completion of the training of His followers. Not until His final moments with His eleven disciples did He pronounce that they would receive *all authority*. This was the moment of delegation. However, the passage in Matthew 28 is called "the Great Commission"—He planned to go with them. In Christ's relationship with His followers and with us, He demonstrates the trust aspect of delegation. In 2 Corinthians 5:20, Paul says, "We are ambassadors for Christ, as though God were making an appeal through us" (NASB). On the other hand, we must continue to support those to whom we delegate, just as the Holy Spirit guides and directs us.

Whom Do You Select?

A significant question in the minds of most leaders is, Whom do I select? Moses receives excellent advice from his father-in-law in a well-known passage in Exodus 18:17–27. Moses was God's man for the job, but he was trying to do everything himself. The result of his actions is brought to his attention by Jethro: "What you are doing is not good. You and these people who come to you will only wear yourselves out. The work is too heavy for you; you cannot handle it alone" (17–18). Jethro recommends that Moses select leaders who have the following qualifications:

1. Leaders must be able men (have demonstrated ability and experience).
2. Leaders must fear God (be spiritually minded).
3. Leaders must be men of truth (possess integrity).
4. Leaders must hate dishonest gain (be honest and not capable of being bought).

A similar list of qualifications appears in Acts 6:3 when the disciples charge the congregation with the responsibility of selecting seven men who could assist with serving tables. They establish these guidelines:

1. The men must have a good reputation (have proven ability).
2. The men must be full of the Spirit (be devoted to the Lord).
3. The men must be full of wisdom (have discernment).

In his discussion on "Identifying Potential Leaders," John Maxwell lists these ten qualities (1995, 47–60):

1. *Character.* The recruit must have qualities such as honesty, integrity, and a strong work ethic.
2. *Influence.* The potential recruit has two characteristics: he or she is going somewhere and is able to persuade others to go.
3. *Positive attitude.* Does the recruit have the enthusiasm of Eeyore, the Winnie-the-Pooh character? This famous cartoon donkey is in the habit of saying, "Why, oh why, does it always happen to me?"
4. *Excellent people skills.* Excellent people skills involve a genuine concern for others, the ability to understand people, and the decision to make positive interaction with others a primary concern.
5. *Evident gifts.* Everyone God creates has gifts, but not everyone is gifted for leadership. What most young leaders lack is *opportunity.*
6. *Proven track record.* An important thing to look for is not so much success but rather learning from mistakes. Unfortunately, in my career, I have observed some teachers who have 20 years of experience yet have been a first-year teacher for 20 years!
7. *Confidence.* People are naturally attracted to people who project confidence. It is contagious and creates in others the desire to attempt new projects.

8. *Self-discipline.* Is the potential leader able to control himself or herself—emotions, reactions, and personal desires? Is the potential leader disciplined in the way that balances his or her use of time and other resources?
9. *Effective communication skills.* All the other skills and abilities the person has can be derailed by poor communication skills. He or she must be able to articulate ideas in a way that can be understood by others and be able to listen carefully to receive information back from others.
10. *Discontent with the status quo.* A potential leader is someone who is dissatisfied with the way things are and who is genuinely interested in seeing things change for the better. He or she must be a risk taker, not one who is foolhardy but one who trusts God while leading people in the direction of a better future.

Where Do You Start?

How can you help a young person who has leadership potential get started? Leighton Ford encourages the following approach (1991, 116–17):

When I talk with young leaders about developing their vision, I often put it in this simple paradigm: Observe—reflect—act.

Observe. Look carefully around at what God is doing, at the needs of the world, at what you see happening until you are attracted to some area of need and opportunity where you can make a difference.

Reflect. Prayerfully read Scripture and other pertinent literature related to what you have observed. Think about it, pray about it, and journalize about it.

Act. In small ways, begin to act on what you observed and reflected and, in that way, your vision and your leadership will develop.

When Crisis Comes

A young school leader who had studied with me throughout several years, a man I greatly respect, called one morning to say he was simply overwhelmed with his new position as the head of a large and well-established Christian school. He wondered aloud if he was the man for this job, if he could get back his joy for ministry, and if he should go back to the classroom full-time where he knew he could get the job done. He explained that he was careful to spend time alone with the Lord and in devotions with the other administrators on his team. He recounted occasions when he took his family to a theme park or other spot for recreation, but he could not shake the weight of the new position and could not rekindle his joy. Perhaps you have been there or someone you are training has confided in you that he or she was drowning in the details and stress of a leadership position. King David was well acquainted with extraordinary stress and difficult odds, and God gave David an exceptional talent to describe his anguish and reveal God's eternal wisdom for continuing in ministry. (My student explained that he felt as if he were standing in front of a tennis ball machine that is used to fire practice balls at you, except in his case, the controls were stuck on the fastest speed and the stop button was not working! Not exactly the poetry of David, but it certainly makes a vivid statement.) Here is what I discussed with my good friend:

1. *Control.* Psalm 46 reminds us that our God is still in charge of any ministry that He has called into existence. We must not be overcome by fear of anything—failure, personal attacks, inadequacy, unfaithfulness of others.

2. *Cease striving.* In Psalm 46:10, the Word tells us to "be still" (NIV) or "cease striving" (NASB). I was often guilty of thinking I had to do something in every situation, and such thinking led to exhaustion and discontent. Develop the discipline to stop and pray when the knots of life become frustrating.

3. *Comfort.* In Psalm 131, we receive the comforting image of a child on its mother's lap. David confesses his inability to conquer his problems as he says, "I do not concern myself with great matters or things too wonderful for me." He goes on to say, "But I have stilled and quieted my soul; like a weaned child with its mother, like a weaned child is my soul within me." If David, the king and warrior, can seek comfort at God's throne of grace, we should follow his example and call on our Father.

4. *Cleansing.* In Psalm 26, David calls on the Lord for a thorough examination of his heart. He asks God to sift him like flour to seek out any impurities and reveal them. When we ask the Lord to examine our mind and heart, we are looking for any impure motives in our relationships or carnal attitudes in our approach to ministry.

5. *Confidence in the future.* Psalm 20 is David's prayer for victory. He prays, "May he give you the desire of your heart and make all your plans succeed…. May the Lord grant all your requests" (4–5). We should pray with genuine hope and confidence that He holds our future in His hands.

6. *Consideration of times of trouble as seasons of testing.* Psalm 105:18 explains that in God's plan for Israel He sent Joseph, who was sold as a slave: "They bruised his feet with shackles, his neck was put in irons." God had specially chosen His representative, but he was not ready and had to wait on the Lord's timing. During this waiting period, he was imprisoned for a crime that he did not commit. Verse 19 says, "Till what he foretold came to pass, till the word of the Lord proved him true." Another translation for *proved* here is "refined." The Lord allows times of difficulty in our lives to test our mettle, and if we accept these trials with a spirit of humility, we will be strengthened as the Lord removes any impurities that will prevent us from being useful to Him in the future.

Has God provided you with the special privilege of preparing leaders for the next generation? I believe that He has. Are you taking the opportunities seriously, as you build your faculty for kingdom work? Consider the *tremble* factor as you pray about leadership development. Every time an arch was constructed in ancient Rome, scaffolding was first prepared. The supporting columns took shape as the stones were cut, fitted, and stacked higher and higher. The space between the columns was filled with an earthen or timber scaffold that bore the great weight of the gradually closing arch. Finally, after the keystone was set in place, completing the arch, the scaffolding was removed, and the arch became load bearing as the stones settled in place. During this process, the engineer was placed directly beneath the completed arch, so that if it failed to hold he would be buried beneath his last construction. The soundness of the arch was not a matter of indifference to the engineer. He experienced the tremble factor; it guaranteed his careful attention to all the details of design and construction. The tremble factor kept the Roman engineers on their toes.

Are you prepared to stand beneath the organizational archways you are constructing?

V. The Helmsman as Steward:
1 Corinthians 4:1-2

Finance and Facilities

10

Principle for Guiding Principals:

The effective administrator oversees the financial practices of the school to ensure integrity and stability.

The school year was progressing smoothly, and the administrator was thankful for many answered prayers. As the leader, however, she had to turn her gaze to next year and the financial demands of a growing school. Her school community was unlike some school communities since it was made up of many families who had to sacrifice in order to pay the monthly tuition. She was well aware that a drastic change would make it extremely difficult for many of the faithful families who had helped to establish the school's positive reputation. She thought of Mrs. Johnson, who has three daughters in elementary school. Each month, on the day tuition payments are due, she appears at the office and pulls from her jean pockets a large roll of currency from her previous month's income; she cleans houses in her neighborhood so that her children can receive a Christian education. And there is Andrea, a high school junior, who works after school and on Saturdays to pay most of her tuition. Her parents allowed her to transfer the previous year, but only if she would pay half of her tuition. Yet another burden pulled on the administrator from another direction—the financial needs of her faithful teachers. None of her teachers had gone into the profession because of the need to make a living, but each certainly deserves more than he or she is being paid. Most of the teachers are getting by with modest used cars, particularly compared to a few of the ones driven by some of the seniors. Some are being helped by their parents, and two drive a long distance to get to school because townhomes are less expensive in other areas. This administrator was well acquainted with the tension between tuition rates and teachers' salaries. She was also committed to seeing that the financial health of the school continue to strengthen so that it could achieve its mission. She determined that her first step was a special time alone with the Lord to ask for wisdom, perseverance, and direction. As the steward of God's resources, she knew that she must lead in a way that would ensure financial integrity and stability.

Financial Integrity

Few events will sidetrack or even bring a ministry to its end as will the failure of its leaders to provide careful procedures for handling money. People demand careful procedures for handling money. The law requires it. Most importantly, we owe it to the Lord as stewards of the money that people have given to this work. The apostle Paul understood this concept when he gave the instructions in 2 Corinthians 8. In verses 1–4, he discusses the collection that was being taken throughout the region, including the generous offering made by financially struggling churches of Macedonia. In preparation for this collection, Paul sent Titus (v. 6) and another believer "whose fame in the things of the gospel has spread through all the churches" (v. 18, NASB). Paul goes on to describe the companion of Titus, "And not only this, but he has also been appointed by the churches to travel with us in this gracious work" (v. 19, NASB). In this passage, Paul establishes at least two concepts that must be required for every ministry, including your school. First, he presents a form of recommendation and a type of background check for the person that they are considering hiring. Today, the administrator should require these for anyone handling money. The presence of a sizable amount of debt or a bankruptcy in the applicant's past may be cause for serious reservations.

Second, Paul speaks about a major concept that is found in procedures known as generally accepted accounting principles (GAAP). According to these principles, whenever money is collected, counted, and recorded, a minimum of two adults who are not related need to be present. I will refer to this concept as the rule of two. Paul spoke very powerfully about making sure that these people are trustworthy and that they will perform their duties with integrity. Paul explains that these precautions are necessary so that no one can discredit how a gift is administered: "For we have regard for what is honorable, not only in the sight of the Lord, but also in the sight of men" (2 Corinthians 8:21, NASB). Do you need a justification for spending money on an annual audit? Then look no further than 2 Corinthians 8. Establishing the strongest internal controls places the administrator in the best position to approach a possible donor and discuss the school's stewardship.

Over the years, I have taught these verses in a number of classes and have heard exceptionally painful stories. One church-sponsored school violated the rule of two when it allowed the man who was both pastor and principal to write and sign the checks by himself. At some point, it was discovered that the school had not been withholding taxes for its teachers and that the school owed the federal government over $100,000 in back taxes. Fortunately, the school accepted responsibility for the error and was able to stay open because the government worked out a payment plan for them.

Two pastors I know, who serve in small rural churches, told me similar stories. In one case, the church treasurer would stop by the little church office every week or two to sign checks. This office was open to anyone who wanted to walk through. He would take the checkbook from the desk drawer (which was unlocked!) and sign several checks. The worst part was that he was signing blank checks! The checkbook would be returned to the drawer so that the signed checks would be there for whomever needed them! Another young pastor explained that his church treasurer, who had served for twenty years, would dump all the contents of the offering plates into a grocery bag each Sunday after the plates were stacked at the back of the church. After he emptied the plates, he would walk out alone and place the bag in his trunk, and the contents would be counted later in the week. In each of these scenarios, the rule of two is broken in several ways, and those involved open themselves up for severe criticism. Sloppy handling of money cannot be honoring to the Lord or to the suspicious eyes of men.

In a newspaper article entitled "Parents Find Montessori School Closed," Sherry Jones, a staff writer for the *Wilmington Star* (North Carolina), reported the shock experienced by parents and students who discovered that their private school closed during Easter break and would not reopen. Some parents did not even know about the closing and foreclosure until they were told by representatives from the sheriff's department on the morning of what would have been the students' first day back after the break. Parents lost the remainder of that year's more than $7,000 tuition, along with their deposit of $700 for the next school year. The school was twenty-two years old and owed a local bank more than $660,000. The school's president made a public statement that included her apology: "I never dreamed that this would happen. It wasn't something that I knew and just didn't tell you" (Jones n.d.).

Listed below are suggestions from *Management Principles for Christian Schools* (Deuink 1996, 123) that should be implemented as a part of your administration's internal controls that are based on the rule of two:

Cash Controls for Christian Schools

1. Have a written, current financial policies manual.
2. Audit all personnel involved in financial activities to ensure that written policies are being followed.
3. Have an internal audit program that verifies all financial transactions periodically.
4. Have an external audit of all financial activities annually.
5. Use prenumbered receipts for all income. Deposits should indicate the receipt numbers. All numbers should be accounted for. Deposits should be noted in the receipt book and referenced to the bank statement when it is reconciled.
6. Whenever possible, two people should count all cash. They should prepare it for deposit and present the deposit to the bookkeeper intact. The bookkeeper should not handle cash receipts.
7. Someone other than the bookkeeper should open and prepare for deposit all receipts received by mail.
8. All checks should be restrictively endorsed and deposited daily with other receipts. No part of the cash receipts should be used to pay expenses.
9. All disbursements should be made by check, and supporting documentation should be kept whenever possible.
10. Instruct your bank in writing never to cash a check payable to the school.
11. A specific individual(s) should be assigned to approve payment of accounts payable.
12. Someone other than the bookkeeper should sign the checks and approve them for release.
13. Someone other than the bookkeeper should receive and reconcile the bank statements.
14. Someone other than the bookkeeper should authorize the writing off of any unpaid tuition.
15. Excess cash should be kept in a separate interest-bearing account.
16. Specific instructions should be written for transferring money from one account to another.
17. All personnel regularly handling cash and signing checks should be bonded.
18. Student activity funds should be kept in a separate account. Deposits to the account should be prepared, given to the

bookkeeper, and deposited. All expenditures should be approved in writing by the principal and the person responsible for the activity.

A Letter Describing a True Story

Dr. Coley,

Well, I've been at the academy almost five months, and I pray that my surprises for the year are finally over. I had to make some major reductions in the budget area to balance this academic year. The toughest part of that was having to lay off eight support personnel, both full-time and part-time employees. This includes the academy and the early learning center. I also had to close the kitchen on the academy side. We are now brown-bagging lunch. My financial director left (as all of this was coming to light). No hanky-panky has been going on. It appears that the board has just not been doing their supervisory role to the best of their ability. I believe I have that problem corrected, and I am encouraged about the involvement they are now taking. They have been running a monthly deficit in the range of $8,000 to $9,000 for the past *two to three years!* They had a substantial savings account that they were hitting every month to make ends meet. Well, you know what has become of that account? I was looking at a $120,000 shortfall by the end of this academic year. With my budget cuts, I now anticipate a $20,000 surplus (if no major problems arise). The students' parents have been very supportive, and not one student has been pulled from the academy. In fact, I have gained one and have had three inquiries about starting in January. This incident has also brought the church more solidly behind the academy than ever before. Enough of the bad news.

I established a reading goal for the year of 6,000 books to be read by the students, parents, and staff. As of yesterday, we passed the halfway mark. This is about thirty days before the midpoint of the academic year. Students' GPAs are higher than last year. The daily attendance rate is higher than last year. Detentions are in the single digits. I did not receive *one* parental complaint or negative comment after the first grading period. I sent home a suggested monthly reading list for the parents, and I have received some very favorable comments from a few.

So, what are my lessons learned from the last five months?

1. I now have a whole new group of questions to ask the board or pastor if the Lord ever moves me to a new institution.

2. As the captain of the ship, I am responsible for the navigational path. (This lesson is a strong reinforcement from my military days.)
3. He is in charge!

Well, it is time for me to go out to the car line. I pray that all is going well with you and your family. Hope to see you soon.

Take care and God bless,
A former student

You Take the Helm

Design a procedure for the handling of school tuition, money collected in the cafeteria, or gate receipts at a sporting event. Ask a friend in accounting to review your procedures.

Employee Files

Another dimension of integrity and accuracy is the careful maintenance of employee files. Not long ago an administrator who was in his third month of leadership at the school where he was calling from began the conversation by asking, "What should I do about questions regarding a former faculty member?" I asked, "Who wants to know?" The voice on the other end softly said, "The police." He went on to explain that there was an ongoing investigation regarding a former teacher and a female student at the school where the teacher was now working. The investigator had come to speak with the administrator in an effort to get information about the teacher in question and his job performance at the previous school. After I told my friend that the police had a right to see the personnel file, he exclaimed, "That's the problem. There isn't one!" Fortunately, in this particular case, the administrator could not be held responsible for the shortcomings of the administrator that he replaced. Certainly not all occasions requiring a look at a personnel file will be this dramatic, but there are a host of reasons, both legal and practical, to maintain meticulous records. Listed below are some of the documents that must be maintained for every employee:

- Form W-4 (including the state form)
- Withholding allowances
- INS Form I-9 (employment eligibility verification)
- Legal name (as on the employee's social security card)
- Contact information (address, phone, etc.)

- Social security number (sometimes it is best to copy the actual card)
- Job classification
- Pertinent qualification information (transcripts, etc.)
- Date employment started
- Payroll period
- Place at which the employee will work
- Employment status (independent contractor, W-2, etc.)
- Wage rate or salary information (with careful notes that you've kept about years of experience and level of education that influence the employee's placement on a salary scale)
- Tax exemption information (federal withholding, FICA)
- Do they exist under any special group under payroll law?
- Employment contract

Financial Stability

Close to the core of every successful Christian ministry is a well-thought-out philosophy for how the administrator and board approach the establishment of the price tag that will be placed on the services that they provide. In a presentation to Christian school leaders attending an Association of Christian Schools regional meeting in Greensboro, North Carolina, Brian Carpenter (1998) described the decision-making process. Carpenter, who has served as an administrator at Gastonia Christian School, argued that there are three simple ways of thinking about managing and leading a Christian school: education, ministry, and business. If you have the business and education legs only, you will have a *private school*. If you have the business and ministry legs only, you will have a well-funded *youth group*. If you have the education and ministry legs only, you will have *no school*.

Carpenter strongly urges leaders not to minimize the importance of the *business* dimension of the school. He believes that *tuition should be set at a rate that is needed to appropriately fund the entire operating budget of the school*. In addition, a primary factor in determining this rate is teachers' salaries, which should be near the salaries of their public-school counterparts. He encourages schools to provide adequate benefits for employees and to establish procedures to monitor the efficient collection of tuition payments. On the other hand, Carpenter strongly discourages the use of fund-raising as a means of keeping tuition rates low. For families needing assistance with tuition payments, he recommends an endowment program to assist in the annual expenses of the school (1998).

Few spokespersons on the topic of tuition rates for Christian schools articulate these issues as clearly as D. Bruce Lockerbie, chairman of

Paideia, Inc., in Stony Brook, New York. In ACSI's *Leadership Academy 2004 Report*, Lockerbie describes the preceding approach as a "cost-based" philosophy. Supporting the idea of funding the operating budget with tuition income, he states, "In order for the *ministry* of Christian schooling to exist at all, it must be funded by some means adequate to fulfill the promise made by our mission statement" (2004, 92). He charges administrators and board members with the responsibility to consider carefully the average "cost-to-educate" as they set their school's tuition rates. Another significant point he wants school administrators to consider is the perception the community has about a particular school, when its tuition rate is artificially suppressed so "everyone can afford it" (92–93). He makes a powerful philosophical statement about whether or not a Christian school should raise its tuition to a level that is closer to its cost-to-educate: "A Christian school should raise its tuition if the board recognizes that the *mission/budget* test reveals a disparity between mission claims and available funding to fulfill those claims" (94).

However, there are opponents to this approach to establishing the tuition rate. Randy Ross, the director of the ACSI Ohio River Valley Region, presents the argument that a higher "cost-based" tuition does not lend itself to achieving the goal of helping as many parents as possible to obey the mandate of providing a Christ-centered education for their children. Ross is concerned that ever-increasing tuition rates create the perception that Christian schools are elitist and exclusive, as opposed to inclusive. He fears that many families will refuse to take even the first step in the application process. Proponents of this argument prefer the faith-based approach that encourages parents of more modest incomes to seriously consider Christian education. This model requires each participant to have faith that God will meet the needs of the school as all members of the community are made aware of the school's financial needs (2004).

One such example of the faith-based approach is the Neighborhood School in Memphis, Tennessee. The administrator is Jo Walt, and she describes the school as "an elementary and middle school for at-risk children who live in a poverty, drug-infested area of Memphis and who had no hope because no one cared" (1998, 7). At one point in the late 1990s, the school had seventy-three students, six teachers, a reading specialist, and more than one hundred volunteers who performed duties such as serving lunch, teaching reading and art, tutoring, and coaching. The starting salary for a teacher in the school at that time was $25,000. However, some students from the most difficult home environments were paying as little as $11 per month (1998, 7). Certainly, God is at work in schools like these.

Finance and Facilities

Brian Carpenter (1998) provides the following guidelines about tuition:

Calculating Tuition Rates—the Philosophical Framework
1. You must *determine* your mission. *If you want people to invest in children through your school and expect to charge them appropriately, you must to be able to communicate to them what you are about!* (Hint: the Christian school movement has suffered long enough under ubiquitous mission statements such as "academic excellence in a Christian environment.")

2. *Honestly* evaluate how well you are fulfilling that mission statement from one year to the next. This assessment does not have to be complicated. In general, look at (or look for) the following:

   • Standardized test scores in the 3 Rs
   • Outstanding student academic achievements
   • University acceptance, especially from more competitive schools
   • PSAT/SAT scores
   • Program breadth and depth (AP courses, foreign language, art, computer, advanced math and English, dual enrollment, etc.)
   • Alumni successes
   • Student body character (especially grades 7–12)
   • Student scholarships awarded
   • Staff turnover
   • Increase in enrollment (all things being equal)

   In a nutshell, if you are not fulfilling your stated mission, you have no right to ask parents to pay tuition, much less *higher tuition.*

3. Communicate the fulfillment of the mission to your constituents! *This is a crucial step.* Your school could conceivably earn As in *all* the above criteria; however, a majority percentage of parents may not know it. This principle is similarly stated by Mark Twain, who said [that the man who can read good books, but doesn't, has no advantage over the man who can't.]

   A school that is fulfilling its mission, but not communicating it, has no advantage over the school that isn't fulfilling its mission.

   An *indispensable* tool in communicating the fulfillment of your mission is a *quality* annual report.

4. *Realize* that approximately 75% of any school's operating budget is usually appropriated for salaries and benefits. Thus, the following is

an irrefutable rule: As tuition goes, so go salaries. (And as salaries go, so goes the program.) Generally speaking,

Low tuition = poor staff retention = poor quality program
Appropriate tuition = better staff retention = high quality program

* Note that tuition is *calculated*. It is not guessed at, held low so "as many people can afford it as possible," or arbitrarily raised in $5–$10 monthly increments. *It should be calculated to fund the entire operating budget for the year.*

Uncollected Tuition Means Lost Income

Which is harder? To say to a parent, "I'm sorry, your child is no longer eligible to attend here until your obligation to pay tuition is fulfilled," *or* to say to a teacher, "I'm sorry, the school can't pay you today because I feel uncomfortable in expecting parents to pay their tuition." (After all, we are a ministry.)

1. All tuition is due and payable on the first of each month. A grace period of ten days is granted from the first to the tenth of the month.

2. If the tuition has not been received by the tenth of the month
   a. A $20 late charge is assessed to the account
   b. A polite reminder is sent by the business manager
   c. The head of school is given a late list/amounts

3. Two weeks later, on or about the 25th of the month
   a. The head of school is given an updated list
   b. A second letter is sent by the head requesting payment before the end of the month

4. On the last working day of that month or the first working day of the next month
   a. The head of school is given a final update
   b. A third letter is sent by the head, offering a final opportunity for the parents to keep their children enrolled by paying the past due amount immediately

Brian Carpenter goes on to say, "The administrator should be vested with authority to use his or her discretion in working with families to make reasonable arrangements for tuition payment for unusual circumstances (for example, loss of job, catastrophic incident)."

He presents some assumptions to consider when preparing the budget:

Income
- Economic conditions in your community prior to determining increases
- The school's track record for operating at capacity
- The school's ability to collect 100% of tuition from families (see policy discussion)
- Finance committee and administrator's ability to track spending

Expense
- Age of the building, equipment, etc., which may need repair, maintenance, or replacement
- Community's present-versus-potential attitude toward giving to scholarships or a capital fund
- Number of students/families receiving discounts

Personnel
- Adequacy of teachers' salaries
- Finances for continuing education
- Escalating costs of benefits
- Expansion of staff for growth of student body or new course offerings
- Number of administrators

Resources
- Rotation of textbook replacement
- Expansion of curriculum or extracurricular activities

Transportation
- Changes in federal/state law for licensing, testing, equipment changes

Other
- Adequacy of insurance coverage
- Adequacy of audit/finance audit

You Take the Helm

Obtain a copy of a budget from a local Christian school and review its figures. Begin by comparing the anticipated income with the expected expenditures. Next, compare the personnel expenses to the total expenses. As you analyze other line items, list areas that you think are perhaps out of balance.

In *From Candy Sales to Committed Donors*, D. Bruce Lockerbie (1996, 47) presents some weaknesses of product sales:

> Fund-raising by product sales demeans the very idea of mission....

> Fund-raising by product sales enables the school's board and administration to avoid asking anyone to give....

> Fund-raising by product sales relies on the public's desire for a tangible exchange of goods in return for money, rather than the intangible benefits of good work to the glory of God....

> [Conclusion:] Christian school leaders need to help their donors recognize how their gifts support personnel and programs essential to a school.

Budget Analysis

Does Your Tuition Cover Your Operating Expenses?
Goal: Tuition covers 100 percent of a school's operating expenses (depending on your board's response to the issue of tuition-based budgeting versus faith-based budgeting). If your school's tuition is not covering 100 percent of its operating expenses, consider increasing the percentage it does cover each year. I have seen a school's budget depend on fund-raisers to supplement over 10 percent of the annual budget. This plan included the expectation that the school would earn over $10,000 at the annual sale of Christmas trees. What if it rained for two weeks in December and no one bought a tree? The leaders of the school would have to go through an entire budget year uncertain of whether they could meet their obligations for the *fixed* costs they had taken on. Serious and prayerful consideration should be given to planning a budget that is tuition-based and to communicating to parents the importance of their support.

What Percent of the Total Budget Are Salaries and Benefits?
Goal: Salaries and benefits make up 66 percent of the budget. David Roth advises: "Salaries and fringe benefits are important variables in the budgeting process. Compensation may comprise up to 75 percent of the costs on the expense side of the ledgers, a major factor to be reckoned with when creating a budget. Expect annual tension between appropriate teacher compensation and affordable student tuition. Every administrator deals with this challenge" (2002, 251).

Are There Portions of the Budget, Such as Cafeteria or Athletics Expenses, That Ought to Be Close to Self-Sustaining but Demand More from Tuition Income?

Goal: Expenses and income represent a wash. Do the cafeteria expenses exceed the income from the cash collected by those who choose to buy their lunch? Are non-eaters paying for this service? Extra expenses such as paper goods supplied for class parties add up quickly. Another issue is the benefit of allowing teachers to eat at no charge. Does the athletic program require a disproportionate amount of the operating fund when compared to the number of students who participate? Should Booster Club activities or participation fees be expected to offset these expenses? Are bus transportation expenses covered by the students who ride the bus, or are other students who are non-riders subsidizing the cost with their tuition?

Consideration for Cost Cutting or Cost Control

Have tuition collection done by a third party to reduce office expenses and increase collection. Outsource payroll to reduce office expenses and increase accuracy. Contract building maintenance to increase efficiency and to pass on costs such as supplies, machines, and personnel benefits. Competition bid for health insurance. Recruit a board member or faculty member who is willing to invest time and energy into the annual activity of "shopping" for the best health care for the money.

One school responded to the inevitable announcement of major increases by putting their health care out to bid. The staff member who was responsible then invited the representatives from each provider to make a presentation to the full faculty. The catch was that the other representatives were present during the competitor's presentation! Reduce full-pay discount (suggestion: the discount for those who pay the entire year's tuition should not exceed 2 percent). Most families who are able to pay in full will appreciate the value of the reduction.

Table 10.1 and table 10.2 feature a basic budget template that could be helpful in establishing your school's first budget. It would be wise to establish a format that allows notations to be included in the right margin. This sample budget has numerous comments to assist you in knowing where the dollar amounts come from.

Table 10.1

New Start Christian School Profit and Loss Draft for 2005–2006			
Note: 250 Students			
Income			
Account Number	**Line Item**	**Financial Assets**	**Assumption**
21000	Fees	$125,000	$500 x 250 students
22000	Tuition	$1,100,000	$4,400 x 250 students
23000	Tuition discounts	($40,000)	Teachers' children free Pastors' discount 50%
23500	Scholarship	($50,000)	Fund for financial assistance
24000	Lunch	$0	Income and expense wash
25000	Program revenue	$5,000	Low estimate for activities income, such as gate receipts, vending
26000	Other income	$5,000	Low estimate: gym rental, etc.
27000	Contributions	$100,000	Used primarily for scholarships
28000	Booster Club	$5,000	Low estimate for fund-raiser
Total Income		**$1,250,000**	

Table 10.2

New Start Christian School Profit and Loss Draft for 2005–2006			
Note: 250 Students			
Expense			
Account Number	**Line Item**	**Financial Assets**	**Assumption**
50000	Salaries	$730,000	Consider the average teacher's salary in your community
51000	Benefits	$0	In salaries
52000	Books	$50,000	$200/student
53000	Supplies	$10,000	$40/student
54000	Maintenance	$60,000	$.66 x 90,000 sq. ft
54500	Utilities	$100,000	$1.00/90,000 sq. ft. + $10,000 water/shower
55000	Purchased services	$20,000	Repair, advertising, testing
56000	Student activities	$5,000	Varies with student interests
56500	Athletics	$25,000	See table 10.3
57000	Equipment	$10,000	Copier leases, etc.
57100	Bus	$30,000	One team bus
57200	Cafeteria	$0	Wash with income
57400	Insurance property and casualty	$10,000	Varies
58000	Travel, education	$5,000	Tuition assistance for continuing education
Total Expense		**$1,055,000**	

Table 10.3

New Start Christian School Athletic Expenses Year Ending 9/30/06				
Category/ Sport	Expense Item	Number Needed	Cost Per	Total Expense
Middle School Boys				
Soccer	Uniforms	16	$100	$1,600
	Balls	8	$20	$160
	Officials (2 per game)	10	$100	$1,000
	Coach stipend	1	$1,000	$1,000
Total Soccer				**$3,760**
Basketball	Uniforms	12	$100	$1,200
	Balls	12	$40	$480
	Officials (2 per game)	10	$50	$500
	Coach stipend	1	$1,000	$1,000
Total Basketball				**$3,180**
Baseball	Uniforms	16	$100	$1,600
	Equipment			$1,000
	Officials (2 per game)	10	$100	$1,000
	Miscellaneous			$400
	Coach stipend	1	$1,000	$1,000
Total Baseball				**$5,000**

Continued

Table 10.3 *continued*

Category/ Sport	Expense Item	Number Needed	Cost Per	Total Expense
Middle School Girls				
Volleyball	Uniforms	16	$100	$1,600
	Balls	8	$20	$160
	Officials (1 per game)	10	$50	$500
	Coach stipend	1	$1,000	$1,000
Total Volleyball				**$3,260**
Basketball	Uniforms	12	$100	$1,200
	Balls	12	$40	$480
	Officials (2 per game)	10	$50	$500
	Coach stipend	1	$1,000	$1,000
Total Basketball				**$3,180**
Softball/Soccer	Uniforms	16	$100	$1,600
	Equipment			$1,000
	Officials (2 per game)	10	$100	$1,000
	Miscellaneous			$400
	Coach stipend	1	$1,000	$1,000
Total Softball/Soccer				**$5,000**
Total Athletic Expense				**$23,380**

The Budgeting Process

Below are some suggestions for the budgeting process:

- Determine major capital needs that will be addressed in the upcoming fiscal year.
- Review current salary information along with projected new personnel needs.
- Project enrollment increases or decreases to determine tuition income.
- Project the need for additional expenditures, such as increases for more resources and inflation adjustments.
- Create an expenditure buffer to handle any overages.
- Finalize the budget for review.
- Present the budget for approval to the organization's board or church group.

Budget Management

A procedure needs to be developed to manage the budget (capital and expenses) changes that occur each year. Since budgets are developed prior to the beginning of the year and since certain items may change during the year, the administration needs the ability to manage "between the banks." This procedure would allow the administration to reallocate dollars from one account to another as part of their daily management process. This procedure would also allow the administration to reallocate funds on the basis of a certain percentage- or dollar-change maximum without coming back to the board for approval. An example would be the need to hire new teachers each year. If the school loses a teacher who has two years of experience and hires a teacher who has ten years of experience to fill the vacant slot, there is not a change in head count, but there will be an impact on the salary budget. This procedure would provide a way for the administration to manage this process within a board-designated percentage or dollar amount each year (for example, 3 percent or $100,000).

In *Called to Lead*, David Roth offers some insight into budget management:

> One of the most difficult areas to manage is budget flexibility. The budget *must be kept*, but within certain flexible guidelines. Ultimately though, the grand total *must not be violated!* Here, confidence in and respect for your CFO (chief financial officer) becomes critical (John Thomas, personal communication).

Respect for the CFO makes possible the effective accomplishment of the school's mission within the boundaries of its resources, because even a one-year budget is only a projection. Managing actual as opposed to projected budgets becomes the "art work" of the CFO. If he or she does well, the mission will be accomplished, the budget balanced, and cash flow adequate. However, that scenario does not mean that areas dictated by mission will never go slightly over budget. (2002, 249)

Building Depreciation

In most cases, the building is depreciated over a 40-year life. If your school is a 501(c)(3) and therefore has no tax liability, the depreciation does not have a cash effect on the ministry.

Table 10.4

Financial Commandments for Administrators
Thou Shalt Not ...
1. Handle cash
2. Write checks
3. Sign checks
4. Spend money outside the scope of your authority
5. Promise lower tuition in exchange for volunteer service (barter)
6. Promise a tax deduction in exchange for a contribution made for scholarship for a specific family
7. Require a "contribution" and see that it is tax deductible
8. Fail to pay state or federal withholding
9. Miss or delay payroll (federal laws)
10. Spend money from a "slush fund" for which there is no accountability or use the school's credit card for personal expenses

Financial Development

A growing area of emphasis for school leadership is the need for financial development to garner funds and resources that will reduce the pressure on the need to increase tuition each year. "Development is a leadership process that articulates the vision and goals of the school and secures the necessary resources to implement those goals through a planned program of prayer, marketing, and fund-raising" (Dill 2002, 260).

Christian schools throughout the Southern Baptist Convention are experiencing overwhelming success and rapid expansion. However, most of these schools are also dealing with the inevitable challenges and growing pains that accompany such growth. More than 600 Christian schools are now affiliated with a Southern Baptist church, and most of these schools have escalating enrollments. Their influence is vital as they partner with parents and churches to teach a Christian worldview to our next generation.

The information reported below was collected in a survey of pastors and administrators at the annual meeting of the Southern Baptist Association of Christian Schools (SBACS) in July of 1998. Leaders from twenty-two schools responded to survey questions focusing on different aspects of development. Three trends related to growth and development emerged from the survey of member Southern Baptist schools.

Numerical Growth
An amazing 80 percent of the schools indicate they are growing, and half of these have waiting lists. Only 20 percent report a pattern of no growth, and no schools are in decline. It comes as no surprise, then, that over half the schools say they are out of space. Of the schools responding, only 13 percent report they have room to grow. In fact, two-thirds of these leaders say they are either in a building program, in the planning phase to build, or in the process of looking for property to respond to current and future demand.

Financial Challenges
Tuition dollars are being stretched as never before and, in most cases, fall short of providing the school with the income it needs to achieve its goals. Given this shortfall, what are their leaders doing to make up the difference? Over half of the schools ask for contributions from students' families, in addition to tuition. Why ask for donations beyond tuition costs? In addition to the constant concern for improving teachers' salaries, one-third of the schools report being in the midst of a capital fund-raising campaign. Most administrators have determined that increasing tuition costs significantly to cover these expenses would eliminate many of their students and families from participation in the school.

Beyond families of students, member schools turn to their own alumni and to the sponsoring church. Of these, 66 percent indicate these are two outside sources. Only 12 percent receive contributions from other churches, and none of the schools surveyed receive money from a local association of churches.

In short, over two-thirds of the schools report depending on tuition and fees for 90 percent or more of the income that it takes to meet their budgets. And most schools expect another 5 percent to be collected by fund-raising, which usually means more money from their families.

Why Do Administrators Continue Fund-Raising Rather Than Ask for Gifts?

Many school administrators lack confidence in their ability to ask for financial support....

Many schools' constituents have become accustomed to the steady cycle of sales and treat them as a necessary nuisance....

Few schools have yet begun to tie their reason-for-being to their reason-for-asking to be supported by those who believe in their mission.

(Lockerbie 1996, 49–50)

The concept of employing a development director whose responsibility it would be to raise money from other sources has not caught on in these schools as it has with most independent schools. Of member schools, 72 percent have not hired such a person. Only 13 percent have a full-time director of development. Consequently, principals are expected to fulfill this responsibility, but 55 percent report spending very little time (less than 5 percent of their workweek) pursuing other sources of income.

Unfortunately, one category that suffers because there is no development director is scholarship grants and aid. Though member schools discuss wanting to help families who have financial needs, 48 percent of member schools grant 2 percent or less of their total budget for this purpose. The number increases to 86 percent for those granting 10 percent or less for financial aid.

Why Do Christian Schools Lag Behind Other Ministries in Obtaining Gift Support?

Parents of current students ... are assumed to be overburdened by tuition payments and are either underrated or ignored as potential donors....

The Christian school is failing to affirm its mission and seeking merely to raise funds rather than win lasting support from committed friends of the school and its mission....

The typical head of a Christian school is taxed by having to serve not only as chief executive officer of the school but also as manager of several necessary departments.

(Lockerbie 1996, 60–61)

Implications

The responses by the leaders of these twenty-two schools indicate that some of the resources that are vital to the success of a school are being stretched thin by the continual expansion. As a former principal, I believe the following concepts must be given serious consideration:

Leadership training. The continued training of current administrators and the recruitment and training of new ones is vitally important. Christian colleges, universities, and seminaries must play an aggressive role in developing leaders who are prepared to meet the expanding demands of our Christian schools.

Financial support from other churches. Churches that do not sponsor a school need to actively support the Christian schools in their area. One such approach would be for every church to establish a scholarship program for families in their congregation. This support would allow schools to continue to increase tuition rates to meet growing financial demands without eliminating families who have difficulty paying these higher rates.

Training in financial development. School board members and administrators who lack skills in the area of financial development need training to discover and cultivate other sources of income beyond tuition and fees. Only the schools that do this will keep pace with the demands that will come with maturation and expansion.

Table 10.5

Contents of an Annual Report
• A message from the administrator • A chart summary of the annual revenue and expenses • A description of ways of giving to the school: cash gifts, appreciated assets, will trust, life insurance, real estate • Annual fund participants • A breakdown by amount or by constituency (parents, faculty, etc.) • Special projects or organizations, such as the Booster Club
This document must clearly communicate the school's successes in light of its mission in the previous year. The layout, printing, pictures, and paper quality will say a lot about the quality and expectations of the school and its leadership.

Table 10.6

Testimony from a Development Director

Coming from the business world to a Christian ministry, I was keenly aware of my dependence on the Lord. I knew He had shaped me and made me to fit the new opportunity before me. Fourteen years of full-time ministry coupled with ten years of non-ministry business training have yielded a unique perspective that can provide a refreshing viewpoint.

First of all, it is important to delineate my part from God's part. God is Master and Controller. He has promised to provide, and because of His sovereignty, I can trust Him to be right on time, every time, with just the right resource. Everything belongs to Him, and He knows more about my situation than I do. My job is to be a good steward of His resources. He encourages me to be faithful in the management of His resources and to integrate total stewardship into my life. Total stewardship involves the transformation of my thinking into God's thinking. Total stewardship is just that—total. The time, talent, and treasure God has entrusted in me are to ultimately be used for His glory and for the advancement of His kingdom. I am to be an example of His transformational power. The director of development is a servant leader who leads by being obedient to God's call for total stewardship. There is no pressure to produce results—no need to deploy trickery or come up with a scheme to manipulate giving. All I have to do is be a faithful steward telling the story with excellence and precision and trust God to do His part. The plan is simple—believe God and His Word, let Him do His part, and be faithful in doing my part for His glory and honor.

God is at work on several different levels simultaneously. In a particular situation, God is at work in my life, your life, and everyone who is observing the situation. Every event, no matter the size or shape, should be viewed as an opportunity for redemption. As a director of development, I must be a conduit of His grace and mercy. I listen and understand while I pray and apply God's wisdom to every event. It must be more of Him and less of me. Every person matters to Him, and every person is a part of His eternal plan. Often I am His feet and His tongue, so my eyes must be His eyes, so my heart beats with His beat. Asking someone to give is one of the highest callings of humankind. Giving is an act of worship, and we are most fulfilled when we are giving. So, I encourage people to give as it has been given unto them. This is not equal giving but giving that is proportional to one's capability to give. No pressure, no strain, just present the truth through God's wisdom, and trust Him for the results. If God called you to a task, He will provide what you need in accordance to His call. The tendency is to press, when the goal should be to trust. Relax in Him and watch as He transforms your life and then uses this transformation to transform another.

Facilities

Many administrators are experiencing the challenges of allocating classroom space for growing educational programs. Unfortunately, the joy of expanding ministries can sometimes be dampened by conflicts between those who are asked to share the same classroom space at different times of the week. In such cases, administrators have seen otherwise calm, loving saints act more like temperamental toddlers who do not want to share their toys. An unwashed tabletop or a row of desks and chairs out of place may result in tears, resignations, or running gun battles. However, an administrator who is diligent and who plans carefully may significantly reduce the frequency of these problems and the hard feelings that often accompany them. Let's examine some specific steps and procedures that can be implemented by a wise leader.

Articulate a Common Vision
An effective administrator will unite and inspire his coworkers to work together for a common cause. Every ministry should have as its primary goals winning the lost to Christ and discipling them as they grow. Each individual and ministry needs to know how others relate to this overarching mission and respect fellow members as coworkers in Christ. Such an understanding is possible if the leader clearly and concisely communicates the interrelatedness of the various ministries.

How can this Herculean task be accomplished by anyone less than Sampson or Solomon? One way to build esprit de corps is to sponsor celebrations in which the various ministries that must struggle to use the same classrooms come together to cheer for each other as they share what God is doing in the lives of the families that they minister to. In this festive atmosphere, the leader can review previously arranged procedures, answer general questions, and encourage a spirit of cooperation. My experiences have led me to the conclusion that people who share in praise and prayer will stay together.

Allocate Resources
Even the most mature and flexible teachers work better when they have materials and space they can call their own. Here are some options for administrators to consider, especially when the classrooms are being used by weekday programs such as a Christian school or preschool, Wednesday night church meetings, and Sunday morning Bible study:

• Provide a locking closet, cabinet, or high shelf for each group that uses the room.

- Provide trained staff to convert the furniture when the need arises and to take care of any custodial needs.
- Provide separate storage areas where educational supplies are stocked for each ministry. If separate areas are not available, make sure ample supplies are maintained.
- Provide a "focal wall" in each classroom for each teacher to be able to post visual aids for units of study.
- Provide bookshelves or toy bins on wheels that can be easily turned around to face the walls when not in use. If these are not available, cover the shelves with easel paper.

One large church designed its new educational space with its Christian school and Sunday school classes in mind. At the end of each school week, a custodial staff stacks all the children's tables and chairs neatly next to the teacher's desk and then pulls a folding curtain across that end of the room. About 80 percent of the classroom space remains and can be used throughout the weekend. From a nearby storage area, stackable tables and chairs are moved into the room on Friday afternoon and returned on Sunday evening.

Accept the Realities of Joint Use
Some teachers might think that an ideal situation is one in which each room has only one user and is frozen in time until the next class session after the teacher closes the door at the end of each week. Is this truly good stewardship of a facility that belongs to the Lord?

Those who are involved in sharing classroom space must make necessary adjustments in relationship to the age group (or groups) that also use the space. For instance, in most cases neither teacher will be able to leave behind large displays or student projects. Students' work will have to be completed during the allotted time or taken home with them for completion, unless suitable storage is available. Leaving them on display is an invitation for disaster.

As previously mentioned, every user of the room must have the option to display announcements, schedules, or class-related materials. The primary user, such as a Christian school teacher, must be courteous and reserve some space.

Finally, all those involved need to have a spirit of love and forgiveness, knowing that there will be times when things will not be perfect or be done according to routine. I recall the time an enthusiastic Sunday school teacher came in on Saturday morning and wrote an entire outline on the chalkboard. That afternoon the Christian school teacher who used the room during the week came in and erased the Sunday school teacher's work. Needless to say, sparks were flying on Sunday morning!

In this section, I have presented three leadership concepts for church administrators to follow so they can effectively inspire those around them to work together in a spirit of appreciation and cooperation. God wants to use us to strengthen harmony and coordination in His Body so that He will be glorified as His children serve Him.

You Take the Helm

Read the following letter from a young administrator requesting advice on finances and facilities. Discuss possible solutions that you would recommend.

> My wife and I came into this church with excitement and concern. I know God led me here because of the positive response and results from my work. The church has a Sunday school enrollment of more than 1,200 and an attendance of more than 700. So, on average more than half of the people actually attend. The church also has a primary school that occupies the church property.
>
> The majority of the church members have personally expressed concern and anger about sharing the church property with the school. I am going to ask some questions, and if you could provide me with some advice or a resource that may help me, I would appreciate it.
>
> We have a money issue and a handful of custodians to help. Our problem is that we don't know who should be responsible for moving the school desks on Friday and setting up for Sunday school. Right now, the teachers are doing the setup on Fridays and the breakdown on Mondays!
>
> We are building a family life center that will be ready next September. The school just started a ninth grade, with seven students enrolled, and they want to add a grade every year to create a full high school. The new building will provide ten large classrooms. The school wants the rooms, and the church people say no! The church people, the senior adults, want space in the church all to themselves. With senior

adults representing the majority of this church, how can I get around this problem?

In addition to the space-sharing issue, the church will be starting dual Sunday schools in six months. So one day, three separate groups (the school and two Sunday schools) will use every classroom.

The headmaster of the school has been here for a very long time. Since I am new, I have started a good relationship with her and the staff separately. Now, with some major decisions coming across my plate, I must step on some toes. The church policy has given me authority over her and the school. I have seen schools and churches that do not work well together and some that do this very smoothly. I know this can work, but I need advice.

Legal Issues

Principle for Guiding Principals:

The effective administrator demonstrates wisdom and discernment in legal matters in order to protect the name of Christ, the safety and well-being of the students and faculty, and the resources of the ministry.

The phone call came just after the administrator had arrived. His secretary said that the police were on the phone reporting an accident involving one of the school buses that made a morning pickup. No other information was given, but he knew he must get to the scene as soon as possible. As he drove in the direction of the intersection where the collision occurred, he noticed a very eerie sight. The lanes on the other side of the street that would normally carry hundreds of commuters were completely deserted. Something severe must have happened to cause the apparent closing of all the oncoming lanes. His prayers for everyone's safety were intermittently interrupted with pangs of fear. Had there been a mechanical failure on the bus? Was its inspection up-to-date? Were the maintenance records complete? Was the teacher who was driving the bus injured? Was his commercial driver's license (CDL) in his wallet with him? Who caused the accident?

As he prayed for the students who were passengers, the administrator remembered the drills he had overseen that taught the students how to deal with an accident. Had they all been properly seated, and were they now in a safe location awaiting adult instructions?

As the school leader crested the hill, he could feel the blood drain from his face. A cohort of emergency vehicles was blocking the street, and traffic had come to a complete standstill. He feared the worst when he observed the school bus at rest on the side of the road underneath a broken telephone pole. A nearby midsize car had a crushed front end and flattened roof. After parking on a side street, the administrator found a police officer who recounted the events that had just unfolded. The bus had been struck by the sedan when the sedan's driver misjudged the speed of the bus and illegally made a left turn in front of the bus. The bus was forced off of the road and clipped the telephone pole just before it came to a stop. The good news was that all the students had exited the rear of the bus, just as they had practiced, under the watchful eye of two high school students who assisted the younger students. The bus driver only received a minor ankle sprain, and the elderly driver of the car would make a full recovery after a short hospital stay.

As the fiduciary head of your organization, have you taken the proper care that a wise and diligent helmsman must do in order to protect the well-being of all who are involved in the ministry? In addition, are the necessary policies and procedures in place to protect the assets of the school in case legal action should occur after an accident or incident such as the one described above? The purpose of this chapter is not to present an exhaustive list of potential legal issues with some corresponding counsel on how to handle them. In a comparatively brief discussion, I hope to motivate you to become a serious observer who diligently looks after the safety of your flock and who is constantly searching for appropriate ways to provide financial security and protect your ministry from legal action that may threaten the future of the school.

Nine Categories That Should Be Considered

A Legal Memorandum, a publication of the well-known professional organization the National Association of Secondary School Principals (1996, 2), listed the following topics as nine areas of importance that may need to be considered in tough moral decisions. I would argue that each of these makes perfect sense when a school leader pauses to reflect on Christ's behavior in similar circumstances, though this concept is not a dimension of the publication's theme.

Legal Issues

1. Respect

Does your action show the proper respect and dignity for those involved? The Golden Rule should be the basis of all decision making by a leader. In addition, the leader must be constantly aware of the scrutiny that he or she is always under. Though another person, such as an unhappy faculty member, is acting in an unprofessional or disrespectful way, the leader must realize that before the Lord and others, the leader's attitude and behavior must consistently reveal "Christ in us." I always knew that no matter how unruly or disrespectful a member of the community became, what would be remembered most would be my response to the situation.

2. Safety

What is the best course of action to protect all those involved? Over the years, my biggest concern in overseeing other faculty members was their lack of awareness in this area. To make matters worse, some adults are by nature risk takers who would do well to heed, or even to have, an internal warning that tells them something is not safe. I know of a situation in which an adult leader had plans to take two dozen teens on a short trip for roller skating. When the group arrived at the bus, the leader discovered that he lacked a key for a small padlock that had been installed on the front door of the bus to keep neighborhood kids out. (The lock was a bad idea to begin with.) An industrious member of the group managed to open the back door of the bus and encouraged his friends to climb aboard. The driver joined them in the vehicle, and they proceeded on the trip, with the front door of the bus still padlocked! What was he thinking? What if a police officer had happened by and noticed a loaded bus with the door locked shut? Even worse, what if the bus had been hit from the rear and the students needed to get out quickly?

You Take the Helm

What course of action would you have taken if you had been the supervisor of the adult leader in the preceding scenario? Can you recount a similar situation in which a group leader exercised poor judgment when it came to the safety of children or teens under his or her care?

3. Student Welfare

What is best for the student involved in the particular situation? This may be difficult, especially when what will help one student may appear to be at odds with what is best for the entire group. This is where prayer is vital. As the Lord gives the administrator peace and a sense of the proper direction or solution, then the administrator can trust Him for the events that follow.

4. **Fair Warning**

Did the student, parent, or staff member know the policy or procedure before it was violated, and is the person in a position to receive some type of punishment? Obviously, the careful construction of handbooks for teachers and students is essential so that those involved will not be blindsided by sudden correction. I was always chagrined every spring when a new style of clothing came out that was not referred to in the student handbook. In situations in which students have an enormous amount invested in an activity, such as with an athletic team or with long-distance travel on an overnight trip, administrators must carefully think through potential situations and prepare a clear-cut warning for a violation of the announced rules.

5. **Due Process**

Did the adult or student involved have an opportunity for due process before a final decision was made and a course of action determined? This process in a school setting should not be viewed as a type of Miranda standard that grants them the right to an attorney. But can we not agree that any child or adult has a basic right to hear the charge that has been brought against him or her, tell his or her side of the story, and be informed of the process for appeal to a higher authority, if one exists? I believe strongly that even the person with the worst history of veracity deserves a brief period of time to react to the accusations and present his or her version of what happened. I believe Christ calls us to such consideration and such a level of professional behavior.

The story of an administrator who carefully executed due process before the dismissal of a staff member illustrates the importance of this concept. A bright young man who was a well-trained mathematician appeared to be the right hire for teaching the advanced math courses for a Christian high school. However, students alerted their administrator early in the year when they did not understand anything the new teacher was presenting. After numerous observations, conferences, and professional assistance, the administrator reluctantly terminated the new instructor before Thanksgiving, the earliest he had ever made such a move. Because of the due process that had been extended to the teacher, the administrator received a lengthy letter from him a few months later thanking him for the way in which the dismissal had been handled and expressing the awareness that the decision had been the correct one.

Goss v. Lopez, a famous court case, is often quoted when there is a legal discussion involving due process. The case involved several students who demonstrated in a high school and junior high school in Columbus, Ohio, damaging property and disturbing classes. Particularly egregious was the attack by one student on a police officer. The students were suspended for ten days without any discussion or conversation between the administration and the students involved. They argued in court that their Fourteenth Amendment rights had been violated: "Nor shall any State deprive any person of life, liberty, or property, without due process of law." The plaintiffs argued that the students should have had some basic hearing before being dismissed. The Supreme Court agreed in a 5 to 4 decision. Justice White said, "Students facing suspension and the consequent interference with a protected property interest must be given … some kind of hearing…. Fairness can rarely be obtained by secret, one-sided determination of the facts…. Secrecy is not congenial to truth-seeking…. No better instrument has been devised for arriving at truth than to give a person in jeopardy of serious loss notice of the case against him and opportunity to meet it" (*Goss v. Lopez*, 519 U.S. 565, 1975). An especially troublesome example of violating this concept occurred at a church school in New York in 2002. *New York Daily News* (December 20, 2002) reported that two staff members were frustrated about discovering feces on the bathroom floor and subjected eight boys, who were in grades four and five, to a strip search in an effort to find the one who was responsible.

6. Consistency
Is the administrator's action consistent with what has taken place in similar circumstances? As an administrator of a large faculty, I made it my practice never to make private or secret agreements with any faculty member or family. For example, it is extremely difficult to anticipate every potential request by a teacher for the appropriate use of personal leave. I found that no matter how lengthy the list of approved reasons published in the handbook, legitimate situations not listed would occur. I would occasionally approve these with the words, "This is not a secret between us. When your colleagues ask, and they will, I want you to tell them …"

There are numerous aspects of the school leader's responsibilities that, if carried out inconsistently, can call into question the leader's integrity, his or her attention to detail, or perhaps worse, the potential for accusations of discrimination. For example, as discussed later in this chapter, it is vital that all employees be required to agree to a background check prior to employment. In a recent issue of the *Legal/Legislative Update*, published by the Association of Christian Schools International, it was noted, "Although you need not perform the same background check on every applicant or employee, any differentiation should be based on legitimate business interests and an investigation policy reasonably calculated to further these interests. You may be held liable for unlawful discrimination, regardless of whether it's intentional, if your investigation practices result in unequal treatment regarding race, national origin, religion, sex, pregnancy, physical or mental disabilities, or any other legally protected category or activity" (Carney 2003, 38).

7. Public Relations Test

What will be the impact of this decision on those not directly involved? What would the community's reaction be if this situation were made public in local media?

Of the nine "tests" published in the secular journal, this issue would probably rank last or not at all on a list of concerns of Christian leaders, and rightfully so. Provided a Christian leader is pursuing God's will in any given situation, the potential for disagreement in public debate should certainly not cause him to change his position. However, I agree that it is worthwhile to pause for a moment and ask "How would my actions make an impact on the cause of Christ if they were reported in tomorrow's newspaper? Can I approach this in such a way that I maintain my integrity before the Lord, but at the same time lessen the negative impact of public perception?"

8. Consultation

What are the reactions of the board chair, your pastor, other administrators, or former mentors? It is certainly well established in Proverbs that "iron sharpens iron" (27:17) and that "plans fail for lack of counsel, but with many advisers they succeed" (15:22). After school leaders have a season of thoughtful prayer, I encourage them to consult with experienced colleagues and/or advisors provided at ACSI regional offices.

9. Law and Policy

What laws, rules, and policies apply? An attorney named Robert who has spent much of his time in practice consulting with school administrators shared with me that one of the most frequent calls he receives always starts out with the question, "Can I fire a teacher that I am unhappy with?" Robert always responds with a question, "I don't know, can you?" What he means by this is simply to direct administrators back to contracts, bylaws, handbooks, and related documents that must be followed if we are to deal with situations with integrity and righteousness. In addition, only in the rarest situation should an administrator consider not following local or state law.

At this point, a significant distinction needs to be made about the sources of law that influence legal issues in Christian schools. Those schools called public schools, which are established by local or state governments, must follow a host of legislative regulations enacted by federal, state, and local governments. Their financial existence is almost completely dependent on tax revenue, and therefore, each school and each school system is obligated to follow laws, policies, and procedures enacted at various levels. (In numerous cases today, many public schools receive private contributions for special projects. For example, corporations wishing to provide extra resources give money for the improvement of technology.) The employees of these schools carry out their duties "under the color of state law," so they are considered employees in much the same way law enforcement officers are.

An example of such requirements would be the recent federal legislation entitled the No Child Left Behind Act. Each school must provide evidence of the successful advancement of its students or risk penalization by being put on probation or even being forced to close. Another example would be the passing of laws at the state level requiring the teaching of creationism as a viable approach to the discussion of the origin of the universe. Private schools are not under such obligations or requirements because they do not receive public money. They are not required to submit to such regulation, for the most part. The organization and operation of private schools must obey some federal laws, such as the use of student records, the treatment of people with handicaps, and the establishment of nondiscriminatory practices. At the state level, regulations are present that establish requirements for the length of the school year and minimum standards for high school graduation. Local governments have laws for fire safety standards that must be followed.

The vast majority of the governance and regulation of Christian schools rests on another source of law called contract law. The legal standard or requirement in most of the legal activity in our schools depends on contracts or agreements between the parents and the school. This necessitates the writing and implementing of carefully crafted documents such as admissions procedures, student and teacher handbooks, and teacher contracts. In the case of a disagreement or legal action, the judge would examine the wording of the policy in question (or lack of policy)! For example, First Amendment expectations for the freedom of speech may present an administrator in a public school some headaches and allow students a broader spectrum of latitude in a student publication. However, the administrator in a private school can exercise total control over what is written and published in his or her school but would do well to establish his or her authority up front in the student handbook.

Another source of law, which is perhaps the most fascinating, is called common law, and it consists of the decisions or rulings made by juries and judges. Once again, most of the decisions do not have an impact on Christian schools because the jurisprudence was based on issues involving public schools. Nevertheless, Christian school leaders would be wise to stay up-to-date on legal discussions and issues. For example, as an educator trained in the public sector, I was coached on the legal standards for what is called search and seizure. In general, an administrator needs some justification for searching a locker or asking a student to empty his or her pockets. The mere fact that something is missing does not give a teacher or an administrator the authority to search everyone indiscriminately. As the leader of a Christian school, I chose to continue this standard of behavior because I not only thought it was wise to adhere to the legal standards of other schools, but I thought it demonstrated a fairness and dignity I felt students deserved.

You Take the Helm

Your school is considering corporal punishment, the spanking of students who have broken school rules. What, if any, regulations exist in the following:

Biblical standards	Is this type of punishment meant to be administered by parents only?
Constitutional issues	Is it cruel and unusual punishment?
State law	In your state, are public schools allowed to administer this type of punishment?
Common law	What have courts established?
Contract law	How should your policy be worded?
Insurance protection	Are you covered if there is legal action against you?

Of course, all employees of Christian schools are obligated to follow all laws regarding criminal law. This is an area, needless to say, that administrators must be familiar with. There are federal statutes regarding sexual harassment (employer-to-employee, teacher-to-student, and student-to-student) that are extremely important.

Sexual Harassment

Definition
- Threatening to impose adverse employment, academic, disciplinary, or other sanctions on a person, unless favors are given
- Conduct containing sexual matter or suggestions that would be offensive to a reasonable person

Example Behaviors
- Sexual proposition
- Off-color jokes
- Inappropriate physical contact
- Innuendos
- Sexual offers, looks, and gestures

In a number of recent cases, female students alleged that male students made sexual statements to them and that school officials, after being informed, declined to take action and stated that "boys will be boys." Case law is suggesting that supervisors who ignore such behavior or do not take it seriously can be held liable.

Suggested Policies
1. Establish clear descriptions for behaviors such as the following:
   - Verbal conduct such as derogatory jokes or comments
   - Unwanted sexual advances or touching
   - Visual contact with sexually oriented photographs or pictures
   - Retaliation for having reported or threatened to report harassment
   - Hostile or intimidating environment
2. Establish procedures for reporting:
   - A statement such as "all allegations will be taken seriously and promptly investigated" should be included
   - Concern for both parties should be expressed
3. Print statements for policies and procedures:
   Statements should be printed in a handbook, which has a statement that parents, students, and staff sign saying they have read them

See *Franklin v. Gwinnett County Public Schools* 503 U.S. (1992). The Supreme Court ruled that monetary damages can be awarded to students whose rights under Title IX were violated.

Most states have enacted tough laws for the distribution of illegal drugs in or near schools. Local and state regulations must be followed in the areas of child abuse or neglect.

Negligence

Another critical area of law involves the issue of negligence or torts. The word *tort* comes from the Latin *tortuous* or *twisted* and involves the notion of a wrong or harm done to someone. In the context of school law, a parent could claim that a teacher in specific or the school in general failed his or her child in some way. To establish that negligence occurred, a parent (the plaintiff) would have to prove all four of the points below. (If one of these is missing, then the defendant would be successful in defending himself or herself.)

1. Duty of the Accused
The teacher, administrator, coach, or other authority figure must have a duty to perform related to the claim of negligence. The remainder of the case against the school employee hinges on the concept that the student was in some way under the care of the one accused.

2. Failure to Perform a Duty
Next, the plaintiff must establish that the one accused did not fulfill his or her duty. At this point, there is the important concern of adequate supervision. Special points to consider include the age of the students, the risk of the activity in which they are involved, and the number of students under the educator's care. For example, when taking a group of first graders to a zoo, the age of the children and the risk involved would dictate that a chaperone should have no more than two or three children to oversee. If the trip involved fifth graders, the number can increase to six students per adult. For eighth graders, the number can increase to eight students per adult. And for tenth graders, the number can increase to ten students per adult.

Two important legal concepts are related to failure to perform a duty, or what is termed breach of duty. The person performing the duty will be measured by a standard called the reasonable and prudent man test. One authority defines it this way: "The hypothetical reasonable person standard is an objective attempt to determine whether, in retrospect, a person with the same duties (teacher, administrator, coach) working with the same clientele (varying age and skill level) under similar circumstances (classroom, field trip, athletic event) would have acted in the same way." A second issue is called foreseeability, which involves a complex question of whether the person could have or should have *anticipated* an event that led to a child's injury. Foreseeability is determined by "the age, relationship, and physical characteristics of the parties involved; the gravity and probability of danger presented; and the necessity and utility of the actor's conduct" (Mawdsley 1995, 15). For example, can a classroom teacher leave the classroom for two minutes to go to the restroom down the hall? If there is not a school policy regarding this decision, a reasonable person would consider the age of the students and the activity in which they are involved. A second question would be, Is there a history with one or more students that would lead a teacher to anticipate problems when he or she is out of the room?

3. Proximate Cause

Proximate cause is the most complex of the four points. Did the failure to perform a duty actually lead to the harm that occurred? "Proximate cause is the logical and sequential connection closely related in time, space or order between duty and breach of duty on one hand and injury on the other." If the teacher on the zoo trip turns her back for a few moments (failure to complete her duty,) is it really her fault if an animal escapes its cage and hurts one of her students? The plaintiff would have to prove that the lack of attention in this incident created the situation for the child to be attacked. "There are three basic requirements in establishing proximate cause: (1) the injury would not have occurred if the breach had not occurred; (2) the injury must be the natural and probable result of the breach; (3) there is no efficient intervening cause" (Mawsdley 1995, 17). Case law presents many unusual and complicated cases. A shop teacher can carefully prepare students to use a cutting tool (instruction), create a safe environment (equipment), and be standing next to a student (supervision) when the student's hand slips and an accident occurs.

The parent of a New York City student failed to prove proximate cause in a 1994 case. The court ruled that the school was not responsible for the shooting death of a junior high student outside the school during lunch break. The mother claimed inadequate supervision, but her son was shot by another boy, an intervening cause, whom he had no previous altercation with. The school could not be proven to have foreseeability (*Maness v. City of New York*, 607 NYS 2nd 325, N.Y. App. Div. 1994). On the other hand, if a parent can make the connection and prove proximate cause, the court may rule in his or her favor. In *Toeller v. Mutual Service Casualty Insurance Company*, a bus driver dismissed a student from his bus but failed to inform the parents or administration at the school. The driver was liable for the injuries to the eleven-year-old when he was struck by a truck while riding his bicycle to school (*Toeller v. Mutual Service Casualty Insurance Co.*, 340 N.W. 2nd 923, Wis. Ct. App. 1983).

4. An injury
The fourth aspect that must be established by a plaintiff in order to be successful in a case of negligence is that the person involved in the incident was actually injured.

Defenses to Tort Liability

Often the statement about the value of collecting signed waivers from parents is that "the waiver is not worth the paper it is written on." A related statement goes like this, "You cannot sign away the rights of a minor." Let's take the second statement first. This is true; a parent or guardian, by signing a form that contains "hold harmless" or "exculpatory clauses" language, cannot in effect give another party freedom from liability *if that party commits an act of negligence.* Such rights cannot be signed away. For example, parents may sign forms granting permission for a student to play football, an obviously risky activity. But their approval does not remove the coaching staff from responsibility if they fail to instruct and supervise correct tackling techniques. The parents cannot give teachers, coaches, or other supervisors permission to fail to carry out their duties.

So then, why concern yourself with permission slips and waiver forms? Mawdsley states, "The contractual nature of nonpublic education lends itself to efforts to reduce or eliminate duties of care, and hence, liability for subsequent injury. Such efforts to limit or eliminate (exculpate) liability by one-time releases, hold-harmless clauses, or general contractual language is common in nonpublic institutions and not uncommon in public ones" (1995, 4). Such statements on permission slips attempt to establish informed consent. Most people have encountered similar notifications at amusement parks when they see warning signs before getting on exciting rides that may present "danger to anyone with the following medical conditions ..." Another example of informed consent is written on the back of the ticket used by spectators at professional baseball games. The wording, along with public address announcements, warns spectators about the possibility of balls or bats coming into the stands and injuring spectators. A teacher who was participating in a student-faculty donkey basketball game fell off her donkey and broke her arm. The court determined that she consented to the danger of this happening when she received instructions from the company prior to the game that the animals can buck and put their heads down, causing people to fall off (*Arbegast v. Board of Ed. of S. New Berlin Cent. Sch.*, 490 N.Y.S. 2nd 751, N.Y. 1985).

Legal experts warn administrators not to rely on waivers or permission slips but rather to invest their time and energy on proper preparation, instruction, and supervision. However, it is beneficial to require the parent's signature because it places parents and especially older students on notice regarding their responsibilities. In addition, such notification may become leverage to prevent or limit the amount of damages an injured party believes he or she can receive (Mawdsley 1995, 8).

Constitutional Umbrella

Because of First Amendment rights, church ministries and Christian schools are blessed to have limited government or legal interference. We as administrators in Christian schools do not, for instance, have to concern ourselves with accusations concerning discrimination related to sexual orientation/alternative employment lifestyles in our employment practices. Likewise, we are completely free to discriminate on the basis of religious, denominational, or biblical considerations in our hiring practice. Having said this, we must seriously protect these freedoms by not taking advantage of the special standing that we enjoy. When we act in such a way that is perceived as being mean or stupid, then we not only hurt the cause of Christ, we also threaten the current freedoms we enjoy. Each time a judge is presented with a case that involves the harsh treatment of a former employee, we invite more intense scrutiny and threaten the size of the constitutional umbrella under which we currently operate.

Are Your Records Up-to-Date?

The accuracy of your personnel files is extremely important. You should not consider it a menial task that can wait for another day. Vital payroll records must be current, including such items as a W-4 form, which lists the number of exemptions for withholding purposes. Also, documentation must be filed that clearly states starting salary and notes on future pay increases. Unfamiliar to many administrators is the requirement to have an immigration document (I-9) in every employee's file, regardless of nationality or citizenship.

The initial employment application is a critical document to have if there should there ever be questions raised about the faculty member's history and qualifications to do the tasks assigned to him or her. Most ministries have a policy that states on the application that failure to give accurate, truthful information could result in immediate dismissal. Related to the application are the notes that reflect the checking of background references. Failure to carry out such a background search and the inability to prove that references were checked could result in an administrator's exposure to liability if a tort were committed and the parents claimed negligent hiring practices. During my years as an administrator, I received a call from an administrator in a nearby city who was doing a reference check on one of our teachers who had applied for an opening at his school. As we reviewed the basics of her age and teaching experience, we discovered that the age she had recorded on her application to my school was several years younger than the truthful information she recorded on the new application. A brief investigation brought out that there had been a gap in her employment that she had not wished to discuss with me. Nothing inappropriate or damaging had occurred during that time, but I learned an important lesson about checking details.

Clearly a must for every employee today is a legal and financial background check. Often individuals involved with child abuse or sexual abuse will simply leave one area or state and seek a position elsewhere with hopes that the new ministry will not require such a check. Those involved with the care of others' children must accept the spiritual and ethical responsibility to make sure that no one with a history, suspected or convicted, of harming children is allowed to be involved in any way. Let me state that again. No one with such a past is allowed to be involved in any way. Yes, God's grace and mercy apply to all sins and sinners, but a person with such a background has forfeited the privilege to be trusted around children of any age. Failure to adopt and execute a thorough process will not only leave the children unprotected but will also leave the ministry vulnerable to legal action that could defame the name of Christ in the community, cause irreparable harm to the reputation of the ministry, and make the school liable for damages that could bankrupt the organization.

Do I Give Negative References?

- Before giving a reference, ask if the applicant has signed a waiver authorizing references. If not, ask why not.
- Be sure you are talking to someone who is authorized to ask the questions.
- Limit your comments to job-related information.
- Be honest and factual, and avoid any mean-spirited comments.
- Document the conversation and file your note, whether the reference is given on the telephone or is written.

(Chaffee 1997, 129–130)

You Take the Helm

Analyze the true story below, using the points following the narrative and the material presented thus far in this chapter:

A chaperone for a white-water rafting trip has been given his assignment of students, has collected all the liability waivers from his group including required student and parent signatures, and has attended the pre-trip safety session. Because of his familiarity with the rapids, he recalls that there is one particularly dangerous and challenging set of white water. Prior to boarding the raft, the chaperone takes the outfitter's guide aside and offers him a $20 tip if he would flip the raft in the run called Widow Maker. The guide accepted the money and flipped the raft, sending all occupants into the rapids.

Fortunately, no one in this incident was injured, but consider the following for the situation if a student had received a concussion after hitting his head on a rock:

- Foreseeability
- Informed consent
- Duty of care
- Reasonable and prudent behavior
- Negligence/liability of the guide
- Negligence/liability of the chaperone

Table 11.1 (Alexander and Alexander 1985)

Precedent-Setting Supreme Court Decisions	
Case	**Summary of Decision**
Engle v. Vitale (1962)	State-mandated prayer is unconstitutional.
Lemon v. Kurtzman (1971)	Establishment clause issue—3-pronged test.
School District of Abington Township v. Schempp (1963)	State-enforced Bible reading and prayer in public schools is unconstitutional.
Pierce v. Society of Sisters (1925)	Compulsory Education Law requiring all children to attend public school is unconstitutional.
Brown v. Board of Education of Topeka, Kansas (1954)	Separate-but-equal facilities are inherently unequal.
Tinker v. Des Moines Independent Community School District (1969)	Students are free to express their views except when such conduct disrupts class work, causes disorder, or invades the rights of others.
Goss v. Lopez (1975)	Suspension from school requires some form of due process for students.
Wood v. Strickland (1975)	A school board's ignorance of the law regarding due process is no excuse for not following it.
Ingraham v. Wright (1977)	Corporal punishment is not cruel or unusual punishment and is permitted where allowed by state law.
New Jersey v. TLO (1985)	To be constitutional, searches of students and students' property must meet a two-pronged test.
Franklin v. Gwinnett County Public Schools (1992)	School personnel are responsible for protecting students from sexual harassment.
Pickering v. Board of Education (1968)	Public school teachers have a constitutional right to speak out freely on matters of public concern.
State of Wisconsin v. Yoder (1972)	State cannot compel Amish children to attend public school.

Shore Leave

Principle for Guiding Principals:

The effective administrator cares for his or her own spiritual, physical, and emotional health.

He sat on the edge of his bed after a particularly long day. Sensing his mood, his wife suggested that he take a much-needed vacation. It was long overdue. Some time passed before he responded to her because his fatigue made it difficult to even speak. When he finally summoned the energy to voice his troubled thoughts, he explained, "Though I have never had any military experience or any reason to be imprisoned, I feel as if I am like the prisoners of war who are enclosed in a bamboo cage and then lowered into a hole. I can't believe I am saying this. I love my job and ministry. I am blessed with a lovely wife, a comfortable home, and two great kids. But I feel trapped and exhausted. My responsibilities have caved in on me." He paused to consider the notion of time off to regain his energy and perspective but had difficulty putting his thoughts into words. Regaining his strength, he continued, "If I had a blank check and unlimited time to spend away from the school, I can't think of anywhere I would want to go or anything I would really want to do." At that moment, the reality of his condition swept over him and he had to struggle to maintain his composure. His dream opportunity in ministry had taken on the bars of a prison, enslaving him with the multitude of burdens he felt obligated to carry. Could God allow him to lay them down for a much-needed rest?

Perhaps it is best left to theologians and Bible scholars to unravel the complex issues of sin in the life of the administrator above; however, I think we can all agree that he had ignored many channel markers that were placed there by God to warn him of coming disaster while he sped full speed toward the rocks. Can we also agree that the words of the angel who visited Elijah apply here? The angel of the Lord touched him and said, "The journey is too great for you" (1 Kings 19:7, NASB).

Warning Signs

Here are some of the common signs that have been positioned in our lives by God to protect us from reaching the point of exhaustion described above and in 1 Kings 19, which details the near collapse of one of God's great servants. It is important to note that the preceding chapter concludes with the statement, "Then the hand of the Lord was on Elijah, and he girded up his loins and outran Ahab to Jezreel" (1 Kings 18:46, NASB). Did he do this with supernatural energy? Certainly his body was enlivened by the adrenaline that remained from his victory at the "Super Bowl of the prophets." Imagine his emotional state after participating in the slaying of the 450 prophets of Baal earlier that day (18:40). For whatever reason, Elijah was vulnerable the following day and responded to the threat of Jezebel by choosing flight over fight. He ended up seemingly alone in a cave, filled with pity, despair, and self-doubt. Consider these warning signs:

Change in Exercise
One of the first schedule changes that takes place in the life of a busy administrator is the exclusion of established times for exercise. Despite frequent warnings from health insurance providers, doctors, and media, we succumb to the pressure to fulfill all our obligations to the point that no time is left for personal exercise. The result is loss of cardiovascular efficiency, increased stress, weight gain, and mental fatigue.

Change in Eating
Hard on the heels of decreased exercise is the increase in eating. It is well known that an increase in stress often triggers a desire for overeating.

Combine this negative change in lifestyle with less exercise, and you experience a downward spiral in overall health accompanied by excessive weight gain. Dr. Melissa C. Stoppler (n.d.), who serves on the medical editorial board of Medicine.Net.com, explains:

> Up to two million Americans suffer from the most recently described eating disorder known as binge eating disorder, and psychological stress may actually precipitate episodes of binge eating in those affected.

> Described by doctors more recently than the eating disorders anorexia nervosa and bulimia nervosa, binge eating disorder is likely the most common of all eating disorders, affecting approximately 2% of adults in the US, or 1 to 2 million people. Persons suffering from this condition have recurrent episodes of binge eating, which is characterized by

> - Eating unusually large amounts of food
> - Eating rapidly
> - Feeling "out of control" when eating
> - Eating whether or not one feels hungry
> - Eating alone or attempting to hide the amount of food consumed
> - Continuing to eat even when one is full
> - Feeling ashamed of the eating episodes

Change in Sleeping

Another companion of the change in exercise and eating habits is difficulty getting a good night's rest:

> Three-quarters of adults say they have a sleep disorder but refuse to do anything about it. Two of the strongest symptoms of a sleep problem are snoring and waking up a lot during the night. Six in ten motorists said they have had an accident or near-accident because they fell asleep while driving.

> When sleep is poor or inadequate, social and intimate relationships suffer. Work productivity is negatively affected. But rather than continuing to suffer the consequences of sleep deprivation, experts say this is one problem people could choose to resolve. (CNN 2005)

An article in *Medical News Today* reports the following:

> In fact, nearly 70 percent of all women in the U.S. report sleeping less than the recommended average of eight hours a night. Women ages 40–60 average a meager five hours of sleep per night, and divorced or separated women, African American and Hispanic women, and Northeasterners/West Coasters suffer the most from lack of sleep, the 2005 poll reports.
>
> Sleepless nights have been linked to many health risks including obesity, heart disease and even car accidents. To address this distressing trend, the Better Sleep Council is teaming up with the Department of Health and Human Services' Office on Women's Health to help women improve the quantity and quality of sleep they get each night. (2005b)

Another article in *Medical News Today* reports on the impact of sleep deprivation on the nation's health:

> Work-related sleeping disorders have proliferated rapidly in recent years with increases in occupational stress and abnormal working hours. "Sleep deprivation affects a person's emotional and mental faculties and increases the risk of, for example, cardiovascular diseases. Work-related sleeping disorders and changes in lifestyle due to occupation are key factors affecting national health," says Finnish Institute of Occupational Health Senior Researcher, Mikko Härmä. (2005a)

Insomnia is a growing health concern for our nation:

> Insomnia is estimated to affect more than half of the U.S. adult population. Insomnia can take many different forms: difficulty falling asleep or staying asleep, waking up too early, or waking up feeling unrefreshed. In a survey by the National Sleep Foundation, 58% of adults reported having insomnia at least a few nights a week. And the vast majority of those surveyed agreed that sleep loss can have a major impact on their lives:
>
> • 93% agreed that sleep loss can impair work performance
> • 92% felt that sleep loss can increase one's risk of injuries
> • 90% agreed that not getting enough sleep makes it difficulty to get along with others
> • 86% believed that sleep deficits can lead to health problems
> (Sanofi-avent n.d.)

Change in Personal and Corporate Worship
In your rush to complete tasks and serve those whom God has called you to minister to, have you bypassed the sweet fellowship with Him that you once enjoyed? I realized that this had become the case in my life after I had been in administration for about twelve years. I shared my concern with my wife, who directed my attention to a special weekend sponsored by a group called Promise Keepers, which was unknown to me at the time. After arriving at a stadium in Boulder, Colorado, which was filled to capacity with men from all walks of life and every state and continent, I suddenly realized that I had left my large ring of keys behind and no one was interrupting my focus on God to ask me for assistance to open a classroom or to help find a projector. In those precious hours of worship, I was free from mundane roles and obligations and able to worship with other saints who, like me, had shed all emblems of titles, status, or position.

Change in Personal Relationships
As your calendar fills with activities and obligations for your school, church, and family, are you losing contact with meaningful relationships that are devoid of the tensions from work? Perhaps a tougher question would be, Do you spend time with anyone who is not a believer, providing an opportunity to be used by the Holy Spirit to lead someone to the Lord?

Change in Patience
The Lord has used my German shepherd to help me identify when I am overstressed and at the end of my rope. My ninety-five-pound dog, my best friend in the world, greets me eagerly every time I arrive home. If I groan and try to avoid his demands to play, I realize that I am overtired and that I must regain my energy and perspective. A good friend has taught me a wise expression, "Land the plane with fuel left in the tank."

Jesus powerfully demonstrated this concept in the Gospel of Luke when He was in the midst of a throng that was crowding and pressing in on Him. A woman touched just the hem of His coat and He was aware that power passed from Himself (Luke 8:43–48). When I consider our Savior's reaction, several questions come to mind: Would I have even noticed? How often do we rush past the hurting, unassuming individuals that God places in our path? Would I have taken the time to seize the opportunity for ministry? Jesus insisted on revealing her identity and used the occasion to help define for her why she was healed—not the touching, but the believing (v. 48)! Would there have been God's power within me to help someone, even if I did stop and take time to respond? Would I have anything to share with a person in need? Am I so exhausted from running from one thing to the next that I end up trying to do ministry through my own power?

Change in Energy

Perhaps we have all experienced what Peter described in the preceding story: "Master, the people are crowding and pressing in on you" (Luke 8:45). I have had the experience of a well-meaning but desperate faculty member knocking on my car window to get my attention when I arrived at the school, before I had turned the engine off! Consider these characteristics of burnout (Neils n.d.):

1. Chronic fatigue—exhaustion, tiredness, a sense of being physically run-down
2. Anger at those making demands
3. Self-criticism for putting up with the demands
4. Cynicism, negativity, and irritability
5. A sense of being besieged
6. Exploding easily at seemingly inconsequential things
7. Frequent headaches and gastrointestinal disturbances
8. Weight loss or gain
9. Sleeplessness and depression
10. Shortness of breath
11. Suspiciousness
12. Feelings of helplessness
13. Increased degree of risk taking

Yet another indicator of coming disaster is found in 1 Kings 19. After two incredible days of physical exertion, Elijah finally sat down under a shade tree and declared, "It is enough" (v. 4, NASB). Do you think that you are a twenty-first-century version of Superman or Wonder Woman, just without the costume? Prolonged periods of fatigue can lead to serious consequences, most of which would be more damaging to the ministry that you are worried about than if you walked away and left some things for tomorrow.

Change in Perspective

The scenario at the beginning of this chapter concluded with our school leader on the edge of his bed, hopelessly adrift from the clear perspective he had when he began ministry. And Elijah—just two days after being mightily used by the Lord—moans under his shade tree, "O Lord, take my life, for I am not better than my fathers" (1 Kings 19:4, NASB). Once into the maelstrom of a loss of perspective, the helmsman is in the gravest danger of helplessly taking the ship and the crew into the rocks.

You Take the Helm

Reread the narrative of the events in Elijah's life in 1 Kings 18 and 19. Is the Lord speaking to you about your lifestyle habits that need to be changed in order to avoid a prolonged period of withdrawal?

Are there other channel markers in your life not discussed here that God has used in your life to warn of coming disaster and steer you back to safe waters? Share these with your classmates.

Confronting Sin in Your Life

During a period of intense Bible study, the Holy Spirit revealed to me a genuine weakness in my personal relationship with my Heavenly Father. It was the issue of trust, and He used a passage in Proverbs to highlight my need: "Trust in the Lord with all your heart and lean not on your own understanding; in all your ways acknowledge him, and he will make your paths straight" (3:5–6).

That was it! At that moment, I recognized what had been stealing my contentment. I could never seem to come to grips with what was robbing me of my joy in ministry. This was particularly evident in two areas in which I lacked control: staffing and finances. No matter how much I invested in the faculty, no matter how much they succeeded individually and collectively, no matter how much I tried to meet their needs, some still left! Can you believe that one of my teachers decided to resign when her husband was transferred out of state? After all that I had done for her, their marriage commitment was more important than the school. And now, I would have to invest the time and energy to train someone new, with the fear that the replacement could never measure up. I was blind to the Lord's design and had a short memory for all He had done beyond our greatest expectations.

The area of finances was also a spiritual battleground. Despite record attendance each year, annual salary increases for the faculty, and a supportive church and school community, it seemed as if I could never outrun the jezebel threat of financial ruin. When other schools and ministries had generous donors on the sidelines that were willing and able to finance major projects, our ministry jogged along at a marathoner's pace. Was the problem youthful impatience? Was it envy or covetousness? In my case, I determined that it was a lack of trust. Because of this sin, I could never find rest. I could not do as the Lord commanded the psalmist,

"Be still, and know that I am God" (46:10). The New American Standard Bible says, "Cease striving." That was exactly what I needed to do.

Trust in Hebrew indicates confidence or hope placed in an object. It also conveys the idea of throwing oneself down. This is the first of three imperatives in Proverbs 3:5–6. The remainder of the phrase from the verse in Proverbs has been especially challenging: "With all your heart." It seemed that I was delighted to talk about God's provision, but when the pressure was turned up, I thought that I had to work harder to make things succeed. At that point, I would invariably "lean on my own understanding." The concept in the second imperative uses the metaphor of a crutch used to assist a person when he or she stands and tries to walk. Do you have personal gifts, special resources, or other people such as a close friend or colleague whom you place your trust in? My experience has been that the Lord will break or remove these crutches somehow in an effort to make me completely dependent on Him.

The third imperative in the passage is the exhortation to "in all your ways acknowledge him." Once again, as I meditated on the passage, I had to admit that on occasion I would move ahead with plans that seemed correct or appropriate, but ones that I had not bathed in prayer. The concluding phrase of verse 6 is a promise concerning God's activity: "He will make your paths straight." Once again, Solomon employs a metaphor that was familiar to his contemporaries. Prior to a journey by a king, the servants would go ahead of their master and make sure the road that the king intended to travel would be passable and cleared of debris that would hinder safe passage. These verses assure us that God intends to assist us in traveling the path He desires for us, if we are careful to "trust," "lean not," and "acknowledge."

You Take the Helm

Is the Lord showing you sin in your life that is hindering your usefulness? Perhaps you are fearful of failure, emotionally drained because of some loss or unfulfilled expectation, or prideful because of the power and authority associated with your position? Ask the Holy Spirit to direct you to passages of Scripture that will provide the instruction that you need.

Shore Leave

Is now a time when you need to consider stepping away from the overwhelming demands of your ministry? I have noticed over the years that leaders who persevere in ministry and remain faithful "in season and out of season" balance an extremely demanding schedule with much-needed time away. Interestingly, those I am thinking of have spoken frequently of the myth of burnout, while consciously or unconsciously setting aside special time away from their ordinary rigors to clear their heads, recharge their energy, and regain much-needed perspective. One such leader of a very large church takes one day a week to chop wood and complete other demanding tasks in his yard. Another is an avid hunter and a scuba diver. A third finds his escape in camping with his family. I find that kayaking and white-water rafting are exhilarating pastimes that renew me in every way.

How about you? Can you put your keys, cell phone, and calendar in your desk drawer and walk away from your ministry role as a helmsman?

Chart a New Course

Once you are back on board, perhaps you need to chart a new course and establish some new channel markers. Here are some that have helped me over the years:

Worship. Make meaningful worship, both personal and corporate, a priority. Remember how frequently Jesus withdrew to spend special time alone with His Father. How much more do we need this time in our relationship with Him? Are you serious about staying filled with the sweet honey of His Word? " 'Son of man, eat this scroll I am giving you and fill your stomach with it.' So I ate it, and it tasted as sweet as honey in my mouth" (Ezekiel 3:3). Suggestion: Consider reading one psalm and one proverb each morning.

Break a sweat. Even if you do not like to exercise, find some activity that requires your heart rate to increase to a level that your doctor approves. Suggestion: Get out your bike, pump up the tires, and tour your neighborhood.

Communicate your need for more deckhands. Many leaders refuse to ask for additional help, even when the size of the ministry has changed drastically. Suggestion: Begin to mentor someone who can help relieve some of your stress.

Schedule breaks. In your schedule, write in short periods of time for mental breaks. Avoid turning every lunch into a meeting to conduct business.

Suggestion: Set aside time every day when you practice MBWA: management by walking around.

Commit valuable time to your family. I worked on my dissertation at night from nine o'clock to midnight, after my son and daughter were in bed. I also committed myself to attending every game that my son played in, and he played three sports. Suggestion: Commit to no more than one night out per week, in addition to Sunday and Wednesday evenings at church.

Why would a bright, spiritually sensitive, and self-controlled leader ever place himself or herself in a position of being fatigued to the point of exhaustion, or even beyond to the point of physical breakdown? Perhaps the motivation is the deep sense of responsibility that administrators have to perform as good stewards. The concept is spoken of often in the New Testament, ten times from Luke to 1 Peter. The Greek word *oikonomos* is used to describe the position of steward or manager. Paul describes himself as an *oikonomous* (Gangel 1997, 55) in 1 Corinthians 4:1–2: "Let a man regard us in this manner, as servants of Christ and stewards of the mysteries of God. In this case, moreover, it is required of stewards that one be found trustworthy" (NASB).

The disconnect comes in our failure to trust God to help us with our burdens along the way. Or even worse, we take on the responsibilities in such a way that we begin to personally identify with every high and low in the ministry. Worse yet, our ego or assessment of our own self-worth gets caught up in the successes or failures of our school. Can we agree that this is not God's plan for our lives? Instead, we must view our own spiritual relationship with the Lord, as well as our own physical and spiritual well-being, as an important dimension of our stewardship that we should care for as we care for all other aspects of the ministry.

References

ACSI. *See* Association of Christian Schools International.

Alexander, Kern, and M. David Alexander. 1985. *American public school law.* St. Paul, MN: West Publishing Company.

Anderson, Leith, Don Cousins, and Arthur DeKruyter. 1990. *Mastering church management.* Portland, OR: Multnomah Press.

Andringa, Robert C. 1998. Basic responsibilities of school boards. Table quoted in Kenneth O. Gangel, ed., *Called to lead: Understanding and fulfilling your role as an educational leader* (Colorado Springs, CO: Purposeful Design Publications, 2002), 22.

Andringa, Robert C., and Ted W. Engstrom. 1997. *Nonprofit board answer book: Practical guidelines for board members and chief executives.* Washington, DC: National Center for Nonprofit Boards (NCNB).

Anthony, Michael J., and Warren S. Benson. 2003. *Exploring the history and philosophy of Christian education: Principles for the 21st century.* Grand Rapids, MI: Kregel.

Argyris, Chris. 1964. *Integrating the individual and the organization.* New York: John Wiley & Sons.

Association of Christian Schools International. 2004. *Building on basics: Essential elements of an effective Christian school.* Brochure. ACSI Matrix for Effectiveness. Colorado Springs, CO: Association of Christian Schools International.

Austin, Gilbert. n.d. Process evaluation: A comprehensive study of outliers. Baltimore, MD: State Department of Education, Education Resources Information Center (ERIC): ED, 160 644.

Barna, George. 1992. *The power of vision: How you can capture and apply God's vision for your ministry.* Ventura, CA: Regal Books.

Bass, Bernard M. 1985. *Leadership and performance beyond expectations.* New York: Free Press.

Bass, Bernard M., and B. Avolio. 1989. Potential biases in leadership measures: How prototypes, leniency, and general satisfaction relate to ratings and rankings of transformational and transactional leadership constructs. *Educational and Psychological Measurement* 49, 3:509–27.

Bennis, Warren. 1999. *Managing people is like herding cats.* Provo, UT: Executive Excellence Publishing.

Blanchard, Ken, Bill Hybels, and Phil Hodges. 1999. *Leadership by the book: Tools to transform your workplace.* New York: William Morrow.

Bolin, Frances S., and Judith McConel Falk, eds. 1987. *Teacher renewal: Professional issues, personal choices.* New York: Teachers College Press.

Braley, James, Jack Layman, and Ray White, eds. 2003. *Foundations of Christian school education.* Colorado Springs, CO: Purposeful Design Publications.

Brown, Gordon B. 2002. *Guiding faculty to excellence: Instructional supervision in the Christian school.* 2nd ed. Colorado Springs, CO: Purposeful Design Publications.

Burns, James MacGregor. 1978. *Leadership.* New York: Harper and Row.

Carney, Burt, ed. 2003. Background checks are important. *Legal/Legislative Update* (ACSI) 13, no. 3:37–40.

Carpenter, Brian. 1998. Presentation at the ACSI Convention in Greensboro, NC (February).

Carver, John. 1997. *Boards that make a difference: A new design for leadership in nonprofit and public organizations.* 2nd ed. Jossey-Bass Public Administration Series. San Francisco: Jossey-Bass.

Carver, John, and Miriam Mayhew Carver. 1997. *Reinventing your board: A step-by-step guide to implementing policy governance.* Jossey-Bass Nonprofit and Public Management Series. San Francisco: Jossey-Bass.

Chaffee, Paul. 1997. *Accountable leadership: A resource guide for sustaining legal, financial, and ethical integrity in today's congregations.* Religion-in-Practice Series. San Francisco: Jossey-Bass.

References

Christian History Institute. 1999. March 28, 1592—Comenius: Born to learn, born to teach. http://chi.gospelcom.net/DAILYF/2001/03/daily-03-28-2001.shtml.

CNN. 2005. Survey: 3 in 4 have sleep problems. *CNN.com*, March 30. www.cnn.com. Referenced in http:/www.lifeway.com/myextra/mainsection (accessed May 18, 2005; site no longer available).

Cogan, Morris L. 1973. *Clinical supervision*. Boston: Houghton Mifflin.

Coley, Kenneth S. 1993. *Transformational and transactional leadership and the school principal: An analysis of selected private secondary school principals in Maryland*. Ann Arbor, MI: UMI Dissertation Services.

Collins, Jim. 2001. *Good to great: Why some great companies make the leap … and others don't*. New York: HarperCollins.

Deuink, James W. 1996. *Management principles for Christian schools*. Greenville, SC: BJU Press.

Dewey, John. 1964. *A common faith*. New Haven, CT: Yale University Press.

Dill, Stephen. 2002. Nehemiah and the Golden Rule: Finding friends and funds. In *Called to lead: Understanding and fulfilling your role as an educational leader*, ed. Kenneth O. Gangel, 259–70. Colorado Springs, CO: Purposeful Design Publications.

Eakin, Sybil. 2000. Giants of American education: John Dewey, the education philosopher. *Technos Quarterly* 9, no. 4 (Winter).

Estacion, Angela, Teresa McMahon, and Janet Quint. 2004. MRDC working papers on research methodology: Conducting classroom observations in first things first schools. Massachusetts Rural Development Council, Inc (MRDC), June. http://www.mrdc.org.

Ford, Leighton. 1991. *Transforming leadership: Jesus' way of creating vision, shaping values and empowering change*. Downers Grove, IL: InterVarsity Press.

Fortosis, Anthony. 1984. Principles of supervision. In *Administration of the Christian school*, ed. Roy W. Lowrie Jr., 99–111. Whittier, CA: Association of Christian Schools International.

Foster, William P. 1984. Toward a critical theory of educational administration. In *Leadership and organizational culture: New perspectives on administrative theory and practice*, ed. Thomas J. Sergiovanni and John E. Corbally. Urbana: University of Illinois Press. Quoted in Ubben, Hughes, and Norris 2001, 18.

Frantzreb, Arthur C. 1997. *Not on this board you don't: Making your trustees more effective*. Chicago: Bonus Books.

Fullan, Michael. 2001. *Leading in a culture of change*. San Francisco: Jossey-Bass.

Gaebelein, Frank E. 2002. *The pattern of God's truth: Problems of integration in Christian education*. Colorado Springs, CO: Association of Christian Schools International. (Orig. pub. 1968.)

Gangel, Kenneth O. 1997. *Team leadership in Christian ministry: Using multiple gifts to build a unified vision*. Rev. ed. Chicago: Moody Press.

Gangel, Kenneth O., and April L. Moreton. 2002. Managing mountains and molehills: Developing executive skills. In *Called to lead: Understanding and fulfilling your role as an educational leader*, ed. Kenneth O. Gangel, 39–52. Colorado Springs, CO: Purposeful Design Publications.

Garrick, Gene. 1984. The administrator as philosophical leader. In *Administration of the Christian school*, ed. Roy W. Lowrie Jr. Whittier, CA: Association of Christian Schools International.

Gibbs, Ollie E. 1999. *Administrative priorities: Straight talk to school leaders*. Nashville, TN: LifeWay.

Glatthorn, Allan A. 1984. *Differentiated supervision*. Alexandria, VA: Association for Supervision and Curriculum Development.

———. 2000. *The principal as curriculum leader: Shaping what is taught and tested*. 2nd ed. Thousand Oaks, CA: Corwin Press.

Glickman, Carl D., Stephen P. Gordon, and Jovita M. Ross-Gordon. 1997. *Supervision of instruction: A developmental approach*. 4th ed. Boston: Allyn and Bacon.

References

Goldhammer, Robert, Robert H. Anderson, and Robert J. Krajewski. 1980. *Clinical supervision: Special methods for the supervision of teachers.* 2nd ed. New York: Holt, Rinehart, and Winston.

Gutek, Gerald L. 2000. *Historical and philosophical foundations of education.* 3rd ed. Upper Saddle River, NJ: Merrill/Prentice Hall.

Hallinger, Philip. 1992. The evolving role of American principals: From managerial to instructional to transformational leaders. *Journal of Educational Administration* 30, no.3.

Hartzler, Hubert. 2004–05. The biblical mandate for Christian schooling. *Christian School Education* 8, no.1:26–28.

Herzberg, Frederick. 1966. *Work and the nature of man.* New York: World Publishing.

Hord, Shirley M., and Gene E. Hall. 1983. *Three images: What principals do in curriculum implementation.* Austin: University of Texas, Research and Development Center for Teacher Education.

Hoy, Wayne K., and Cecil G. Miskel. 1982. *Educational administration: Theory, research, and practice.* 2nd ed. Ed. Jack Nelson. New York: Random House.

Hughes, Sandra R., Berit M. Lakey, and Marla J. Bobowick. 2000. *The board building cycle: Nine steps to finding, recruiting, and engaging nonprofit board members.* Washington, DC: National Center for Nonprofit Boards.

Jones, Sherry. n.d. Parents find Montessori School closed. *The Wilmington Star.* http://www.wilmingtonstar.com/news/stories/10734 newsstorypage.html (accessed on April 4, 2002).

Keenan, Derek J. 1998. *Curriculum development for Christian schools.* Colorado Springs, CO: Association of Christian Schools International.

———. 2003. Seminar presentation at ACSI Board Administrator Conference in Lake Lanier, GA (August).

Kienel, Paul A., Ollie E. Gibbs, and Sharon R. Berry, eds. 1995. *Philosophy of Christian school education.* Colorado Springs, CO: Association of Christian Schools International.

Kittel, Gerhard, ed. 1985 *Theological dictionary of the New Testament*, s.v. "Kubern EQ Kubernesis." Trans. G. W. Bromiley. Grand Rapids, MI: Eerdmans Publishing, 1036.

Kouzes, James, and Barry Posner. 2002. *The leadership challenge.* 3rd ed. San Francisco: Jossey-Bass.

Kynerd, Byrle. 2002. Training a terrific teaching team. In *Called to lead: Understanding and fulfilling your role as an educational leader*, ed. Kenneth O. Gangel. Colorado Springs, CO: Purposeful Design Publications.

Layman, Jack. 2003. Modern educational philosophies. In *Foundations of Christian school education*, ed. James Braley, Jack Layman, and Ray White, 37–49. Colorado Springs, CO: Purposeful Design Publications.

Leithwood, Kenneth A. 1992. The move toward transformational leadership. *Educational Leadership* 49, no. 5:8–12.

Leithwood, Kenneth A., and Doris Jantzi. 1991. Transformational leadership: How principals can help reform school cultures. *School Effectiveness and School Improvement* 1, no. 3:249–81.

Leithwood, Kenneth A., and Rosanne Steinbach. 1991. Indicators of transformational leadership in the everyday problem solving of school administrators. *Journal of Personnel Evaluation in Education* 4, no. 3:221–44.

Lewis, Phillip V. 1996. *Transformational leadership: A new model for total church involvement.* Nashville, TN: Broadman and Holman.

Lezotte, Lawrence. n.d. Effective schools process: A proven path to learning for all. http://www.effectiveschools.com.

Likert, Rensis. 1961. *New patterns of management.* New York: McGraw-Hill.

Lipsitz, Joan. 1984. *Successful schools for young adolescents.* New Brunswick, NJ: Transaction.

Lockerbie, D. Bruce. 1996. *From candy sales to committed donors: A guide to financing Christian schools.* Milwaukee, WI: Christian Stewardship Association.

References

———. 2004. Should tuition be cost based or ministry based? Point. In ACSI's *Leadership Academy 2004 report*, 92-95. Colorado Springs, CO: Association of Christian Schools International.

Lowrie, Roy W., Jr., ed. 1984. *Administration of the Christian school.* Whittier, CA: Association of Christian Schools International.

MacCullough, Martha E. 2001. *How to develop a teaching model for world view integration.* Langhorne, PA: PCB Graduate School, Center for Leadership Development.

Marzano, Robert J. 2003. *What works in schools: Translating research into action.* Alexandria, VA: Association for Supervision and Curriculum Development.

Mawdsley, Ralph D. 1995. *Legal problems of religious and private schools.* Topeka, KS: National Organization on Legal Problems of Education.

Maxwell, John C. 1995. *Developing the leaders around you.* Nashville, TN: Thomas Nelson.

McEwan, Elaine K. 2003. *Ten traits of highly effective principals: From good to great performance.* Thousand Oaks, CA: Corwin Press.

McGregor, Douglas. 1960. *The human side of enterprise.* New York: McGraw-Hill.

Medical News Today. 2005a. Sleep deprivation also has impact on nation's health. March 17. http://www.medicalnewstoday.com/medicalnews.php?newsid=21419.

———. 2005b. Stress, sickness and an uncomfortable mattress keep nearly 70 percent of U.S. women up at night. May 3. http://www.medicalnewstoday.com/medicalnews.php?newsid=23767 (accessed on May 25, 2005).

Meeks, Gregory B. 2004. The curriculum connection: Building biblical principles into a quality academic program. *World Report* (ACSI) (Spring): 1–3, 18–22.

Mendez-Morse, Sylvia. 1992. Leadership characteristics that facilitate school change. Southwest Educational Development Laboratory. http://www.sedl.org/change/leadership/.

Montana, Patrick J., and Bruce H. Charnov. 1993. *Management*. 2nd ed. Barron's Business Review Series. Hauppauge, NY: Barron's Educational Series.

Nason, Janet Lowrie. 2002. Protecting your quiddity: Emphasizing Christian school uniqueness. In *Called to lead*, ed. Kenneth O. Gangel, 3–15. Colorado Springs, CO: Purposeful Design Publications.

National Association of Secondary School Principals. 1996. *A legal memorandum*. Reston, VA: National Association of Secondary School Principals.

Neils, Henry. n.d. Thirteen signs of burnout and how to help you avoid it. http://www.assessment.com/mappmembers/avoidingburnout.asp (accessed on May 25, 2005).

Oliva, Peter F. 1997. *Developing the curriculum*. 4th ed. New York: Longman.

Ornstein, Allan C., and Frances P. Hunkins. 1998. *Curriculum: Foundations, principles, and issues*. 3rd ed. Boston: Allyn and Bacon.

Ornstein, Allan C., and Daniel U. Levine. 2000. *Foundations of education*. 7th ed. Boston: Houghton Mifflin.

Overman, Christian. 2003. *Think again!* Materials presented at the Think Again! workshop in Bellevue, WA.

Overman, Christian, and Don Johnson. 2003. *Making the connections: How to put biblical worldview integration into practice*. Puyallup, WA: The Biblical Worldview Institute.

Ross, Randy. 2004. Should tuition be cost based or ministry based? Counterpoint. In ACSI's *Leadership Academy 2004 report*, 95–98. Colorado Springs, CO: Association of Christian Schools International.

Roth, David L. 2002. Turning vision into reality: Managing school budgets. In *Called to lead: Understanding and fulfilling your role as an educational leader*, ed. Kenneth O. Gangel, 243–55. Colorado Springs, CO: Purposeful Design Publications.

References

Sanofi-aventis. n.d. About insomnia. http://www.shuteye.com/insomnia.asp?engine=adwords!3626&keyword=%28sleep+disord (accessed on May 25, 2005).

Santos, Fernanda. 2002. "Potty cops" at private school made 8 boys strip. *New York Daily News*, December 20.

Schimmer, John, Jr. 2002. Who's in charge here? Working with the board. In *Called to lead: Understanding and fulfilling your role as an educational leader*, ed. Kenneth O. Gangel, 19–36. Colorado Springs, CO: Purposeful Design Publications.

———. 2004. *Board governance: Understanding the roles and responsibilities of Christian school board members*. Colorado Springs, CO: Association of Christian Schools International.

Schindler, Claude E. 1979. *Educating for eternity*. Wheaton, IL: Tyndale House.

Schultz, Glen. 1998. *Kingdom education: God's plan for educating future generations*. Nashville, TN: LifeWay.

Sergiovanni, Thomas J. 1991. *Value-added leadership: How to get extraordinary performance in schools*. New York: Harcourt Brace Jovanovich.

———. 1992a. *Moral leadership: Getting to the heart of school improvement*. Jossey-Bass Education Series. San Francisco: Jossey-Bass.

———. 1992b. Why we should seek substitutes for leadership. *Educational Leadership* 49, no. 5:41–45.

———. 1995. *The principalship: A reflective practice perspective*. 3rd ed. Boston: Allyn and Bacon.

Sergiovanni, Thomas J., and Robert J. Starratt. 1993. *Supervision: A redefinition*. New York: McGraw-Hill.

Shakespeare, William. 1974. *Macbeth*, act 1, scene 7, lines 58–61. In *The riverside Shakespeare*. Boston: Houghton Mifflin.

Smitherman, Ken. 2004–05. Is Christian schooling essential? *Christian School Education* (ACSI) 8, no. 1:5.

Stoppler, Melissa C. n.d. Binge eating disorder. http://stress.about.com/ (accessed on May 25, 2005).

Stronks, Gloria Goris, and Doug Blomberg, eds. 1993. *A vision with a task: Christian schooling for responsive discipleship.* Grand Rapids, MI: Baker.

Sweet, Leonard. 1999. *AquaChurch.* Loveland, CO: Group Publishing.

Swindoll, Charles R. 1978. *Hand me another brick.* Nashville, TN: Thomas Nelson.

Taba, Hilda. 1962. *Curriculum development: Theory and practice.* New York: Harcourt Brace Jovanovich.

Tyler, Ralph W. 1949. *Basic principles of curriculum and instruction.* Chicago: University of Chicago Press.

Ubben, Gerald C., Larry W. Hughes, and Cynthia J. Norris. 2001. *The principal: Creative leadership for effective schools.* 4th ed. Boston: Allyn and Bacon.

Van Brummelen, Harro. 2002. *Steppingstones to curriculum: A biblical path.* 2nd ed. Colorado Springs, CO: Purposeful Design Publications.

Walberg, Herbert J., Diane Schiller, and Geneva D. Haertel. 1979. The quiet revolution in educational research. *Phi Delta Kappan* 61, no. 3:179–83.

Walt, Jo. 1998. The Neighborhood School. ACSI regional publication (Winter). Colorado Springs, CO: Association of Christian Schools International.

Additional Resources for the Development of Your Schoolwide Observation Rubric

Berry, Sharon. 2000. *Classroom perspectives: Strategies for student management.* Nashville, TN: LifeWay.

Borich, Gary D. 2006. *Effective teaching methods: Research-based practice.* 6th ed. Upper Saddle River, NJ: Prentice Hall.

References

Braley, James W., and Ollie E. Gibbs. 2000. *Classroom perspectives: Teachers committed to excellence.* Nashville, TN: LifeWay.

Brown, Gordon. 2002. *Guiding faculty to excellence: Instructional supervision in the Christian school.* Colorado Springs, CO: Purposeful Design Publications. (Note: Contains reproducible forms for observations and evaluations.)

Marzano, Robert J., Debra Pickering, and Jane Pollock. 2001. *Classroom instruction that works: Research-based strategies for increasing student achievement.* Alexandria, VA: Association for Supervision and Curriculum Development.

Orlich, Donald, ed. 2004. *Teaching strategies: A guide to effective instruction.* 7th ed. Boston: Houghton Mifflin.

Wong, Harry K., and Rosemary T. Wong. 2004. *The first days of school: How to be an effective teacher.* Rev. ed. Mountain View, CA: Harry K. Wong Publications.